Training by Objectives

GEORGE S. ODIORNE

AN ECONOMIC APPROACH TO MANAGEMENT TRAINING

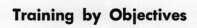

Training by Objectives

Training by Objectives

AN ECONOMIC APPROACH TO MANAGEMENT TRAINING

George S. Odiorne

Dean, College of Business Administration, University of Utah

THE MACMILLAN COMPANY
Collier-Macmillan Limited, London

118017

6 5 8.3
O 24

THE MACMILLAN COMPANY
866 Third Avenue, New York, New York 10022

COLLIER-MACMILLAN CANADA, LTD., Toronto, Ontario

Library of Congress catalog card number: 78–91586

First Printing

Preface

SINCE 1960 the field of training has been subject to considerable attention, unmatched since the early days of World War II. The emphasis upon manpower development as a method of eradicating unemployment, the demand for more technically trained persons for high-technology businesses, the decentralization of firms, earlier retirements, shorter work weeks for many public servants such as policemen and firemen, and the development of numerous new forms of training have combined to produce a training revolution.

It became apparent early in the 1960's that unemployment at levels above 4 per cent was becoming unacceptable and politically explosive. It became further apparent that unemployment could be socially explosive as the civil rights movement turned from passive to active means. Riots in the cities were quickly attributed to unemployment and poverty in the ghettos, and the cause of the poverty and unemployment was attached equally firmly to lack of skills. The solution adopted for all of this was more training.

This conclusion produced a drastic change in training objectives. In management development and management training, learning theory has become the slave and instrument of economics. In this book we shall look at these two influences in that order, first economics of training and then applied learning theory. They will then be integrated into an approach to training.

For most managers of training, learning theory has all too often been the master plan around which training is prepared, planned, and presented. This does not mean that training has been wrong but rather that it has often misguided itself by asking the wrong questions. "Which form of training should be applied to work best?" has often been answered in favor of the most effective form from the viewpoint of learning theory, rather than from the viewpoint of whether the training was designed to serve a specific end, to achieve a needed objective.

Although the economics of the training program is probably easier to figure out in the corporation where profit is a form of economic discipline that is easy to understand, the same limiting conditions exist in nonprofit organizations and government. As Robert McNamara and the recent trend toward program budgeting (PPBS) in government have pointed up, there is an economic dimension to public service that sets the limiting conditions on activity in that sector as well.

Thus this book is for corporate and governmental trainers and management development experts.

Is there a theoretical justification for this arrangement of priorities—economic first, then learning theory? Clearly this arrangement adopts the assumption that intention, goals, and objectives determine the *effectiveness* of the means used. The motive for the training becomes a matter of some moment when we consider it from such a viewpoint. The firm has a charter that justifies all of its activities. The government agency has a limiting condition that comes to the same conclusion in many cases. The motive for government to train people, however, is less clear, and the forms of training and applied learning theory will not be centered in its limiting condition, even though they cannot be ignored. Political scientists have often chosen power as the major motive. Senator William Fulbright proposes that a genius of our system is an ability to start with man as he actually exists rather than as he should be. The major realities the Senator proposes are the goals of profit in economic matters and ambition in governmental and political life.

The 1960's have seen a rather close alliance between the ambitions of politicians and the profit of economic institutions. Unemployment, poverty, and underemployment have become issues in politics as well as matters of direct concern to corporations. Part I of this book deals with the economic approach to training, pointing out the fruitlessness of many past training efforts in today's environment. Part II presents the systems approach to training as a means of reorienting training to economic objectives. Part III outlines the various kinds of learning theories, classified with hard criteria and soft criteria, and shows what the demands of the 1970's will be for hard criteria training. It then goes on to illustrate how these will look in terms of training methods and action training.

Special note on use of cases: When this book is used as a text in a class in training administration, both teacher and students should read Chapters 13 and 14 before starting the course. This will equip them to study each of the chapters using the cases at the end of each chapter. Suggestions for using case study and action training methods include reading the text and applying it in order to streamline class learning time considerably.

Salt Lake City   G. S. O.

Contents

PART **I** The New Look in Training

1
Economic Objectives of Training

Reason governs men far more imperiously
than any master.

—PASCAL

FOR many years the training profession has been
strongly influenced by psychologists, especially
learning theorists. Their influence has been a rich
one and has often led industrial trainers into the fore-
front of experimentation and testing of new teaching
methods, whereas the more conservative and stable
college and school faculties have dragged their heels over introducing
such change. The use of role playing in changing behavior has made
small impact on the campus but is commonly used in supervisory and
management development programs. Training directors in the military
services, for example, have led in training trainers, with such schools as
the trainers school of the 11th Naval District doing a far better job of
teaching teachers *to teach* than any school of education. More recently
the largest strides in the application of programmed instruction for
teaching machines and auto-instructional methods have taken hold in
industry at a far greater rate than on campus.[1]

Despite the gains in learning theory that have been made by this near
domination of training by learning theorists, there is still a persuasive
case to be made for a turn now toward more intensive economic
orientation in training.

[1] Geary Rummler, "Programmed Learning—A Progress Report," *Management of
Personnel Quarterly*, 2:3 (Fall 1963).

Is Training an Economic Function?

Most training programs are considered successful by the people who attend them, especially the management development programs.[2] Almost any well-planned and competently executed course will draw a favorable response from those who attend it. In fact, there is some nagging doubt whether or not the questionnaires normally circulated at the end of training courses are worth very much because they are uniformly laudatory, with a minor spattering of "suggestions for improvement." For example, at the University of Michigan in 1968 such opinion surveys were circulated among 1,400 managers who attended two-day seminars; the responses were most flattering to the instructors. Based on a rating scale of 1 to 5 indicating degrees of satisfaction with the course, the average ran about 4.5. More interesting were the free responses that were given to the question "Of what value was this meeting to you?" A typical sampling of such comments ran as follows:

"One of the greatest I have ever attended."

"I had my eyes opened."

"I had a chance to get a good look at myself and my job, and plan to make some changes."

These three comments, incidentally, were typical of all those received. They came from a single seminar on cost reduction. They would have made a glowing testimony for a course in human relations, sensitivity training, or "How To Win Friends and Influence People." As objective measures of the behavior change or actual worth of the course to the man on his job and the company, they are not very useful. Flattering to the staff, yes. An indication of enthused teaching, yes. Useful, no.

As every experimental psychologist knows, there are some definite rules for measuring behavior change. (1) You must have an experimental group that is to be trained and a control group that is not to be trained. (2) You measure behavior in specific actions that can be seen or counted in both groups before and after the training of the experimental groups. (3) You measure the changes in each group and infer meaning from the results by T-test, Chi square, multiple correlation, and the like.

Such a procedure takes some special training, and even if all trainers in industry had the ability to conduct such measures, as well as the time and money, it would not be necessary. It is better perhaps to keep abreast of experiments that have been conducted along such lines to

---

[2] Kenneth Andrews, "Is Management Training Effective?" *Harvard Business Review* (Jan.–Feb. 1957).

find guides as to which training methods will most likely change behavior. One of the problems that confronts trainers is that many of the widely used methods of training have no basis for use in the firm because they do not change behavior. The training of managers in human relations, for example, has an exceedingly poor record in this respect.[3]

Line managers have arrived at some of the same conclusions about training in their firm but by a different method. They have asked what contribution to profit, growth, or efficiency has been made by the expenditures made for training and all too often have concluded that the gains have not justified the expense. Accordingly, training department budgets are often the first to suffer when a downturn in business or an economy drive is under way.

In the light of the latter, it might be well for the trainer to re-evaluate his learning practices from an economic viewpoint.

In fact, it may be necessary to his survival as a trainer to do so continuously. It is becoming reasonably apparent by now that industrial training has a poor record of survival when the earnings of the business decline. When profits disappear, so does the training department in many cases. Although this can be explained in part by the limited vision of the general manager, this cannot be a complete explanation. It is also possible that much of the training being done is prosperity-based and under intense economic scrutiny comes out looking like so much purposeless nonsense. The time to turn an economic light onto training is before the crisis of survival of training (and trainers) is at hand. As a result we may eliminate a lot of the pretentious nonsense that some of the more experimental schools of social scientists have been selling to trainers. *Learning theory and psychology can tell us how to teach. Economic analysis can tell us whether or not we should train at all.*

The Future Demand for Training Is High

Labor market statistics are all in favor of the training function being an important one in the future. The work of the trainer is an important one to the firm and should be accorded status and function in keeping with it. Let us look at the big training jobs that lie ahead for our profession during the coming decade:

1. The induction training of 26 million people will be required simply to get new persons in the jobs to replace those leaving the labor force in the next decade.

[3] E. Z. Fleischman, "Leadership Climate, Human Relations Training and Supervisory Behavior," *Personnel Psychology*, 6 (1953).

2. The training of 6 million new skilled craftsmen to replace those retiring, as well as training present men in new crafts, will have to be done.
3. The upgrading of an additional 3 to 4 million managerial people faces us. One report states that 40 per cent of the present managers will be replaced during this decade and that another 20 per cent will move into lateral positions requiring new skills. The average age of company presidents is 59, and the average age of their assistants is slightly higher.
4. Job content is changing rapidly and this means that much retraining must be done to keep abreast of the changes.
5. The urban crisis of the 1960's has highlighted the explosive potential of two societies: one white, educated, and employed; the other black, uneducated, and unemployed. Retraining is a key remedy here.

The total cost of such training in all its forms for on-the-job training has been estimated at around $30 billion annually.[4] In the face of such a challenge the training professional has every reason to be optimistic about the economic potential of his field both as a career site and as a professional challenge.

Where does the economics of this field find its roots?

Investment in Human Capital as a Base Point

The president of the American Economic Association, Theodore Schultz, has pointed up the necessity for a new look at on-the-job training. In his presidential address in 1961, he said:

Although it is obvious that people acquire useful skills and knowledge, it is not obvious that these skills and knowledge are a form of capital, that this capital is part of a deliberate investment that has grown in Western societies at a faster rate than conventional (non-human) capital, and that its growth may well be the most distinctive feature of the economic system.[5]

This provocative idea has had a sizable impact on the thinking of others since it was stated. Some have concluded from this view of investment that companies should therefore never fire anybody. Others

---

[4] H. F. Clark, "Potentialities of Educational Establishments Outside the Structure of Higher Education," *Financing Higher Education, 1960–70*, D. M. Keezer, ed. (New York: McGraw-Hill, 1959).

[5] Theodore Schultz, "Presidential Address," *American Economic Review*, 51:1 (March 1961).

have concluded that because the tax man and the accountants' procedures do not accommodate themselves to this kind of thinking, then it really is not an investment at all. Galbraith points out that because companies do not hold title to the men (since Abraham Lincoln freed the slaves) then government training must take over.[6]

Vuaridel points up quite reasonably that only part of the investment in educational expenditures has tangible effects but that we should not overlook the intangible effects that have benefits as well. Although the tangible effects of education, such as more productivity, can be equated to producer's goods, it may well be the intangible ones (better citizens) that have the greatest impact.[7]

For one thing, education is good for the whole economy, as many studies have shown. In agriculture, for example, the higher educational level of farmers through land grant colleges has been credited with much of the improved agricultural productivity that characterized this country from 1940 to 1960.[8] Southern economists have studied the effects of human capital investments on the economic health of the region.[9]

The training director has an important argument to present to potential trainees in the studies showing that great personal benefits accrue to the trained that are denied the untrained. David and Morgan estimate that investment in education by the individual pays 4–6 per cent return, as figured on a national basis.[10] Hansen reports that the return to individuals from schooling as private beneficiaries actually exceeds the social return.[11] Yet far too few training directors have shown any awareness of this important economic facet of their work— that it does indeed add to the capital of the firm in the form of investment in human capital—and far too few guide their efforts to accelerate this growth.

How does one begin? Table 1 is a worksheet to help you make a quick economic classification of your training programs. It can help you

[6] J. K. Galbraith, *The Liberal Hour* (Boston: Houghton Mifflin, 1960).

[7] Roger Vuaridel, "Human Capital and the Economics of Education," *Schweizwische Zeitschrift fur Volkswirt und Statistik*, 99:2 (June 1963).

[8] Ziv Griliches, "Sources of Productivity Growth: U.S. Agriculture 1940–1960," *Journal of Political Economy*, LXI:4 (Aug. 1963).

[9] Marshall Colberg, "Human Capital as a Southern Resource," *Southern Economic Review*, XXIX:3 (June 1963).

[10] Martin David, and James Morgan, "Education and Income," *Quarterly Journal of Economics*, LXXVII:3 (June 1963).

[11] W. Lee Hansen, "Total and Private Rates of Return to Investment in Schooling," *Journal of Political Economy*, LXXI:3 (April 1963).

Table I

Part I:	Estimated total costs		
	1. Direct expense (paid out)	$_____	
	2. Indirect expense (staff salaries, space, and so on)	_____	
	3. Participant salaries	_____	
	Total cost of program .... $	_____	

Part II: Economic classification (state as percentage of costs in Part I)
    1. Profit improvement training (one-year period)
      (a) Sales: increase volumes;
          cut selling costs .... _____%
      (b) Manufacturing: cut costs .... _____%
      (c) Service: lower unit costs .... _____%
      (d) Staff: improve program, lower
          budget expense .... _____% _____%
    2. Added human working capital .... _____%
    3. Investment in human capital .... _____%
    4. Fails to fit any economic classification .... _____%

classify your training costs into economic categories. It has two major sections: In part I, identify the major segments of costs; in part II, by percentage, identify how much of the costs would be classified into profit improvement, human working capital, and investment in human capital. This is done as follows.

PROFIT OBJECTIVES AS A TAKE-OFF POINT

The reason so many training departments find themselves in hard times, even when it is apparent that they are necessary and will continue to be in the future, often lies in the specific economic relation they hold to their organization. (Not all organizations are profit-making, but all are economic in part.) The training function is not necessarily an organization of reform, but it *is* an organization of change. Of all the personnel and industrial relations functions, the training function alone has the function of being a *change agent*. (The failure of many especially created change agent programs is probably explainable in their failure to adopt and be consistent with the training staff role.)

What is the economic take-off point for training? Figure 1–1 spells out economic objectives for different parts of the firm. Figure 1–1 represents the different kinds of economic measures of organization performance. Each organization unit has a unique economic characteristic. Thus the general manager level is the lowest possible level

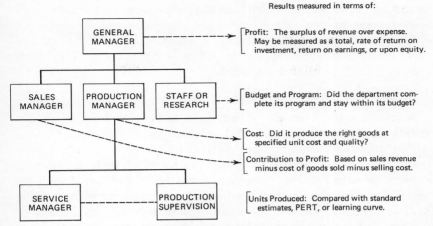

FIGURE 1–1   Economic Measures of Organization Performance

at which "profit-producing training" is of immediate importance, because it is the lowest level that has responsibility for profit. It is the lowest level that controls *both* revenue and expense. Sales personnel are contributors to profit through the control of two variables under their control: sales volume and selling expense. (The combination of these variables is *contribution to profit.*)

The work of the manufacturing manager is primarily measured by cost of goods sold, with side conditions of quality, delivery, and the like. The work of his subordinates in manufacturing or service supervision are measured by units produced as compared with certain engineered or historical standards.

Training or change programs that unqualifiedly purport to "improve productivity" are naive in many respects. They are not attuned to the economic end measurements or the specific language of the firm in its economic division of labor. Sales training programs should produce new volume or cut selling expense. Manufacturing management courses should aim primarily at cost reduction. Little else is significant in this branch of the business. Manufacturing supervision courses or programs should increase units produced against standards, reduce scrap, eliminate accidents, reduce downtime on machines, or prevent machine damage. Service supervision should provide units of service at standard costs or below.

It should be noted that all these kinds of training objectives are profit-centered and probably will pay off for the firm within the immediate accounting period. Such training should be classified as *profit improvement training.*

Not all training is in this category; it is merely the take-off point and basic program for training that is economically oriented. Two other economic kinds of training are possible.

TRAINING AS ADDITION TO HUMAN WORKING CAPITAL

A second major economic classification is training from which the results can be converted to profits in a relatively short time but not within the usual one-year period. Returns on the costs of training in a period of from one to three years would include such training. Training expense for such purposes as training understudies for people going on vacation and for managers who will retire in a couple of years, training to have backstops for key personnel, or prior training for planned expansion of the plant or sales force would be expense that would not contribute to profit during the immediate accounting period at hand, yet it would be a sound economic expense for the firm because it would enhance profit and pay back the costs within a one- to three-year period. Such training expenses are in the same category as inventories and receivables.

TRAINING AS CAPITAL BUDGETING

The third category of training is that which falls into the economic category of major replacements or additions to the plant and that which takes several years (up to ten) to return the cash outlay. Included are such programs as sending executives to Harvard, rotation of junior executives through various departments in preparation for key jobs many years in the future, upgrading workers in key crafts, and many other executive and managerial development programs on which immediate cash return in a current accounting period cannot be predicted.

Capital Budgeting for Investment in Human Capital. Having thus classified our training plans and programs as to how each will ultimately contribute to the profit of the firm, we shall probably discover that we have created some new problems in handling the long-range human investment portion of the budgets. To adequately prepare and sell such expenses the training director must be prepared to answer the following four questions as they apply to his training programs for the forthcoming year.

1. *How much money in total will be needed for expenditure in long-range investment in human capital during the coming period?* The need here will be weighed against the prospective profitability of the alternative possibilities that are available. Shall we send three executives to executive development schools and rotate six others at a cost of $25,000

or should we run 40 weeks of education in political action for supervision for 300 foremen at the same cost? Should we make young Mr. X assistant to the president for training purposes for 2 years at $25,000 *or* should we conduct a cadet training school for 15 college recruits at the same cost? The answers to such questions of investment alternative must always be based on a comparison of alternative profitable uses. It also competes with demands for capital for physical equipment and for research and must have some basis for screening alternative uses.

2. *How should funds for investment in human capital be supplied?* Unlike the competing demands for capital funds for conventional training, investments in business are never—to my knowledge—raised through conventional capital-raising methods. Usually such capital comes out of operating income before it goes through profit or reinvested earnings channels. In many instances it may come through depreciation allowances, which are automatically reinvested in the business. Perhaps one of the needs of business in the future will be for the setting aside of allowances for depreciation of human skills caused by obsolescence, technological change, new products, turnover, or other losses of skill.

Tax allowances to corporations for depreciation of the vast investments they make in human capital would have an immense effect on accelerating the rate at which they made such investment. With such allowances permitted by law, the economic effects of skill investment because of automation, technological change, and unemployment would, for other reasons, be poured back into the retraining of people, the building of health services, the transfer of workers from one place to another, adult education, and the support of private education. Rather than funnel all such development (as Galbraith suggests[12]) in personal development through public finance, the government might better accomplish the same aim by arranging tax procedures—under proper controls to prevent private gouging—that spur and pull the private employers not only to increase their investment in personal development but to put the whole thing on a more businesslike basis. Galbraith suggests the audacious thought that perhaps companies might even float bond issues to underwrite personal development and investment in human capital if it really pays off. Such possibilities would place immense responsibilities on the executive in charge of training if he were required to pay off a bond issue from the income attributable to his training efforts and expenditures. Perhaps many existing encumbents of training positions would find their work unsuitable under such an

[12] J. K. Galbraith, *The Liberal Hour* (Boston: Houghton Mifflin, 1960).

arrangement, which leads us further to hypothesize that perhaps much of what is now being done under the guise of personal development really is not worth very much after all.

3. *How should training expense be rationed?* If the long-range training expenditures are to be handled realistically as investments, they will automatically run into the same kinds of rationing problems that any conventional capital investment does. The alternative use of investment capital among the places where it might be spent is a matter of business strategy. Should the company be spending money on supervisory training when it might be running professional development programs for its engineers? Should staff training of accountants in electronics take precedence over the other uses for the same investment in money for training? This means that the director of on-the-job training and personal development must be more sophisticated than he customarily is today in setting up standards for the rate of return on different kinds of personal development investments.

4. *How should timing be handled?* One of the most troublesome problems that plagues training directors is a lack of understanding on their part of the manner in which the timing of training expense control is handled. All too often they respond to curtailment of investment-type expenditures for personal development caused by recession by "pouting." They tell me they "aren't understood." They rail at the "blindness" of management. Yet the blindness—if it exists—is two-sided, for they fail to see realistically that capital financing problems are different in bad times than in good. Timing of investment is something about which they actually know little but about which top managers often know little more, and if general managers are to learn about investment in human capital, then it must be the training directors who educate them.

WHAT IF A TRAINING PROGRAM DOES NOT CLASSIFY ITSELF ECONOMICALLY?

Perhaps you have listed one of your actual training programs in the worksheet listed earlier and have found that it simply cannot, by any stretch of the imagination, fit into any of the economic categories listed. At this stage you should ask yourself seriously whether it should be conducted at all.

Economic analysis of your training should answer the question as to whether the training should be conducted. After this question has been answered affirmatively, then the skills of the learning theorist can be effectively brought to bear to execute the needed training with maximum skill.

Many of the present offerings of management training will fall into this category of "impossible to identify economic return" and should probably be abandoned. It would be a better investment in human capital for such firms to calculate the costs of such programs and make a donation of an equal amount to the United Negro College Fund or some other general aid to education than to conduct exorbitantly priced, esoteric, and useless extravagances that provide emotional entertainment and in some instances cause actual damage to the organization.

Such vaguely defined training, which cannot be identified as profit improvement, improved human working capital, or added investment in human capital, is risky stuff to build a training program on.

Conclusions

Corporate directors of training today oversee an educational effort in this country that nearly matches in dollar cost the expense of the entire formal educational system in the public sphere.

Employees of the modern firm may count on a steady return to school, either in company classes, in man-to-man coaching, tuition refund support for adult education, or guided experience on their jobs, for the rest of their working lives. Not only is this true of mechanics and salesmen but of staff experts and company presidents as well.

The field of manager education is especially crucial for the company training staff at this time because so many conflicting theories of management are being promulgated as being the proper style for the manager of the future to adopt. In seeking the solution to the proper kind of behavior to teach managers in their firms, there are seven guides for today's industrial educator:

1. Remember that the training manager is the major change agent for the firm and accordingly that he should be broadly aware of the entire scope of the business and the major forces that are bringing about change. The necessity for economic growth of firms means that he must be constantly oriented toward those behaviors that will accelerate growth and profit.
2. Training directors should avoid forms of training that would perform psychotherapy on the personalities of managers. Not only is there no uniform executive personality, but even if there were, the tinkering into any employee's personality by the firm is an unwarranted invasion of his privacy. This should limit not only the courses conducted by company staff, but also those conducted by consultants and experts from outside the firm.
3. The basis for training should be changing job behavior. Behavior is

activity that can be seen or measured for which the company rewards the man. The trainer of the future will service his firm, the employee, and society best by limiting himself to that context.

4. Company trainers can do much to alleviate the distress of structural unemployment by constantly upgrading people. Such upgrading from within by internal training would alleviate the shortage of skilled people and would also free the lower-level positions vacated by promotion for those persons in the labor market who through limited capacity simply cannot be retrained for the more complex job.

5. There are certain techniques of training that have been proved effective in changing behavior. Such methods should be applied, and other methods for which no research evidence exists that shows behavior is changed should be avoided. Among the methods that have proved effective are lecture-discussion, role playing, case method, management games, programmed instruction, and the incident process.

6. Training managers today must move more in the direction of economic evaluation of their training efforts and shun those kinds of training that merely entertain, excite, or flatter the student. The investment expense in human capital is becoming big business, and as manager of that expense item the training manager must think equally as businessman as well as educator.

7. Industrial trainers and educators should move ahead cautiously in applying behavioral science research in changing management behavior. Many social and behavioral researchers who perform excellent research are simply out of their field when they try to prescribe how the research should be used. In aeronautical engineering it is not the inventor who insists on flying the passengers and collecting the tickets, as many social scientists attempt to do with their findings. The training director should be aware of all the latest social research but should make his own economic decisions on its usefulness to business.

THE NU BANK CASE

After his discharge from the Navy in August 1960, Jonathan Cox Tweed, III, applied for a job in the credit department of the Nu Bank, one of the larger banks of Central City, an important Midwestern financial center. During his initial interview with the personnel director, Mr. Reynard, Jonathan was told that the bank had a formal training program and that soon the credit department would begin its program, which consisted of lectures, case studies, and outside assignments. Later in the day, Jonathan talked with several of the younger loan officers, who explained the internal workings of the bank. All expressed enthusiasm for their work and loyalty to the bank. Moreover, they assured him that he would be happy if he accepted the job. In the final interview, Mr. Reynard told Jonathan that the bank's training program was one of the best in the country. Two weeks later, Jonathan began his new job with enthusiasm and high expectations.

Prior to his new employment, Jonathan had served a three year hitch as a Navy Supply Officer aboard the U.S.S. Gut Bucket in the Atlantic. His resumé showed that he was graduated from Stanford University in 1954 with honors in classical studies. Between graduation and his naval duty, Jonathan had worked for one of the largest commercial banks on Wall Street. While with this bank, he had completed the six-month advanced training program for college graduates, had done special work as an installment loan representative, had compiled a constructive critique of the bank's advanced training program, and had spent about six months in the credit department. The critique of the training program was done in conjunction with three contemporaries and at the request of a personal friend, who was a senior member of the top-management group. The credit department training program was to last approximately two and a half years and consisted of many special lectures and classes, case studies, and on-the-job assistance from the department head or one of his assistants. The areas covered were statement analysis, working capital loans, secured loans, terms loans, finance company loans, and foreign loans. However, before Jonathan could complete the entire program he began his naval career at Newport.

The credit department at the Nu Bank consisted of Assistant Vice President I. M. Rock, two elderly senior clerks who assisted Mr. Rock, and Miss Medulla, who supervised training and credit analysis. She had nearly 20 years of analytical experience. There were 12 senior analysts and 12 junior analysts, all of whom were located in the same large work area as Mr. Rock and his staff.

As an introduction to the department, Rock told Jonathan that he could expect an accelerated tour in the department because he had had previous training.

MR. ROCK: I expect that within about two and a half years you should be moving across to the platform because your training time will be less than for most of the boys. As a starter, why don't you begin spreading statements, and then after a couple of weeks we'll move you to analysis.

JONATHAN: Fine. Where will I sit?

After agreeing on this program, Jonathan was introduced to each member of the department and anyone who happened to be visiting it at that time.

That afternoon Jonathan was told how to spread a statement according to the bank's established system. Within several days he had memorized the 60-odd marking lines and knew reasonably well what went where. For the next three months Jonathan marked statements. Frequently, however, much of his time was spent reading the department's copy of *The Wall Street Journal*, for this was the slack season and there were few statements to mark. On several occasions during this period he asked Mr. Rock when he was scheduled to begin his analytical training. To this Mr. Rock usually replied, "As soon as Miss Medulla has a free moment she'll explain the procedure to you and the two other new boys."

Several weeks later when looking for work, Jonathan was told to go over to the supervisor's desk as she wanted to talk with him. The ensuing conversation revolved around the spreading procedure and future plans for analytical training. Beginning the following Monday, Jonathan and the other two newcomers would start the analytical phase of their training.

On Monday, when the three trainees gathered around Miss Medulla's desk, she greeted them and said, "Why don't you have some coffee first?" After the coffee break, Miss Medulla told the trainees she could not talk to them: "I can't talk to you now since I've just been given a rush analysis to do. Go back to your spreading and I'll call you when I get a free moment."

Toward the end of the week the trainees were summoned over to her desk for a preliminary introduction to analysis: "The Nu Bank has a very high set of standards with regard to whom we extend credit. We just don't make loans to any one wanting credit. Also, our analysis follows a definite format. You can begin your training by reading through these five files. Pay particular attention to the analyses, and I expect that most of your questions will answer themselves."

The reading period lasted three weeks, and then there was another conference. At this time, each trainee was given an analysis to do. One of the other trainees protested, "But where do we begin? Aren't you going to explain the analysis to us?" To this Miss Medulla replied, "No, here we believe in the sink or swim approach. Besides, you can learn more from your mistakes than from my telling you how to do it."

Jonathan wrote the analysis in general conformance to the prescribed method, but there were overtones of his previous training. Miss Medulla, after reading the analysis, made the following comments: "Jonathan, here we always refer to the acid test, not 'cash, securities and receivables to current liabilities.' Also, we never refer to a firm's liquidity as such, but rather its 'margin of creditors' protection.' Why have you omitted the receivables to days' sales ratio?"

At this point, he began to question her as to why such language must be used when everybody knew the meaning of his statements and why such ratios were to be included when they were insignificantly small. In this conversation, he cited his past experience and the method of his former employer as a basis for his work and decisions. Miss Medulla concluded the conversation by saying, "Well, we do it differently here, and I don't want you to question my reasons."

Much perplexed and concerned about this situation, Jonathan returned to his desk and rewrote the analysis. He was bothered by the need to use only certain phrases. He was also puzzled as to just what to include in future analyses. At the same time, the other two trainees were struggling with their respective assignments, for neither had any prior training, nor any formal education in accounting, although both were taking accounting courses at night school.

As a supplement to his training, Jonathan was enrolled in the New Credit Officer correspondence course. He protested by saying that he had completed a more comprehensive course elsewhere and that the N.C.O. course was merely repetitious. His arguments did not prevail, and Mr. Rock mailed his enrollment. Other members of the department sympathized.

SCOTT DRAKE: The course is an absolute waste of time, but you'd better do what 'The Rock' wants. It's really designed for high school graduates, but *C'est la guere!* Here are my answers. Go ahead and use them; no one who has taken this course ever did any work.

Throughout the next month an acute tension built up between Miss Medulla and Jonathan. He felt that if the basic philosophy behind the bank's approach had been explained he would have been able to see why certain things were done and that this knowledge would make his work more meaningful. With the approach of the rush season in mid-February the situation was much the same; however, prior to this time Jonathan had been told by one of the senior clerks not to challenge the authority of Miss Medulla.

JONATHAN: I only want to know why I am doing things the way I am told to do them. After all, should not the training program be informative as well as instructive?

In April, at the peak of the rush season, Jonathan was assigned to the finance company desk. He was delighted to be assigned permanently to one area, but at the same time he had misgivings because he had had no training in finance company analyses. Subsequently, he expressed his concern to Miss Medulla, but she told him not to worry because he would surely learn the job in due time. However, this did not satisfy him.

JONATHAN: Well, then what's the primary purpose of the credit department? Is it not to provide analytical service to the loan officers, as well as train the future officers of the bank?

MISS MEDULLA: I don't know. My job is to see that the analyses are written, and written the way the department wants them.

JONATHAN: In that case, wouldn't it be wise to have a booklet describing the aim of the department and the whys and wherefores of our work? Wouldn't this reduce your training burden?

MISS MEDULLA: Certainly not! We don't want anything written, for that implies permanency.

JONATHAN: But. . . .

MISS MEDULLA: Jonathan! Don't challenge me. I'll do my job the way I see fit!

Shortly thereafter Jonathan submitted his resignation, which was not well received by Mr. Rock. When asked why he was resigning, Jonathan said, "I want a broader background." To this Mr. Rock replied, "Why don't you go to night school?"

JONATHAN: I am, but under the circumstances I can get more for my money by going to school full time. Why doesn't the bank reimburse us for our night schooling; the other banks do.

At the termination interview, Mr. Reynard talked to Jonathan about the chances of the Twins winning the pennant and his future plans.

CASE DISCUSSION QUESTIONS

The Nu Bank Case

1. What is the major problem here?

2. If you had to compute a cost of training in Nu Bank, how would you proceed?

3. What kind of program would you construct for trainees to make them junior analysts? Seniors?

4. How could you show comparative costs and savings of your training?

2 | Management Training—
Relating Economic and
Behavioral Goals

Men of the world understand readily
what is commonly met with amongst
mankind.
                    —HENRY TAYLOR (1836)

SUPERVISORY training during the 1930's and
part of the 1940's was a desultory and ill-
aimed business for the most part. Experiments in Western Electric's Hawthorne plant had
led to the conclusion that economic matters were
subordinate to social and cultural considerations.[1]
This led to the further conclusion that the training of foremen was
primarily a matter of teaching them human relations skills so that they
could become instruments for allaying the discontent of workers. The
training of foremen would effectively change the working environment
and social climate in which the all-important worker would function.
Changed supervisor behavior would change the psychological atmosphere and would ease the potential problems arising from troublesome
workers. Under such circumstances foremen training was merely another
procedure, like rest-rooms, guarded machines, coffee breaks, and rest
pauses, to persuade the worker that his magical inner box of "needs"
were being filled daily by the firm, which would in turn trigger his
motives and attitudes in the direction of doing a day's work for his pay.

Management under such a rationale was human relations.

---

[1] Elton Mayo, *Human Problems of an Industrial Civilization* (New York: Viking,
1931).

The worker was a potential saboteur who would withhold his ego involvement unless a tacit bargain was made and kept—he would abstain from goldbricking and cheating his employer if his employer would regularly fill his needs tank with a mixture of 100-octane recognition, belonging, ego satisfaction, social satisfaction, and self-expression.[2] The foreman was trained to serve as the attendant at the pump that kept this needs tank filled. One key ingredient in this system was the instruction that the foreman should use his delegated powers from the owners sparingly and permit wide latitude to workers because they all had a highly developed sense of independence and desire for freedom from orders and directions.

Any consideration that the foreman himself was a resource to be developed and improved (beyond serving his workers' needs for contentment) became more evident during World War II. His greatest point of development in prevailing human relations courses was in becoming an invisible neuter. For a time at the end of the war he himself became an object of compassionate attention, being described as the man in the middle and the victim of benighted upper management.

"Human Relations" Training Evolves

During and after the war drastic changes took place in the composition of the work force and the economics of business. The unskilled worker was replaced by his better-educated children or by a machine. Mechanized plants and more technical products such as electronic devices and chemical products called for more educated people. Such people brought to the job middle-class values that outmoded many of the perfectly apt ideas about what employees expected from the company. The new breed of employee was more success-oriented, stronger goal-oriented, and far more likely to be frustrated than the worker on the bench because his aspiration levels were higher.[3] The new professional middle-class worker was also far less likely to be concerned over having a boss but was able to see that his success consisted of helping his superior succeed rather than in finding simple inward satisfactions on one job forever as his father might have done.

While this steady urgent restructuring of the work force was occurring, the social scientists continued to pursue research that called for

[2] A. H. Maslow, *Motivation and Personality* (New York: Harper & Row, 1954)— perhaps the leading exposition of the "needs theory" of motivation.

[3] Gerald Gurin, Joseph Veroff, and Sheila Feld, *Americans View Their Mental Health* (New York: Basic Books, 1960).

equalized power between boss and worker. Almost universally their studies proved that permissive management was superior to directive styles. Because the masses were diminishing in number and the possibility of their revolt was reduced to negligible proportion, the proofs tended to show that participation would make them more productive. The steady dissolution of the worker class and its vastly improved condition since Hawthorne went unnoticed.

In the early days of human relations training—through about 1950—there was a distinct moralistic and idealistic tone to the findings. The worker who was permitted to participate in the decisions that affected him on the job would be a better citizen outside the plant. The tough question—still unanswered and seldom asked by social scientists these days—"Can a man be a regimented automaton in the factory and a responsible free voter outside?" underlay many of the early human relations training programs. This line was subsequently dropped in favor of the line that "participative management increases production on the job," the latter being far more acceptable to line managers than the former. It became the central theme of social science research. Few companies were sponsoring research and training on company time and money to achieve generalized social uplift theories.

Despite the fact that the "better citizen" argument was the moral position, the social scientists veered sharply toward the pragmatic (and shakier) "production speed-up" base for comparing various styles of management.

The social scientist declared frankly that his findings were production-improving in nature and that in fact he had better answers than the industrial engineers and production people who spent their time on the plant floor working directly with the machines, the workers, and the methods.[4]

Most such studies pursued a pattern along the following lines:

1. A senior social scientist designed a scientific investigation (one that would produce measured results) and assembled a team to execute the study.

2. Two major tools were used in such studies: the interview and the questionnaire. ("Our researchers actually went out into a real factory and spoke to the real live workers who worked there.") The workers always called the researchers "Doc" and said such things as "the Goddam boss" and other workerlike terms.

---

[4] For example, see W. H. Whyte, ed., *Money and Motivation* (New York: Harper & Row, 1955).

3. The raw data were brought back to the campus where the senior investigator conferred with the research associates (usually graduate students) and checked their data.
4. Complex statistical tests were applied to relations (T-tests for significance, Chi square for variance from expected values, and multiple correlation for more complex relationships).
5. Where correlations of high scores were found, one of the variables was determined as being cause and another as effect. Which was which was not entirely important. Workers governed by permissive foremen had 22 per cent fewer cavities than those who were autocrats. Nobody got back to the plant to ask the manager to explain the *reasons* for the correlations.

The end product of much of this research was a vast torrent of economic ignorance and much of this ignorance found its way into supervisory and management training during the 1940's and 1950's.

The prior misconception that was corrected in such research lay in the proof that management did not *have* to be harsh and tough to get results. In so doing it sometimes went to the other extreme and proved wrongly that it must *never* be tough.

1. It devoted all the energies it could muster toward training managers on techniques of being "soft," participative, permissive, or democratic.
2. It devoted none of its effort toward showing the manager on those remaining occasions where hard-nosed management was called for how he could carry such practices off.
3. The social sciences declared that it discovered a new method of managing that pre-empted older previous styles and that present practices were wrong.
4. Its general line assumed that if management acted autocratically that the resulting worker resistance was continuing and inexorable and could not itself be treated as a new separate problem subject to dynamic remedial action.
5. It was out of touch with the engineering and economic facts of the two decades since the end of World War II on which operating managers have had a firm grasp.

A perfectly available remedy for troublesome workers was to replace the worker with machines and devices. This remedy was as easily done as attempting to change their attitudes and was far more permanent.

6. The great contribution of the social sciences—which cannot be overestimated—was the insights they brought to the management of the fast-growing segment of the labor force comprised of engineers, managers, and professionals.[5] Such persons, steeped in middle-class values and expectations, have been a fertile field for modern behavioral methods of managing democratically.

Which Type of Management to Teach?

From the ensuing discussion it can now be seen that the training director must, in designing a course in supervision, determine which style of management to train his supervision in.

Most supervisors should be trained both in methods of being firm (or tough) and being soft—and furthermore must be trained in when to use which style.

TRAINING IN TOUGH MANAGEMENT

The basic element is discipline and the control of persons by the use of authority to obtain compliance to the will of the boss. It means strict selection standards, developing work standards, using reprimands effectively, changing employee behavior by ordering the change, working within the union contract, avoiding reversal by the arbitrator through fairness, using key steps in decision making and problem solving, using corrective discipline as a form of behavior change, using reward and punishment, and using methods of checking and correcting employee behavior. Training is also pertinent here in avoiding certain undesirable supervisory behavior in the process, such as being discriminatory, prejudiced, unfair, inequitable, intemperate, hasty, profane, inconsistent in application or using physical coercion.

TRAINING IN PERMISSIVE MANAGEMENT

Methods of getting participation, listening, counseling, leading conferences, letting subordinates set their own goals, joint management-labor committees, motivational factors, attitude changes without coercion, and similar matters should be made part of every supervisor's repertory of skills.

The supervisor who is untrained in *either* set of skills may be unarmed for every kind of problem he will face in executing his duties. Even in

[5] L. E. Danielson, *Characteristics of Engineers and Scientists Important in Their Motivation and Supervision* (Ann Arbor: Bureau of Industrial Relations, University of Michigan, 1960). The research of Pelz and others is notable.

research laboratories there may be frivolous young secretaries who need a firm hand. In the roughest shop there may be skilled and sensitive people who require a feather touch to obtain their cooperation.

Hard Line, Soft Line—When to Use Each

It is popular today to polarize the styles of supervision into hard line versus soft line. We have theory X versus theory Y, autocratic versus permissive styles.[6] For the most part the evidence is becoming clearer that no such polarizing is genuinely worthwhile as a prescription.

Likert, for example, has put it this way:

Supervision is always a relative process. To be effective and to communicate as intended, a leader must always adapt his behavior to take into account the expectations, values and interpersonal skills of those with whom he is interacting.[7]

Such a conclusion should not come as a surprise to the experienced and successful supervisor. Current research makes it clear that there are three major ingredients in picking a style of supervision for a particular job, subordinates, and company:[8]

1. The supervisor himself is one ingredient. The chances of developing a whole new personality or background to fit a job is not likely. You can, however, change behavior somewhat. Sensible mature people are capable of discriminatory behavior; that is, we learn to sing hymns in church and raucous songs at smokers and never get mixed up.
2. The supervisor's followers are another ingredient. The management of engineers is different from that of foundry workers or college professors.
3. The third ingredient is a situational environment that can change supervisory methods and practices.

Figure 2–1 illustrates how supervisors may learn the basics of pertinent behavior. The three most common choices in the range of supervisory styles are listed across the top of the chart. In the first column are the limiting conditions in choosing the style. The important point, of course, is that there is no right or wrong style for its own sake. The

---

6 Douglas McGregor, *The Human Side of Enterprise* (New York: McGraw-Hill, 1960).

7 Rensis Likert, *New Patterns of Management* (New York: McGraw-Hill, 1961).

8 Bernard Indik, in *Personnel Administration*, 1961.

RANGE OF SUPERVISORY STYLES AVAILABLE

	AUTOCRATIC	DEMOCRATIC	LAISSEZ FAIRE
THE LEADER	· Has complete power · No restraints on its use · Has a way of saving matters in an emergency · Has some unique knowledge · Is firmly entrenched in position	· Has limited power · Restraints on its use · Group might reject his authority and succeed at it · Some time pressures · Has some sanctions he can exert	· Has no power to compel action · No time pressure exists · Tenure based on pleasure of group · Has no sanctions to exert on followers · Has no special knowledge
THE FOLLOWERS	· Are leader-dependent persons · Never asked opinion · Lower socioeconomic background · Realize the emergency · A labor surplus exists · Are autocrats themselves	· Expect to have some control over methods used · Middle-class values dominant · Engineers, managers, staff persons, typical types · Scarce skills · Like system but not authority · Rather scarce labor supply but not drastic	· Have more power than the leader · Dislike orders · Will rebel successfully if they so choose · Choose own goals and methods · Are volunteers, loosely organized, or in short supply · Scientists—rare skills needed for typical jobs
THE SITUATION	· Tight discipline is normal · Strong controls are ordinary · Time pressures are constant · Low profit margins or tight cost is prevalent · Physical dangers present · Low skill required of workers · Frequent changes must be made quickly	· General goals understood · Controls self-imposed but checked · Some time pressures · Gradual or regularly spaced changes · Occasional hazards · Moderate skills called for	· No clear purpose apparent · No controls exist · No time pressures · Few or gradual changes · Safe, placid environment · High skill or conceptual ability required

The Limiting Conditions in Choosing a Style

FIGURE 2–1   Some Guides to Supervisory Leadership Practices

supervisor learns that there are three main criteria for choosing a style: himself, his followers, and the situation in which all are operating.[9] In choosing a style, he makes an estimate of all three.

The autocratic style, close analysis shows, is probably useful only in unusual situations with typical followers, situations that are rapidly disappearing in industry. Yet numerous such situations continue to exist in real life, and in many factories they can be considered a normal pattern.

Similarly the laissez-faire style is useful only in special circumstances that are not widespread with people at work in the present-day world. In college faculties in those universities where faculty dominance of administration exists, in a few research laboratories, and in all voluntary associations where the followers are unpaid amateurs working under an elected chairman, this style is *de riguer*.

Democratic leadership (widely mistaken for the laissez-faire style) is a median style that is probably most typical of the present-day employment condition. Technical, managerial, and professional employees; skilled persons; teachers; and other white collar workers are probably best managed when this middle of the road approach is employed.

Because the opportunities for applying a style in the wrong situation with the wrong followers are obviously quite numerous, it is not especially surprising that so many supervisors have troubles in their relations with subordinates and in getting their job done.

Can Pertinent Behavior Be Taught?

The question of whether or not such mature behavior that calls for discriminatory judgments can be taught in training sessions is germane. Any kind of supervisory skill that is unteachable may depend on staffing our first- and second-level posts with supermen, which creates an impossible problem in logistics and manpower procurement. Hearteningly enough, there is evidence that training does change supervisory behavior.[10]

How could such sophisticated behavior as recognizing kinds of followers and situations be taught to a supervisor?

1. A rudimentary kind of training would simply be to teach him the content of a chart such as the one in Figure 2–1. He might memorize and recite its content, for example. The limitations here are that no

[9] An expansion from R. Tannenbaum and I. Wechsler.

[10] Norman Maier, *Creative Management* (New York: Wiley, 1964).

guarantee that it would be translated into action could be reasonably made.

2. There should be some kind of assurance that if the supervisor learns such pertinent behavior skills he will have a chance to apply them. For example, if his boss is rigid in demanding permissive management, his chances of cracking the whip with any degree of effectiveness are small. On the other hand, if his boss is a "hard nose" and judges his subordinates by his own standards, any attempt to apply democratic behavior is probably futile.[11]

3. If the man's peers or company policies are designed to create one kind of style in the organization, training to change supervisory behavior is nothing more than an exercise in frustration.

4. The techniques of training should rely on methods that have some research-based evidence that behavior change can be expected. Role play, discussion, lecture, cases, and simulation could be used. In all these action training methods there must be some feedback of success or failure to diagnose the followers and the situation correctly. A major limitation of the uses of role play, cases, and discussion in the past has been that their purposes have been limited to teaching a soft line. They can also be used to teach effective autocracy and autocratic methods that work.

5. The very idea that managers should be trained in techniques of autocracy on the job is so unorthodox to trainers that it may seem heretical. Indeed there may be some dangers in doing so unless it is done hand in glove with instruction in democratic and laissez-faire methods. The objective should be to develop a repertory of behaviors along with analytical skills in choosing the time and place for the use of each.

Some trainers may be aghast at the idea that supervisors should be given a mastery of autocratic methods. "They already know that style too well. It is natural." Such a jaundiced viewpoint toward the nature of man is apparently widely held by trainers who hold to the view that only training in permissiveness is needed.

Yet as a result of many years of training in human relations to inculcate the permissive nature it may well be that when situations and followers call for temporary or permanent periods of autocratic managerial behavior the supervisor is totally incompetent to cope with the problems facing him. This indeed has been the experience in many factories where conditions have demanded tight discipline.

[11] Robert House, "Management Development Is a Game," *Harvard Business Review*, **41** (1963).

Economics of the Firm as a Base Point

Although the quick reference chart (Figure 2-1) for selecting supervisory styles is a suitable guide for training supervisors, it provides no basic underlying reason for the nature of the conditions or for the composition of the work force of followers. Such explanations must be taken from the economics of the business rather than from whimsical, arbitrary choices or from values that are beloved of the social scientist but that may or may not be consistent with the economics of the firm.

When social science values (democracy, freedom at work, self-actualization) clash with economic values, the economic values must predominate because economic values are survival values for the firm. Social science serves economics in the business firm.

Let us look at the economics of the firm (Fig. 2-2). As an economic unit the firm ingests inputs (A), converts them through the processes of the firm (B), and emits goods and services as outputs (C). To do this it assembles capital, which must be preserved (not used up) in the process. The result of this flow is a profit that is either distributed or plowed back in renewed capital.[12]

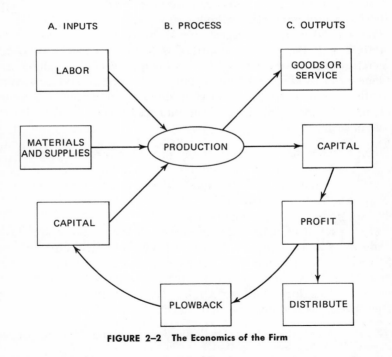

FIGURE 2-2   The Economics of the Firm

[12] Kenneth Boulding, *Economic Analysis* (New York: Harper & Row, 1948).

How Training Serves an Economic Role

This same scheme serves as a focal point for measuring training as a contribution.[13]

1. It can improve the value of the labor input. This can be done by making the labor dollars more effective in terms of output, or it can reduce labor dollars through training higher managers in labor-saving methods.
2. It can maximize the utilization of materials and supplies through teaching supervisors and staff better methods of planning, control, and management of resources.
3. It can reduce capital required (especially working capital such as inventories, receivables, and cash) through training technical, managerial, and professional people in management technique and business practice.

It can also add to human capital through enlarging the skills inventories of people, or making them more available for different positions, and enhancing their power to contribute to the firm.

Such an economic structure may on occasion call for one style of supervisor, or it may call for another. It may call for alternating applications as the economic functioning of the firm demands it.

For example, we can see the firm that has a general climate of good human relations and permissive management. Profits decline seriously and studies show that people have a lax way of handling inventories and that the inventories are swollen. Supervisors have permitted excess personnel to remain on their staff when they are contributing little. There is little attention being paid to cost reduction. First attempts at seeking cooperation through permissive methods meet resistance and threats of "lowered morale" if such pressure continues. Profits continue to slide. The present management expresses confidence in the people and in their style, which borders on laissez-faire in many parts of the firm. Increasing pressure from outside fails to change their easy-going style.

In company after company the effects of rigid management leadership styles have led to such a circumstance. In many, this rigidity of style has required that *different management* (with different behavior) be brought into the firm to exercise the required autocratic behavior to tell and not request cost reduction and more effective control of costs. Recent experience in a large aircraft company, an automobile

[13] G. S. Odiorne, *Personnel Policy* (Columbus: C. E. Merrill, 1963).

company, a midwestern paper company, and a milling firm have been widely described in the business press.[14]

Inflexible adherence of management to a permissive style of management in the face of economic evidence that it is no longer pertinent is a dangerous rigidity. Equally dangerous is rigid adherence to autocratic and dictatorial styles in firms where more permissive styles are needed to free the talents of able men.

In short, the economics of the firm demands that supervisors and managers be trained in a repertory of pertinent skills and a knowledge of when to use which.

Is it not time we started such training?

[14] *Fortune*, Oct. 1962, p. 118; Sept. 1962, pp. 102ff.; Jan. 1962, pp. 64ff.; Feb. 1962, pp. 120ff.

THE SIMPLEX ELECTRONICS COMPANY CASE

Mr. Tasmin, president of Simplex Electronics, was talking to a professor from the state university.

"I've got a management problem here that you might be interested in," he said. "This company has been very successful and has grown considerably since I took it over three years ago. I came back to the company after being with a competitor for several years. I left here in 1951 after ten years in sales and marketing because of a disagreement with the manager of sales here on marketing policies. I took my ideas over to a competitor and gave this company lots of trouble. In fact I proved that I was right in my original argument and became executive vice president of the competing firm. When the presidency of Simplex opened up, the board of Simplex asked me to return as chief executive, and I did so. I came back in 1958 and we've really moved since then. We've clarified the organization, and removed several levels of excess baggage in management. I've got authority and responsibility well defined, and we've put in an executive incentive plan.

"My major problem is that the major executives here don't seem to be really hitting the ball on all counts. They are all good men, and I guess a couple of them wanted my job, but I think they are satisfied that I'm qualified for the job, and nobody left since I was appointed president. Briefly let me give you my organization:

President:
Mr. Tasmin

VP Sales: Joe Ourbach	VP Manufacturing: Clem Bratt	Controller: Fred Bux	Chief Engineer: Mac Hansen
Marketing	Assembly	Accounting	Design
Advertising	Purchasing	Finance	Research
Sales	Quality Control	Personnel	Manufacturing
Contracts			Engineering

"We plan some further changes in the organization, but since we've become accustomed to the present form we will continue it for a while and make changes slowly. That isn't my major problem, however; it's simply that they don't pull in harness.

"Take the manufacturing manager, for example. A terrific pusher, but he rouses some hackles with his insistence that the whole place hinges around his problems. He's always throwing words around like "overhead and burden" when he's discussing a problem with one of the other departments. He seems to feel that engineering and sales are a special cross he has to bear. Now you know he's a good man, but it's hard to get him to play on the team. He is always pushing for something from the others, and it's all take and no give from his viewpoint.

"The sales department follows Joe Ourbach pretty closely in the same kind of lead. Joe feels that since he's producing the income he should be able to stomp on people. He gets into some heated disputes with Bratt, and I end up as referee. When he comes in with a fat contract, he thinks the whole place should stop everything they are doing and serve him. I'm a sales-minded guy, but this guy just won't play it the team way. If he doesn't get his own way he pouts or gets sarcastic.

"The controller is probably the brightest guy of the bunch but he doesn't get along too well with the others. They call him a figure worshipper. He does tend to act as if they weren't real people, just figures on a chart, and I've tried a few times to get him to go out into the plant or the sales field and get in touch with what's cooking there so he'll be more realistic, but so far he hasn't moved. The personnel man reports to him and I understand that on a couple of occasions they have had a row over labor relations matters, and I may have to do something about that.

"Mac Hansen, the chief engineer, is a designer primarily. He gets all wrapped up in a new machine or process and you can hardly speak to him. He really is a genius in this field, but we've been having some trouble over the quality control man and manufacturing and he just lets the poor guy fight his own battles. Our inspectors try to shut something down for bad quality conformance and the foreman in assembly tells them to run it. When the inspector goes to his boss, then the chief inspector gets no backing.

"Take the other day, we had a visual defect on an assembly. The foreman wanted to ship the assemblies and the inspector said they were bad and should be reworked. The inspector took it to the chief inspector who agreed that the assemblies should be reworked. He went to the foreman and manufacturing boss Clem Bratt and got a chewing out for his trouble. The chief inspector then took it to his boss (Mac Hansen) but Mac was busy on a design project and just said, 'You fellows work it out for yourself.' The next thing you know the chief inspector was in my office red-eyed and threatening to quit.

"Another case is that Fred Bux comes to one of the men to find out why costs are rising. The other day, for instance, he wanted to know why the plant was running overtime last month. Naturally he went to the Production Department and Bratt chewed him out—said 'ask the sales department. . . . They are the guys who are overscheduling the plant. . . .' The sales department said that they were merely scheduling against the standards set by manufacturing engineering, and if the standards were too high then Bux should get after Mac Hansen. Mac was in Washington talking to a customer on a design, so the thing ended up in my office.

"In another case a $10,000 account receivable went sour when the customer got in a financial jam . . . in fact his whole company went belly up leaving us with the loss of $10,000. I asked Bux to check out how the credit rating of the guy had been set. He couldn't get an answer. The sales department said that Bux was supposed to check credit, and Bux said that Sales had told him the thing was Triple A. Meanwhile we lost the money and I'm worried that it could be happening again any time because nobody seems to get along.

"Now professor, you've been around a lot and seen a lot of companies. What is wrong with these fellows, anyhow?"

CASE DISCUSSION QUESTIONS

The Simplex Electronics Company Case

1. What do you say in response to Mr. Tasmin's question?

2. Is there a generalized problem here that might be alleviated by training? For whom?

3. Of the specific problems Mr. Tasmin uses for examples, which could be helped by training? For whom?

3 | An Uneasy Look at Motivation Training

Some things which seem virtues would, if followed, lead to one's ruin, and some others which appear vices result in one's greater security and well-being.
—Niccolo Machiavelli

I'M PUZZLED about the training of managers in human relations. We now train them in certain interpersonal skills, like conference leadership and interviewing. That doesn't really suit me however. It seems to me we should also be telling them some of the *inner reasons* people act the way they do. Out of such understanding of behavioral science and scientific knowledge of inward human motivation and applied psychology they should be able to solve their own human relations problems.

Well, the skills courses work. Our conferences are better, and our recruiting and interviewing is better because of the interviewer skill training. But the rest of it doesn't seem to have any effect.

These paragraphs, extracted from a letter from a topflight training director, points up a prevalent problem for trainers.

Has all the talk and work on teaching motivation theory been overdone? I'd like to suggest that it has. Training should change job behavior. It has no useful purposes in teaching managers to probe in private motives.

For more than two decades the training profession has been floundering with the problem of teaching supervisors and managers what motivation is and how to understand it.

Ambiguity, conflicting theory, and lost time and energy in training without much discernible change in behavior in far too many cases suggests that it may be time to take a fresh look at the subject.[1]

The brief made here is that we simply stop talking about the subject of *motivation* theory and turn our attention to something we can accomplish with our own skills—the changing of *job behavior*.[2] This will suggest the following things:

1. The attempt to teach motivation has been a not-too-useful attempt to *teach explanations of behavior*, and it is perhaps time to quit teaching the explanations and focus on changing management behavior itself and the stimuli that shape it. If we cannot identify what behavior we want to change, we cannot change it.
2. We might stop talking about motivation theory as the cure to every problem that besets the company—not because it may not be true but because nobody knows what it is, including the behavioral scientists.
3. Most training aimed at teaching motivation ends up prompting managers to probe into the personal privacy of others and practicing amateur psychology without having a useful effect on job performance or supervisory results. That this pointless and widespread invasion of privacy is resented is increasingly apparent.

Motivation as Proposed Explanation

When we observe a person acting out his role in a job, a society, or an organization, we see several things:

1. We see what he does. His activity (including verbal activity) can be seen, observed, measured, heard, recorded, or even photographed as is done in industrial engineering. He scowls, he smiles, he operates his tools fast or slow, he gets to work on time or late, he remains with the firm or he quits.
2. We also note certain forces that are working on him. His boss is

---

[1] Edward Fleischman, "Leadership Climate," *Personnel Psychology*, 6 (1953).

[2] G. S. Odiorne, "Management Training—The Conflict Between Economics and Social Science," *Training Directors Journal* (Sept. 1964), and "An Economic Approach to Training," *Training Directors Journal* (March 1964).

inconsistent, being a joker one day and a grouch the next. The president is an autocrat or a nice man. His colleagues warmly invite him to play bridge at lunch hour or they let him sit uninvited at his desk. He is urged to join a union or exhorted to remain aloof from it. The organizer does or does not say certain things.

Between these two visible activities (stimuli and behavior) something is taking place, apparently inside the man, that caused (motivated) him to act as he did in the face of such actions. The direction and force of activity is apparently modified by inward forces. In Fig. 3–1 we see these three facets of behavior outlined. In much of our training on

FIGURE 3–1   Stimuli and Behavior Modified by Inward Force of Motivation

motivation we have overemphasized the least manageable of these—that of the inward forces inside the person (organism)—and have tended to ignore the measurement of resulting managerial behavior and more often the controlling nature of stimuli such as organization, boss, peers, and the like.

The temptation to explain these vague inward forces that modify the reaction of persons to the outward and more certain forces that press on them is generally considered to be in the area of motivation theory and most certainly has assumed a much too important and somewhat damaging role in industrial training.

1. For one thing we really do not *know* what goes on inside the person, because "motivation" is merely a kind of abstract concept invented from evidence taken from observed behavior that purports to explain that behavior. St. Augustine put it, "There are hidden deeps in every man which we can never probe." Modern behavioral science is more confident of its ability than Augustine but in truth has done little more than develop imaginative explanations with scant scientific bases. Motivation theory at the present time, then, consists of *proposed explanations* of the behavior of people. Such explanations concern themselves with hidden forces that reside inside the man. They tacitly assume that these inner forces are the major causes of his actions as seen by others. As an exercise, every time you hear the term *motivation* used in management speech or article,

substitute the two words *proposed explanation* and note the paucity of the remainder of the argument.

2. The prevalence of explanations of the inward "needs" of people owe wide acceptance to their plausibility rather than to their verity in fact or their usefulness in action.

3. The body of literature that deals with needs of men is not, strictly speaking, behavioral "science" at all but a rather heart-warming and pleasing kind of philosophical speculation that draws on bits of evidence, combined with personal and private systems of explanation and modes of expression.

CURRENT FASHIONS IN PROPOSED EXPLANATIONS OF BEHAVIOR

The plausibility and clarity of an explanation of human behavior such as the "needs" theory appears to depend on the extent to which it affords satisfaction to the largest number of people. The popularity or fame of the explainer is clearly a part of its value as explanation. Thus motivation theory is best when it meets some demand for assurance on the part of a large number of people. When a "nice man" utters an explanation it is more likely to be accepted as scientific than an explanation emitted by an unpleasant person.

What assurances are met by current motivational theories by the social sciences or behavioral sciences? The first is that democracy in the work place is intrinsically—perhaps morally—better than autocracy or order giving. Thus, if motivation can be explained as consisting of basic needs for physical, ego, and social and self-actualization, arrayed in a hierarchy, the conclusion is obvious. To get people to produce more, you must motivate them by meeting these needs. The logic is irrefutable if we accept their premises about needs as fact. What better way to gain acceptance for such inner-glow-inducing assumptions and moral philosophizing than to garb them in the clothing of "behavioral science"? It is a minor caveat that such speculative postulates are not, in fact, science at all but moral philosophy rooted in the saporous aura of its adherents.

Please be assured that I favor participative management, as I am confident you do (especially for ourselves), over autocratic styles. I think most professors and professional people share this with you and me. I am, however, slightly concerned that your hunch or mine should be disguised as a science, when really it is an assumption that restates an event, theory, or doctrine in terms of my current interests and aversions. I would go further and say that I think that democracy at work is laudable because it prepares people for better citizenship— beating those packaged company courses on "good citizenship" by a country mile for improving our political fiber. I doubt that participative management *always* improves production.

Yet my hunches, assumptions, and private values hardly deserve to be classed as "science," even "behavioral science," which is admittedly at the less tangible end of the science spectrum. If I so classify my philosophies I am perhaps misusing both science and the practitioners who might depend on me to act as broker of the behavioral sciences to the fields of policy and action.

Why then do behavioral scientists vigorously sell their moral philosophies so blithely to the training environment of business management solemnly labeled with the brand name of science? This science posture grows in part out of frustration over failing to really learn very much about motivation. Like the alchemist of the middle ages (an analogy that sadly depicts the present state of much behavioral research) the motivation theorist fondly hopes that the most current explanation is in fact justified by his experiments. Such a hearty desire to succeed leads many of our behavioral scientist friends to realize that an explanation, to be successful, must be stated in terms that seem ultimate and impossible of further analysis.

Many of the senior men in the field, such as Douglas McGregor, Mason Haire, Norman Maier, and others, have warned against over-reliance on current knowledge, but apparently explanation is thirsted after in some kind of search for assurance by trainers and managers. We ourselves have excavated much of the pit into which we fall.

I would not suggest that current explanations are false but merely that they are unproved and may not last. I would further urge that when you rely on training managers in motivation theory you see it for what it really is, a course of proposed explanation that should be regarded with suspicion, be critically evaluated, and discredited where your own experience reveals it to be less than ultimate in explanation.

From the viewpoint of the trainer who hopes to improve the performance of managers in his organization, a more pointed summary might be germane.

If you wish to change managerial behavior, you will do a better job if you define what job result is sought and what behavior you want and give your trainee the knowledge and skill necessary to apply it. The rest is in the hands of his boss, the organizational culture, the organizational climate, his peers, and his subordinates.

If you have concluded that all these forces are arrayed against the use of the behavioral skills you plan to teach your supervisors, I would suggest you forego the training. It will simply prove to be an exercise in conflict creation. The old saying in training "understanding's not enough" can be expanded to cover the situation: "Understanding behavior by having an explanation that is plausible but unproved can be misunderstanding."

The Sparse Knowledge of Motivation

The number of safe generalizations we can acquire from the behavioral sciences is far smaller than we are led to suppose by many of the behavioral scientists themselves. Endless arrays of footnotes attached to positive statements of principles have led many unwary personnel and training men to infer falsely that there is actually a large body of generality for which there is some sizable amount of scientific evidence.

A close examination of the behavioral research on *motivation* is indicative of this condition, although it is probably weaker than some other fields of study. What does the research in motivation really tell us, based on the scientific studies? Here are a few of the more reliable findings of behavioral research:

1. Physical motives are more easily measured, predicted, and controlled than others. Here we learn that
   (a) Food deprivation leads to mass activity of the organism to obtain and eat food.
   (b) Continued intake of narcotics leads to increased activity to obtain and use them.
   (c) Sleep deprivation brings temporary deterioration of behavior.
   (d) Harmful and painful stimuli will increase avoidance of activities.

2. Acquired, social, secondary, learned, or psychogenic motives are less centered in the individual himself and may be considered as true under certain circumstances. (That is, they are not *basic* motives but are situational.) For instance,
   (a) We try to obtain things we like.
   (b) Primates will seek stimulating activity.
   (c) New things get more attention than old.
   (d) Animals expend energy to get variability.
   (e) Children and monkeys like physical fondling.
   (f) All primates associate with one another.
   (g) Some primates dominate others.
   (h) First-born children conform to groups more than those born later and so on.[3]

[3] J. Holland, and B. F. Skinner, *The Analysis of Behavior* (New York: McGraw-Hill, 1961), and Bernard Berelson, and Gary A. Steiner, *Human Behavior—An Inventory of Scientific Findings* (New York: Harcourt, Brace & World, 1964).

The nub of the problem for the industrial trainer is that most of the findings that are reliable are useless because they are so obvious. Those that tackle the real problems lack the precision to definitely state any rules or uniformities that are not situational in nature. Common insights are vested with the cloak of science. Indication is stated as if it were proved. It lacks the requirements of a science that its details be public. "Our findings in three anonymous companies reveal that larger firms have lower morale than smaller firms," for example, never mentions the firms nor the details of the study. The findings are not replicable in another firm or even the same firm at another time. The approach to finding the basic truths of motivation in business is not systematic, does not employ common definitions in the same way from time to time, calls indication proof, and relies excessively on correlations without making it clear that the reasons for the correlation are not readily apparent in the figures themselves.

As an explanation of human behavior on the job, motivation theory is based on the assumption that there is some order and uniformity that characterizes all of that behavior, when in fact nobody has proved such a thesis. Motivation theory is often concerned with right and wrong. However laudable this may be from the viewpoint of biblical or ethical values, it is not a scientific value and for that reason many of the explanations we have been teaching have been useless for prediction and control of job behavior.

Industrial trainers, like management teachers in the colleges, are brokers of behavioral research. In that capacity we have an obligation to the clients—the managers of today and tomorrow—that we train and educate. We must not teach them the uncertain as if it were certain. We must not promulgate plausible explanations as valid scientific truths. Situational findings should not be promulgated as generalities that fit all situations.

Above all, the trainer in industry, like the management teacher in the business school, must be increasingly critical of the caliber of research being conducted by the more fundamental researchers who conduct the experiments. When a behavioral scientist generalizes beyond his data, presuming to report proofs where he may in truth only be reporting indications, it is our responsibility as brokers and policy-shapers to correct his interpretations in the light of what we know of the business situation in our firm and of the world of action.

Most trainers, and unfortunately too many management professors, vacillate between the roles of uncritical acceptance and arbitrary rejection of behavioral research. Perhaps the best guide to the use of behavioral research for the trainer in the coming decade would be *learn more about behavioral research and use it less.*

The Great Assault on Privacy—The End of Uniqueness of Man

Perhaps the most damning case that can be made for the overutilization of the proposed explanations of behavior with which we have become obsessed as laymen is the widespread invasion of personal privacy and the increased scorn for the uniqueness of every man.[4]

This uniqueness in man is made up of all the manifold personal qualities that distinguish him from every other man and from being a number. Pictured as successive stages of human freedom, it might be pictured as in Fig 3–2. The behavioral sciences have strived hard to move us up from the lower level (stage 1) to the second level (stage 2). In the process they have vigorously blocked efforts to achieve the higher level (stage 3) where the *thou* becomes equivalent to *I* in importance.

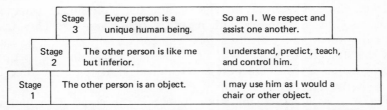

Stage 3	Every person is a unique human being.	So am I. We respect and assist one another.
Stage 2	The other person is like me but inferior.	I understand, predict, teach, and control him.
Stage 1	The other person is an object.	I may use him as I would a chair or other object.

FIGURE 3–2   The Uniqueness of Man: Successive Stages of Human Freedom

Early capitalism and all of the totalitarian countries adhere to the lower levels. Many employment situations today are based on this premise. Modern behavioral science suggests that by understanding behavior we can cause people to become "ego-involved" in their work. They see a scandal in men who see their work as simply a job to be done during the day and who "alienate" themselves from their job at night when they go home. This involvement can be done by the devices of teaching every manager who directs others some ready methods of probing the inner motives of people. This probing gives the manager tools for predicting and controlling behavior. The clever leader thus fixes administrative arrangements to meet these needs and watching expectantly for the higher productivity. Very often, when the boss is watching for the productivity that his amateur psychiatry predicts will be forthcoming, he gets it! The reason for this is not that his psychiatry works; more likely it is because his expectations are worn on his sleeve and everyone rightly interprets this as a polite form of order and hops to it.

Direct orders, autocracy, and demands for specific behavior delivered

[4] Vance Packard, *The Naked Society* (New York: David McKay, 1964).

for fair wages are much more honest than a kind of complex and involuted anxiety game that goes beyond job performance and permits the boss to press into private likes and dislikes, weaknesses, and plain foolishness in his subordinates that bear little relation to the results he is paying for on the job.

CAN CORPORATE EMPLOYEES RETAIN UNIQUENESS?

One of the key questions in suggesting that companies and their training programs eschew imparting skills in exposing individuals is whether or not the corporation and the individual can live together.

If the corporation assumes responsibility for raising mature individuals (whatever that is), it assumes a power and responsibility over private folly and uniqueness that goes beyond even the family, the church, or the university. All our institutions, because they are so defined, provide something to members that the members apparently cannot find alone. The army, the church, and the professional society all have one thing in common with regard to their members: They limit their individual power of discretion. The corporation alone apparently has the strength to make with its employees a bargain that permits a man to retain his uniqueness as an individual at the same time he earns his money.

For such a happy circumstance to occur, the corporation and its officers and managers must see the relationship as an economic one.

1. The company that defines the behavior of people on the job and then pays well enough for that behavior that the individual can be himself off the job is doing more to protect uniqueness in its people than most other forms of institution.
2. The company that teaches its managers to intrude into the motives of its men is arranging for its employees and managers to be controlled in their whole life, not merely at work. Whether it succeeds in this domination or not, the end result must always be a mutual invasion of the individual's privacy by his co-workers slightly above him in the hierarchy.
3. Because the trained psychologist *knows* that he is dealing in proposed explanations and constantly focuses his attention on behavior, his role is quite different from the multitude of amateurs who are taught to ignore behavior and results and leap vigorously into generalities in dealing with people.

LEAVE PSYCHOLOGY TO THE PSYCHOLOGISTS

The latter point brings us to the question of the role of the professional psychologist. Some might interpret the foregoing as a part of the current popular attack on that professional group. Vance Packard and others have attributed the "Naked Society" to the professional activity of this group. I would differ with him in identifying the causes of what he views with such distaste. The professional psychologist is trained to study behavior and uses generalizations as a shorthand for a wide collection of specific behaviors. The amateur product of training programs in "motivation" skips the behavioral content and starts to apply the generalization. The psychologist has standards of confidentiality of information and of reliance on his tools that takes their limitations into account and is suspicious of his own findings. The trainee fresh out of the training department course makes unqualified interpretations, uses his observations indiscriminately, and relies heavily on his lay judgments in a field in which he has had scant training.

The major differences between professional psychologists and amateurs lies in their use of such adjectives as *initiative, drive,* and the like. To the professional, each word implies a repertory of specific behaviors. The amateur merely connects generalizations in which one adjective is defined by another adjective. The first verbalization is explained as a second verbalization with no hard behavioral reference in mind. The result is chaos.

The strong mental illness bias of motivation theory, and the depth to which much training in motivation theory goes, is akin to the first-aid instructor supplementing his course with a few informative lectures on surgery. The temptation to pick up a scalpel and practice may be irresistible to some, especially when they are not warned that there is a difference between applying a small bandage and performing major surgery. Amateur group therapy must fall into the same category.

Summary

The theme of this chapter has been to question the practice of training supervisors and managers in motivational theory. The company has duties to be performed, skills to be applied, and jobs to be done. There are useful economic goals for training.

It is no invasion of privacy to ask that a man behave productively at work for the pay he takes from the firm if he makes the choice freely. Nor is it an invasion of his privacy to ask that he acquire behavioral habits and skills that will help him to perform those tasks well. This is some distance removed from the kind of training that arms him to prove the motives of others and expose his own and to apply to everyone his little repertory of canned explanations.

The ill effects of such training are dual in nature. In assuming that others' inner nature can be so simply explained, he loses his own respect for his private reflections. His taste for the development of uniqueness in himself is stunted by his packaged little dogmas about his inner nature. The enrichment of his own uniqueness is a product of being left alone by those who have some power of persuasion over him and accepting responsibility for his actions.

Is this uniqueness of every man important? I suggest that it is. The training program that helps one man diminish it in others does no service to either party. The right of people to be privately wrong-headed, fuzzy-minded, cantankerous, or brilliant for motives that occur to them at the moment to be suitable is part and parcel of individual freedom and uniqueness that the world all too often suppresses today.

Is it not time we stick to our business and simply teach people how to do their jobs better rather than equipping them—at the same time suggesting to them—that motives are company property?

An Existentialist Model for Training

From the practical business viewpoint, as well as a philosophy that stresses a hands-off label on personal privacy, the doctrines of existential philosophy seem to be most pertinent.[5]

1. Man is responsible for what he is, including his own existence.
2. An individual chooses and makes himself, and it is impossible for him to transcend his human subjectivity.
3. Man is condemned to be free, and once he is thrown into the world he is responsible for everything that he does.

Although we might engage in some disputes over the complete application of Sartre's statement that "man is nothing else than the ensemble of his acts," it is nevertheless a better course of action for the trainer and the manager than its opposite, which we have pursued over the past two decades in training. Its polar opposite would conclude in opposition to the preceding that "The company, not the manager, will decide what he knows, doesn't know, and should know. The company will remove his subjectivity in guiding his behavior by tossing it into a common pot. His dependence will be stressed rather than his freedom, and he is to be relieved of responsibility for deciding whether or not to react to stimuli as his subjective will dictates."

When an existentialist views behavior, he says that the actor is responsible for his acts (and for changing them). If he is given reasons for changing and does so, the responsibility for his acts are still his own.

The trainer becomes less godlike and more mortal in the process.

[5] Jean-Paul Sartre, *Existentialism and Human Emotions* (New York: Philosophical Library, 1957).

THE PAXTON PLANT CASE

Paxton News, April 10, 1958: "Picket lines were established at the Paxton plant of the Anderson Company as 200 workers struck in a dispute over wages."

About a year later, Bill Jones, industrial relations director of the Anderson Company, sat down with the writer at lunch to recreate the major factors in this strike situation. "This was the first and only strike we've had in any of our five domestic plants. Our policy is to deal with union relations at the local level, where problems can be worked out flexibly in accordance with the needs of the particular plant. Except for the Paxton situation, we have enjoyed a harmonious give-and-take type of relationship with each union."

What was the main issue in the Paxton strike?

"It was dispute over wages. We offered flat increases of 12 cents for 1958 and 10 cents for 1959. Including increases in fringe benefits, the total package offered by the company amounted to 28 cents per hour for the two-year contract. The union demanded 15 cents and 15 cents, plus the fringes, and went out on strike."

The company offer seemed to be a generous one. . . .

"It was! Settlements in the area and nationally were running about 9 cents; the same was true in our industry; and we had gotten settlements from 8 to 10 cents in our other plants. Moreover, we were paying above-average wages in the Paxton area, which has consistently been our wage policy for each plant location. The package we offered would have given our Paxton employees wages and benefits well above what other firms were paying in that community. No matter how you slice it, it was a reasonable offer."

Then why do you think they struck?

"I believe the strike took place primarily because the union decided that 1958 was the last chance they had to close the wage differential between the Paxton and Travis plants. Our position was that we were willing to take a strike to avoid the wage differential between the two plants being closed."

Could you tell me more about the wage differential?

"I'll have to go back into the history of the situation a little bit. Paxton was a very depressed area when we set up our plant there about 6 years ago. We set wage rates 10 cents below rates for comparable jobs in our main plant at Travis, which is about 25 miles away from Paxton. We did this on the basis of a survey of average rates in the Paxton area compared with the Travis area. The union in Paxton, a separate local of the same union we have in Travis, has, of course, argued that we should pay comparable rates in the two locations. Actually, the wage differential widened to 15 cents a few years after the Paxton plant got going. There was a lot of unemployment in the area; the demand for our product lines was very uneven; we had a lot of bugs to iron out in our production processes; and we had a significant layoff problem. Consequently, the Paxton local was pretty ineffective in winning wage concessions because the workers recognized this situation and were primarily interested in hanging on to their jobs. As conditions improved in the Paxton area, the differential was gradually reduced to 12 cents at the time of the 1958 negotiations. By demanding 15 cents for 1958 and 15 cents for 1959, the union was trying to wipe out this differential in one negotiation."

You mentioned that the union saw this as their *last chance* to close the differential. . . .

"It appeared to be the last chance because they were aware then of our plans to build another plant that would essentially duplicate the production facilities at Paxton. Construction of this plant began in 1959 at a small town outside of Cincinnati, Ohio. They knew their bargaining power would be reduced once this new plant was in operation, since we could readily expand our production at the new location if having trouble at Paxton. They decided, therefore, to get tough and close the differential while they stood a good chance of beating us. We knew that the differential would eventually have to be closed and committed ourselves to a policy of equalization over a period of time. This was consistent with our long-established wage policy of being above-average in each community, since our surveys showed that area averages in Paxton were gradually approaching those in Travis. This occurred because the Travis metropolitan area was expanding to include outlying communities. But we were not going to have it closed all at once. This was not justified by any objective data, would be damned costly, and would have a tremendous effect on our forthcoming negotiations in Travis because our Travis local couldn't sit by and watch a sister local greatly outdo them. I believe we could have resolved the issue peaceably had we not been dealing with a militant and unreasonable union leadership."

You believe, then, that a further factor in the strike was the lack of responsible union leadership. . . .

"Yes. We were dealing with an international representative who has had a sustained history of being in the middle of strikes. He was a trouble-maker who was about as strongly antimanagement as any union representative I have ever come across. He was completely antagonistic and unreliable, both before and after the strike, and this point of view is shared by other companies and by various people within the union. For example, he made a lot of outlandish statements about our financial position. We offered to have our plant manager and division manager go over our financial records with the negotiating committee but were told that the membership would not believe any figures that were presented. He also distorted our final offer to the press, so we sent out a letter under the president's signature to all Paxton employees explaining our position. He, of course, claimed that we were trying to short-circuit the union. Moreover, we offered to submit the dispute to arbitration in a meeting with the board of conciliation. Our wage policy has been upheld before in cases where we arbitrate wage reopeners, and we were pretty sure our data would stand up in this one. He would not accept arbitration, however, since he needed a face-saver—something he could take to the membership and say 'we won.' He was antagonistic throughout the whole thing and greatly reduced whatever chances there may originally have been of obtaining a settlement."

What about the local union leadership? How did they feel about all this?

"They were pretty amateurish in unionism and played a role of little consequence. Just prior to negotiations, they would run around the plant, find out the gripes and demands of each individual worker, put these all down on paper, and hand them over to the international representative. I must say I never envied him the job of toning down their demands, but the international rep we dealt with before at Paxton was pretty good at this. Perhaps this was a part of the problem, since the local essentially kicked him out before the last negotiations for not getting them what they wanted. I think this helps explain how easy it was for the new international rep to convince the membership to go for broke this last time, even if it meant a strike. He made a lot of promises and trumped up charges and got out on a limb."

You seem to indicate that there were a lot of worker dissatisfactions with conditions in the Paxton plant. . . .

"This was true. In fact, a real sore spot throughout the negotiations was poor union-management relations in the plant. The union, for example, complained that foremen were doing production work, and there were a lot of complaints concerning foremen attitudes toward people. I believe that many of these complaints were valid, since we did have a number of old-line foremen in the plant. They only knew one way to get out production and that was to stand over the men and give orders. And when things didn't go just right, they would either knock a few heads together or barge in and do the job themselves. Another problem was scheduling of work. We had a high rate of absenteeism which resulted in a lot of last-minute requests for overtime work as well as worker complaints concerning the need for more utility men to cover for absentees on the production lines.

The utility men, in turn, were always griping. As soon as they would start one job, they would be asked to fill in on another, and back and forth. There were also a lot of complaints about unsafe working conditions, particularly concerning the running of machinery without adequate safety devices. These conditions had been sources of friction both in negotiations and in our plant union-management meetings for a number of years. It reached the point where there was little trust and confidence between workers and plant management. For instance, when plant management recently decided to pay $5.00 a year toward the purchase of a pair of safety shoes for each worker, many of them complained bitterly that the company did this to make some money off them since they felt they could buy shoes cheaper from another source. This kind of thing was going on all the time."

Do you feel that this situation could have been improved by management action or was it pretty much beyond its control?

"Some of it was inherent in the situation, but a lot of it was our own fault. Right off the bat we did a poor job of screening job applicants, and this had much to do with our absenteeism. And we are still trying to get some of the bad apples out of there. There was little excuse for poor hiring, but it was one of those cases where management was so concerned with getting the plant in operation that they refused the time or expense for reference checks and so on. Another problem was the attitude of one of our two plant managers."

You say two plant managers. . . .

"Yes. You see, we had two district production operations going in two separate buildings with a plant manager over each operation. One of them was a real autocrat from the old school. For example, the working conditions were very poor in his plant because of a formaldehyde solution which was used to treat the products. This coupled with heat during the summer and the fact that the majority of workers worked close to ovens made conditions pretty unbearable at times. We suggested that he investigate a means of ventilating the building and his reply was 'Do you think it bothers them?' While there was a limit to what could be done in this direction, though much improvement has now been made, I think this illustrates his general attitude toward the workers. Our safety experience was also much poorer on his side of the total operation. Another problem was that a worker would receive instructions from his foreman and ten minutes later be told to do the opposite by the plant manager or his assistant. Conditions were much better in the other plant, and it was not too surprising that the union got a strike vote only when the number of workers in that plant became less than in the plant where poor conditions existed. In general, I would say that headquarters permitted too much autonomy in labor relations to the local plant managers. We now have a local personnel department, including a medical and safety program, and have greater central staff and division head involvement in what is going on out there. Relationships have improved considerably as a result."

How was the strike finally settled?

"The final settlement was 14 cents for 1958 and 13 cents for 1959, along with retroactivity on all items. The current wage differential, as a result of this settlement, is 4 cents, and I suspect that it will be closed completely in 1961, at which time the area averages in Paxton will very likely be about as high as those in the Travis area."

How long did the strike last?

"We had decided before the strike that, if it occurred, we would make sure it lasted long enough to hurt in the pocketbook. For this reason, it lasted three weeks, even though it undoubtedly could have been settled before then for the same total amount. I feel sure that this decision was a wise one in that it greatly reduced the likelihood of a strike in either the Travis or Paxton plants since 1958. The memory of three weeks without a pay check is still rather vivid."

CASE DISCUSSION QUESTIONS

The Paxton Plant Case

1. Is there a supervisory training problem here? Define it?

2. What are some possible avenues to solution?

3. What kinds of training would you give? To whom?

4. Are there any nontraining problems that should be solved?

5. Map out a total solution plan.

4 The Trouble with Sensitivity Training

A million zeros joined together do not, unfortunately, add up to one. Ultimately everything depends upon the quality of the individual.

—C. G. JUNG

MANY speaking dates I am requested to make seem to be those in which I am asked to attack something or other. In the past ten years I have been the author of critical speeches or articles on such diverse topics as engineers, appraisals, operations research, college recruiting, industrial training, and college students. It did not surprise me, then, when Cornell University recently invited me to take part in a debate and take the stance "What's Wrong With Sensitivity Training." Such a critical paper on sensitivity training is long overdue. For a form of experimental endeavor to have gone on for more than a decade without more than half a dozen even mildly negative articles or comments being published is somewhat surprising.[1] The absence of criticism of it may account for the fact that there is no research whatsoever that proves its worth in changing behavior. If more criticism had been forthcoming, it might now be on sounder ground. I hope to help alleviate this shortcoming somewhat.

[1] Spencer Klaw, "Two Weeks in a T-Group," *Fortune*, 69 (Aug. 1961), pp. 44–117), and W. H. Whyte, Jr., *The Organization Man* (New York: Doubleday, 1956), pp. 60–61.

Unlike my prior efforts of a critical nature, it has been my experience that one who criticizes sensitivity training is almost certain to incur personal attacks from the adherents. For those who fear arguments *ad hominium* it seems safer to abstain from making critical comments. Often these personalized rebuttals are a highly refined kind of defensiveness that go something like this: "The very fact that you attack sensitivity training indicates that you are in favor of autocratic management and therefore *need* sensitivity training to straighten out your personal inadequacies." The conclusion that is further arrived at is that anybody who sees flaws in sensitivity training is automatically incompetent to be critical because of that. This incompetence could, of course, be overcome if the critic were to undergo such training—or more of it.

The most damaging criticism of sensitivity training is that it has built into its system an automatic rejection of orderly, rational, conscious criticism. This itself is dangerous rigidity, which should be corrected first.

For a field of study to set itself above and immune to the attacks to which every scholar and writer must willingly submit his ideas is prime evidence of weakness. Nor must all such criticism be couched in the rules of the "leaders" in the field. Valid science withstands every attack, including the specious and unfair.

What Is Sensitivity Training?

The distinctive feature of sensitivity training is the T-group. Other forms of training that are sometimes offered concurrently at laboratories are not unique to such laboratories. Role playing, lectures, and action training methods are used in all sorts of training programs of a non-laboratory nature. Most of the comments to which this chapter addresses itself are therefore pointed toward those laboratories that have featured T-group education. T-groups have also been defined as "developmental groups," "laboratory education," and leaderless groups." Their essence is the playing down of an overt behavior on the part of the trainer, with the actions of the group during the sessions being determined by the members. Its emphasis is usually on the "here and now." The group has no purpose assigned it by authority figures, but it is usually understood that it is to be a training session to study interpersonal relations in groups.

This is not a critique of training.
It is not a critique of role playing.

It is not a critique of action training.

It is a criticism of the T-group, its underlying assumptions, and the cultish practices of many of its adherents.

In the absence of major criticism of the method, one must openly inquire "is this because it is perfect or even mostly effective?" The answer here is clearly negative. The suspicion of many who attended that "the king has no clothes" is true.

A detailed study of the periodicals in which research reports on effectiveness of sensitivity training might have been reported between 1948 and 1961 shows that not a single conclusive piece of research has been reported that proves that sensitivity training changes behavior of trainees overtly back on the job. The best rigorously conducted evaluations of sensitivity laboratories have been done by Argyris[2] and Bass.[3] Each of these scholars has studied the behavior of people before and after laboratory experience. Argyris' study showed that the laboratory experience resulted in the class being better able to describe other members of the organization in interpersonal terms before and after training and found that they could do so for those who had been through the training. They did not show improvement in describing behavior of colleagues who had not been through the laboratory, however. His criteria of measurement was the ability to describe others' behavior. No direct tie is made to the training in the sense of showing that it was indeed the laboratory experience that had brought about the change. (Perhaps two weeks together in a submarine would have brought about the same behavior?) This new found verbal skill did not apply at all when it came to describing those people who worked around them who had not been to the laboratory.

Postevaluation questionnaires of the participants showed that the alumni thought that the course was a fine thing. This tells us little. This is a common reaction to all management courses that have been well planned and seriously presented.[4]

2 Chris Argyris, *Interpersonal Competence and Organization Behavior* (Homewood, Ill.: Richard D. Irwin, 1962). This book has undergone serious criticism for its lack of scientific design in *Management Science* (Apr. 1963) in a review by Mason Haire.

3 Bernard M. Bass, "Reactions to 'Twelve Angry Men' as a Measure of Sensitivity Training," *Journal of Applied Psychology*, 5 (Autumn 1965), pp. 157–74; and Bernard M. Bass, "Mood Changes During a Management Training Laboratory," *Journal of Applied Psychology*, 46:5 (Oct. 1962), pp. 361–64.

4 Kenneth Andrews, "Is Management Training Effective?" *Harvard Business Review*, 35:1 (Jan.–Feb. 1957).

Bass' studies showed that sensitivity training alumni were more perceptive of a popular movie's interpersonal relations than a control group that had not been through the course. His other studies showed that mood changes during sensitivity training followed changing patterns.

The important point here is that this is the limit of the factual research evidence that sensitivity training changes behavior. Neither of these evaluations shows anything about behavior change on the job, nor do the 51 books, 68 articles, and 7 pamphlets on the subject published by other organizations. After 13 years or more of laboratory training, then, researchers find that not a single bit of proof exists in published form that laboratory training changes behavior.[5]

We can pass for the moment the criticisms of Lewinian Group Dynamics Theory, which have taken up somewhat more space.[6] They are not especially relevant to the training director, whose principal concern is whether or not he should send his managers to a laboratory to be trained. The context of this discussion deals with sensitivity training as a means of changing management behavior.

Two recent reports have been added to the literature that by their findings might indicate that all is not well with the customary methods of sensitivity training. One study of a group in Denmark concedes that at least one important practitioner has been perplexed by the failure of sensitivity training to change behavior back on the job.[7] His trial solution was to combine coaching back on the job with laboratory experience, which he reported anecdotally did bring change. Another article, frankly speculative, theorizes that any effects of sensitivity training can be attributed to the informal atmosphere accompanying laboratory sessions, casual clothes, name tags, and so on, which brings on regressive behavior in the attendees.[8] This, too, has been untested, but in the absence of other evidence is perfectly germane as an explanation.

Leading figures in the field flatly state that there is no evidence that

---

5 Jon Lowrey, and Robert J. House, "Sensitivity Training—Where Do We Stand Now?" Unpublished ms., forthcoming in *Management of Personnel Quarterly*.

6 Hubert Bonner, *Group Dynamics* (New York: Ronald Press, 1959). Chapter 15 summarizes the gist of many key arguments of a critical nature about group dynamics, including its conceptual basis, its panacean concept of democracy, and excessive veneration.

7 Hjelholt Gunnar, and Matthew Miles, "Extending the Conventional Training Laboratory Design," *Training Directors Journal* (March 1963), p. 3.

8 C. R. Mill, "A Theory for the Group Dynamics Laboratory Milieu," *Adult Leadership*, II:5 (1959–60), pp. 133–34.

sensitivity training changes behavior back on the job. Bass, for example, states:

Whether sensitivity training decreases sensitivity on the job or success as a leader on the job still has to be demonstrated.[9]

Although the same criticisms apply to many training courses, there are empirical studies that demonstrate behavior change from other forms of training that has not been proved of T-groups,[10] especially role play and discussion.

In the absence of any research evidence that demonstrates that sensitivity training changes behavior, we are left with nothing but anecdotal evidence and example drawn from experience. This qualifies any number of people to judge. The anecdotes that follow actually occurred.

Such evidence shows that sensitivity training is enjoyed by many who attend, is viewed with suspicion by others, and on the negative side has had bad effects on other individuals and organizations. Such anecdotal evidence is not hard to collect. This is especially true when one gets into places where the fringe groups of unskilled practitioners have been selling numerous variations of sensitivity training to companies. Nor can the "serious" practitioners avoid responsibility for the numerous persons (of admittedly undetermined numbers) whose careers in business have been impeded, damaged, or diverted by laboratory experimentation that intervenes in the serious business of a man and his boss relating to one another.

In the absence of any firm proof that the people leading the sensitivity training movement are sure of what they are doing, we might well suggest that they retire from the important business of rendering advice about running a firm until they are certain they know what they are doing. Essentially they are outsiders. This role is perfectly acceptable and useful when the outsiders bring new and proved insights. When they bring unproved ideas that they hope to test and allude to their validity and usefulness to the firm when they are actually unproved, they should be rejected. Emerson put it as follows: "He has a right to meddle who has a heart to help." This, too, might be a basis for holding off on the use of sensitivity training for many trainers.

[9] Bernard M. Bass, review of *Leadership and Organization*, by R. Tannenbaum, I. Wechsler, and F. Massarch, in the *Journal of Business*, **XXXV:3** (July 1961), p. 235.

[10] For a typical report, see Norman Maier, "An Experimental Test of the Effect of Training on Discussion Leadership," *Human Relations*, 6:2 (1953), pp. 161–73.

Is Sensitivity Training Really Training?

Training should change behavior. How can we demonstrate changed behavior? We should be able to measure it. One of the most common outcomes of sensitivity training is that the people who undergo it describe the experience as one that "I am sure has had an effect on me but it's too early to tell just how." These are the fortunate ones.

ANECDOTE NO. 1

Not long ago a large engineering company in the Midwest was prevailed upon by a consulting firm to bring a group of their research executives to a lodge in Wisconsin for sensitivity training. The leader of the session had no prior training in the conduct of such sessions. During one horrible weekend he broke down the barriers of formal courtesy that had substituted quite successfully for human relations in this successful laboratory for many years. People spoke frankly of their hostilities. At this point they went back to the laboratory, their dislikes laid bare, with no substitute behavior being provided. Chaos immediately took over. People who had worked in good-mannered pomposity for years, turning out patents and papers at a prodigious pace, began to engage in organized "politicking" to get square. Senior scientists quit in droves and a major purge took place. Candid observations made up at the lake hung heavy between colleagues who had become accustomed to the equilibrium of their Ph.D. status systems, and they became human beings, which of course could ruin any good research organization. People who had learned that they were seen as SOB's were somewhat less than grateful to the colleague who had enlightened them. The duplicating department went on two shifts, turning out resumés of people who wanted out. Several alcoholic conditions became active again.

This is training?

Training should produce changed behavior, which is further justified only by the possibility that this changed behavior contributes more to the goals of the organization than earlier behavior. To qualify as sound training, it would seem that five criteria should be met.

CRITERION NO. 1

In good training the desired terminal behavior can be identified before the training begins. Sensitivity training simply does not do this. It rightfully can state that it will change the verbal behavior of some people who take part. It has little or no idea what any other terminal behavior will be or whether it will be more or less productive than when the man started.

ANECDOTE No. 2

Not long ago I interviewed a young company president who had returned a month before from a sensitivity training laboratory conducted only for young presidents. Here is what he told me:

We sat around the Princeton Inn flagellating one another for days on end. After I graduated from Harvard Business School, I bought a gray flannel suit and some half glasses and went into the family business. Then I went to this thing. Now I have to get it out of my system that I am an incompetent slob who is riding on his ancestor's coattails. A lot of those guys spent the whole time crying about the vice presidents who run the business while they held the inherited stock. A few of them who married the boss's daughter wanted to have a public catharsis over the fact that nobody respected them because they were executives who married their job. One guy got plastered and kept me up until 3 A.M. telling me some horrible tales about his marital problems. I've got to keep busy to shake that horrible mess at Princeton and get back to making a buck for the company.

Here are some typical statements of terminal behavior sought by laboratory training:

1. To achieve authenticity in interpersonal relations.
2. To unfreeze managers' minds.
3. To develop self-esteem in trainees.
4. To improve human relations through achieving interpersonal competence, internal commitment, and the process of conformation.

Three serious questions arise about training that states its objectives in such terms:

1. What is the behavioral definition of such words as *authenticity* or *esteem*. Are they not so lacking in precision as to be immeasurable?
2. Presuming they were precisely defined and could be measured, would sensitivity laboratory training change them?
3. Presuming that the changes did occur, what evidence exists that such a behavior change would be good for the man and the company?

CRITERION No. 2

The course of change is comprised of some logical small steps in good training. In sensitivity training not only are the participants unaware of what the outcome will be, but in many instances, because there are no controls, neither are the trainers. In most laboratories the coordination of what the respective trainers will do at what time is as vague at the middle and end as it was in the beginning. Typically the staff of a laboratory is assembled by mail or telephone from the in-group that conducts such sessions. They agree to gather one day ahead of the arrival of the subjects to be trained. They divide up the chores under the direction of the assembler of the program. There is little chance for any detailed checking of objectives of individual sessions or any careful planning so that progressive stages of training will occur. Accordingly most such sessions lack many of the elements of training that might change behavior simply because they are so ineffectually run. If a general statement of objectives is made, it goes along the line of saying something like "open up their minds" or something equally vague. *How* open, or even what an open mind *is*, is not defined.

If we analyze carefully the sessions that comprise the two- and three-week sensitivity training session we note that the objectives are often stated in such terminology as teaching the student "to recognize," "to feel," "to relate," "to begin to understand," "to gain self insight," "to become aware," or similar phrases. Little if any behavioral terminology is used to describe what the persons will do, do differently, or stop doing in terms of specific actions. Presumably these changes are in the smooth muscles or glands. There is little overt behavior prescribed—not even precise verbal behavior.

Emitted behavior of any specific definition in the laboratory setting is not clearly classified as being required for success, and the only reinforcements that shape behavior are those randomly provided by a group of unknown composition. (The major criterion for admission is that of being able to pay the registration fee. This builds in a reinforcement of middle-class values and little more.)

Value changes are not based on careful analysis of the present values that are to be changed, nor even are explicit statements of desired terminal values sought. Because value changes could be measured only by verbal or written behavior at the end of the course and no such values are clearly defined, the efforts at measuring behavior change run into logical blocks. The few efforts at evaluation of behavior change from laboratories have not been clearly successful and certainly are not wholly reliable.

Because success in the course is not clear, the feedback of reinforcing evidence of achievement of intermediate steps in personal behavior change is impossible. Because the T-group is the major source of reinforcement and its values are mixed, the reinforcement of emitted behavior is just as likely to be for the wrong things as the right things.

Specific causes of changes are unclear. More pointedly, there is no attempt to measure the relative effects of the different parts of the laboratory on the learner. Are the T-groups the crucial variable? How can we be sure the T-group has not changed the trainee in one direction and the lectures in another? Where observation and anecdotal evidence point to behavior change after a laboratory session, how can we know which training method effected the change; the role playing (which has been proved to change behavior even outside laboratory groups), the informal bull sessions, or simply the opportunity to live in a closed community for two weeks with others? Do different T-group leader personalities (or reputations) or marvelously skilled lectures such as Argyris delivers have differential effects in changing behavior? Because we cannot prove behavior change, all these questions are merely speculative.

CRITERION NO. 3

The learning is under control. The major reason that control is not present in sensitivity training is that it is based on creating stress situations for their own sake, which may go out of control and often do. Here is what happened in one group:

ANECDOTE NO. 3

Explosions of angry disagreement were the order of the day. People turned on one member and evaluated him publicly, voicing open disapproval of him. Others wondered why they felt upset when their fellows began to get angry at each other, and tried to cut off the argument before they got it off their chest.[11]

Out of this the trainees are left to "discover for themselves" how this stress can be converted into such things as business meetings, conference leadership, coaching and counseling, and other useful business practices.[12] This transference is a mere detail, it seems, that any person can do. This seems to be a very broad jump and one that my training experience shows just does not take place.

And what if this transference *does not* take place?

Then the trainee has been through an emotional binge that has some totally unpredictable effects. The possibility that uncontrolled experience may be harmful is just as probable as its being helpful. In any event it can hardly be called training.

[11] I. R. Wechsler, "A New Focus in Executive Training," *Advanced Management*, 20 (May 1955), p. 19.

[12] Harvey D. Tchirigi, "The Contribution of Stress to Sensitivity Training," *The Personnel Administrator* (Mar.–Apr. 1961), p. 44.

The lack of control over learning in sensitivity laboratories is further evidenced by the lack of control in the exercises. This is coupled with *too much* control at other times. Add to this a lack of control over facilities and management that could seriously affect the attitudes of registrants, and the end result is chaotic—planned and unplanned, but chaotic.

ANECDOTE No. 4

At Bethel in 1955 during one afternoon of gang-role-play, several of us who were simulating vocational school teachers in a make-believe school system attempted to add reality to the exercise by forming an unauthorized but quite realistic teachers' union. Two immediate reactions followed. First, the staff howled with dismay that this was not part of the exercise, and second, the whole session took on a touch of vitality as the industrial executive playing superintendent of schools started an energetic union-busting campaign. Finally, after an unauthorized mass meeting on the lawn deciding whether or not we would strike the whole training laboratory, we were politely requested by the trainers to break up our union because we were fouling up the whole exercise.

To be a truly controlled "laboratory" there would be more careful matching of roommates, tight limitations on private liquor stores, closer attention to boy-girl relations, and careful attention to the internal management of such mundane matters as meals, lodging, visual aids, and reading inputs. Many of these are handled rather cavalierly in laboratories.

CRITERION No. 4

There are selection standards for admission. The more serious defects of sensitivity training relate to admissions standards. The present condition is such that anybody with the registration fee can attend. He may already be sensitive and aware—in fact may be too much so. You could make a good case that far too many people who are attracted to it are those who are emotionally high strung and overly sensitive. They will, of course, be admitted if they have the registration fee. There is no optimum level of sensitivity defined in such courses—merely that you will probably go away more sensitive than you came. How about the overprotected individual whose pressing need is that he toughen up a bit because he is already a mass of quivering ganglions, thinking and feeling on several levels of perception at the same time, and therefore totally incompetent at the world of business infighting. For this person the laboratory becomes a great psychological nudist camp in which he bares his pale sensitive soul to the hard-nosed autocratic ruffians in the

T-group and gets roundly clobbered. He goes away with his sense of inferiority indelibly reinforced. The bullies, of course, have also reinforced their roughneck tendencies on him. There are more J. Alfred Prufrocks who voluntarily enroll in sensitivity training than there are Babbitts or Cash McCalls.[13]

Anecdote No. 5

In one laboratory I attended, one woman who never should have been admitted because of a prior mental breakdown "went berserk" (as a fellow T-group member described it) and was under psychiatric treatment until she returned home.

Anecdote No. 6

A large food firm directed 60 of its middle managers to attend a "Conference Leader Training Seminar." The actual but not stated intent was to conduct T-groups. A high official attended and noted individual behavior under stress. Several persons who "didn't measure up" had marks placed in their career folders.

Anecdote No. 7

A slick brochure advertising a "Leader Training" course drew several dozen enrollees to a course. Those coming found themselves in T-group training. Shaken badly, two left early, and another broke into tears several months later describing his public humiliation to an interviewer. His T-group had voted him "the worst leader they would like to work for." The specification of their charge? He was "too wishy washy." His job was procurement analyst and he was highly regarded by his superiors for his technical knowledge.

Anecdote No. 8

A large company established a laboratory as one of numerous training courses. Over several years the laboratory's reputation became "a place where the problem managers go to get straightened up." The staff attempted unsuccessfully to allay this fearful image. One successful and able manager was assigned to attend and immediately resigned to accept another job. A quick survey of the past enrollees showed that the terminations among this group was quadruple that of the company

---

13 Prufrock is the principal figure in a poem by T. S. Eliot, "The Love Song of J. Alfred Prufrock," from *Poems Written in Early Youth*, 1909–1925 (London: Faber, 1967). What makes Prufrock pathetic rather than comic is his awareness of his own frustrations. He is repelled by actuality yet longs for the things of the earth.

management as a whole. Others who graduated but did not quit were extremely bitter about this singling out. Others were reported by their managers to have "gotten back on the track and are now doing topflight jobs after the treatment."

CRITERION NO. 5

Evaluation of results. The most common result of taking sensitivity training is that the individual reports that "I really don't know what happened to me if anything but I feel that I have been through an experience." This perfectly accurate statement could be said of an individual who has visited a jail, an insane asylum of the older type, a home for blind children, or the emergency ward of the local hospital. Because the sensitivity trainers do not know what the goal of such training is, any road will get them there, and any outcome is exactly what can be expected. Small wonder nobody has yet done a rigorously executed evaluation of effect.

An experience it is, without doubt. Training, I am afraid, it is not, and the company that spends its cash on sending people to the more esoteric kinds is being unfair to their shareholders. No proof has been shown that it changes behavior on the job.

The escape that is often taken is that "we aren't really practicing therapy but are merely teaching group dynamics"; this is easily said but the end efforts prove otherwise. Couple this opportunity for playing God over managerial styles with hard-sell direct-mail advertising and you have the makings of a most harmful movement.

Group dynamics differs from sensitivity training. The process of group psychotherapy in sensitivity training is not very different from the study group dynamics through action training and role playing. The use to which the process is put is entirely in the hands of the practitioner. In an attempt to achieve dramatic effects and to bring about emotional stimulus that guarantees a sure-fire reaction from the customer, far too many of the sensitivity trainers are indeed playing God with their clients—in some cases without even realizing what a powerful instrument they are tinkering with.

ANECDOTE NO. 9

One team of business school professors will take into any company a one-week sensitivity course that has as an integral part of its package a simulated phone call from the man's mistress, threatening revelation of everything to his wife. This comes in along with calls from customers threatening to cancel contracts and a simulated call from his wife announcing that their oldest child has cancer.

This is management training?

Adapting the processes of sensitivity training into sound training of managers in group processes is not difficult to do. The key ingredient is to identify some terminal behavior that we would like to see in the trainee. Among these are such group related matters as

1. How to lead problem-solving conferences.
2. How to lead decision-making conferences.
3. How to avoid being a blocker in conferences.
4. How to elicit complete participation in meetings.
5. How to identify and use the various roles of conference members.
6. How to gain cooperation between competing groups.
7. How to organize committees and conferences.

Such things might be taught, that is, behavior change effected and perhaps even measured. Yet these could be taught without a T-group.

One of the basic assumptions of laboratory training is that "value changes lead to behavior change, and never the reverse." This is only half true. Skill development leads to attitude and value change if practice of the newly acquired skill brings knowledge of success from parties whose approval is important.

Anecdote No. 10

Managers of a chemical company were (lecture) trained in techniques of political activity for managers by direction of their president. Many were hostile or indifferent to begin. As the course progressed they were required to meet with county and municipal officials and take part in civic affairs. They found that they could understand and question actions of officials intelligently. Over 30 are now serving actively in civic activity, which they had not done before. Their indifference is now changed to zest and enthusiasm as they continue to see good effects in a better community and in personal satisfaction and success. "I used to be a political slob, but now I'm running for Democratic County Committee," one said.

Sensitivity Training and Business Objectives

The real flaw in sensitivity training is that it is not consistent with business and the economic world we live in. We are trapped in our own standard of living. We may struggle through proofs that the new participative styles of management are more productive than autocratic styles, but then there crops up General Motors, which is built on tight technical organization and tight discipline and is the most successful corporation that ever existed.[14]

Business is primarily an economic institution into which the inputs are materials and supplies, labor, and beginning capital. Through the process of production we obtain outputs of goods and services and ending capital. The objective of this output is profit, from which comes growth and survival of the firm, and produces the end product of it all, which is *consumption*.

ANECDOTE No. 11

Even the new utopians are caught in this trap. They are experts at consumption like the rest of us. I once heard of a study that proved that people do not work for money alone. I invited the researcher who had done the study to speak at a conference. I found that he wanted $500 to make the speech, and when I sadly reported that we could not afford it, he would not come. If you have tried to get a good human relations trainer for your company's training program these days, you know that the rates are from a minimum of $250 a day up to $750 (for the man whose researches prove more about the idealistic nature of man than the lower-priced one).

Survival of firms is serious business these days. Of the 4,500,000 companies in this country, the average length of life is seven years; 450,000 will go broke this year and another 375,000 will go inactive. Managers obviously need training in their jobs to help them and their firms survive. All too often they have learned their management by imitation. Behavioral science has much to offer in finding new and better ways of managing. This could be greatly accelerated if the new utopians could become more objective in their science. The great difficulty is not whether they are wrong in their assumptions about participative versus autocratic management—theory X versus theory Y, or liberty versus oppression. The point is that we cannot trust them to be good scientists as long as every research proves one position to which our common experience tells us there are some exceptions that work even better.

Many businessmen know the true value of situational thinking, in which you are sometimes autocratic or downright ruthless, coupled with other times when you are as gentle and refined as a doting mother with people's sensibilities, and the whole range of actions in between.

[14] For two current researches that cast some doubts on proof of the ill-effects of "close supervision," see Martin Patchen, "Supervisory Methods and Group Performance Norms," *Administrative Science*, 7 (1962), pp. 275–94, and Sigvard Rubenowitz, "Job-Oriented and Person-Oriented Leadership," *Personnel Psychology*, 15:4 (Winter 1962), pp. 387–96.

A form of management training that has good guys and bad guys arbitrarily built into it to fit a utopian ideal of panacean democracy is not safe for a business or any other form of administrative organization to experiment with. Until the sensitivity trainers have come forth with a school that takes overly sensitive man and toughens him up into a rough and ready model of man as well as the reverse, I can only suggest to businessmen that they avoid the entire cult.

Back to the Drawing Board

The time has come, I would suggest, when the entire sensitivity training movement should be drawn back to the campus and overhauled by the more responsible behavioral scientists who started it all. My specific recommendations would be as follows:

1. A clearer distinction between group dynamics and group psychotherapy should be drawn in laboratory objectives.
2. People conducting group psychotherapy should be required to be certified and licensed by law, just as psychologists are now licensed or approved by professional bodies and by state law. The conduct of group psychotherapy without a license and appropriate professional qualifications should be outlawed.
3. Group dynamics for business is badly in need of more attention to the actual problems that administrators face in making their organization perform. Training procedures that identify desired terminal behavior and that have an orderly path toward it should be developed. This means that the group dynamics researchers must be supplemented by practical trainers who are fully aware of the training needs of administrators.
4. There should be concerted action by the responsible behavioral scientists to rout from their field the many fast-buck operators who are peddling the many weird variations of basic science by hard-sell direct-mail advertising. The formation of an association of accredited firms and agencies for the conduct of group dynamics training comparable to the association of management consultants is badly needed.

Unless this takes place, and soon, the entire region of behavioral science will suffer badly. The responsibility for this action lies with the serious and able behavioral scientists who comprise the inner circle.

As an advisor to business I can only tell those with whom I talk, wait until this reform is done before you turn any of your successful and mature managers loose in this barren steppe where the wolves lie in wait.

THE ROCKWELL-HAYES COMPANY CASE

THE COMPANY

The Rockwell-Hayes Company is the second oldest publishing house in New York City. At present it maintains a steady, though smallish (Harper & Row, Doubleday, and Random House usually double Rockwell-Hayes' annual volume) output of highclass books—John Updike, J. D. Salinger, James Baldwin, as well as a healthy variety of topical nonfiction. Rockwell-Hayes' current bestseller is a well-documented bombshell on censorship in the public schools of New York State.

As of January 1963, there were a total of 210 employees in all departments of the company. Though employment turnover on the lower levels is fairly rapid, Rockwell-Hayes seldom has difficulty filling its positions. It is, as both employees and outside observers readily admit, a "prestige outfit"; it prints no "pulp," prints and binds its books with quality materials, and occupies four floors of a small, upper Park Avenue office building. The colonial decor of the first-floor lounge and reception room accurately reflect the taste and image that, in general, the firm embodies.

The organization of Rockwell-Hayes is not systematic (see Fig. 4–1). As its president occasionally notes, "Like Topsey, we just seem to have grown. When there's a need, we accommodate it. That's all." The atmosphere of the company, however, in no way reflects the seeming casualness of its organization. New employees are often taken back by the pompous air of

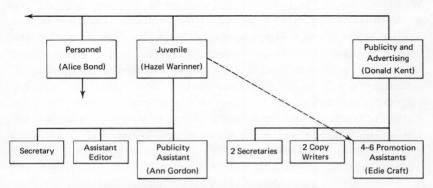

FIGURE 4–1 The Rockwell-Hayes Company's organization chart, showing the relation of the Personnel, Juvenile, and Publicity and Advertising Departments

their superiors and the chill of personnel relations. Almost everyone is addressed as "Mr., Mrs., or Miss." First names are considered gauche for all except the younger secretaries (namely, so the word goes, those who did not attend college). And beneath this austere formality, as the new employee discovers in a few weeks, there are the uneasy tensions of a sometimes almost demonic competitiveness. One young college girl, who worked in the Textbook Department for several months after her graduation—before resigning —gave as her reason for departing: "This place is full of people who are only vying for their own egos. I came to work, not to slit people's throats." And although she was accused of "sour grapes" by those who knew of her leaving, there was more than a grain of truth in her statement.

Most of the younger staff of the company are college graduates, most of them relatively fresh off the campus and eager to work their ways up in the publishing world. Commencing in the mid-winter of each year, the personnel office is flooded with applications and letters of inquiry. The few most promising are answered with acceptances, and the others are simply thrown out after a form letter of regret is returned. As a result of this fat supply, most of the younger staff finds itself occupied with menial and routine work—functioning at levels that are far below those of their full and real abilities. A Stanford girl with a M.A. in creative writing, for example, is now employed as a message girl with promises of an editorial position after two years of employment. She earns $57.50 a week.

THE PEOPLE

HAZEL R. WARINNER, EDITOR OF THE JUVENILE DEPARTMENT

Miss Warinner's resume, as she wishes it known to the public, is shown in Fig. 4–2. It was dictated to her secretary with the appended note. Miss Warinner is now 62 years old and is, for all intents and purposes, a lifelong Rockwell-Hayes employee. Regardless of the adverse criticism that is often directed at her, she is a highly competent business woman with a remarkable, if brusque, ability to cut through extraneous details, dispose of red tape, and so on. In her turns, Miss Warinner is competitive, accusing, and defensive. To most of her employees she is a "slavedriver," but those employees are also aware that she drives herself as hard as anyone else. Most of the dislike she arouses (and there is plenty of it) comes from her substitution of bluntness and rudeness for normal businesslike tactics. Miss Warinner slams phone receivers, writes curt memos (see Fig. 4–3), and when she speaks, it is usually with vituperation. To her current secretary, Miss Warinner is "just a bear." But the fact remains that Miss Warinner gets work done efficiently and well, and for that reason the company president and managing editor are more than happy to have her aboard. Her efficiency has brought Rockwell-Hayes several very lucrative contracts in recent years, including the Latin version of *Winnie, the Pooh* (or *Winnie, Ille Pooh*).

Resume: Hazel R. Warinner (for publicity purposes)

Born in Greenwich, Conn.—still lives there in same farmhouse.

Farmington School for Girls, Farmington, Conn., 1922.

Vassar College, 1926.

Cambridge University Summer Session, 1928.

First job: copy holder, Beaconfield Press, Sept. 1926–Jan. 1927.

Second job: Direct Mail division of Textbook Department, Rockwell-Hayes Company.

With Rockwell-Hayes ever since: in college texts, assistant to Manager of Textbook Department, Assistant Manager of Publicity and Advertising Department, Associate Editor, Editor of Children's Books.

Member: Children's Book Council, Library Committee, WNBA, Boys' Club of New York City.

Avocation: Farmer.

(Miss Warinner asks that you make copies of this and keep them in a "safe place," as she is tired of these requests!)

FIGURE 4–2

Memos from Miss Warinner

I. To: Craft
   From: HRW
   I want the lists for *Mother West Wind* now!
II. To: Craft
    From: HRW
    Forget that Salinger mailing. The Children's Book Council needs a general release on the *Red Wheelbarrow*. See me at 3:00.
III. To: Craft
     From: HRW
     I don't want to be bothered by any more publicity requests.
IV. To: Craft
    From: HRW
    The *Red Wheelbarrow* releases should have been out two days ago. See me.
V. To: Craft
   From: HRW
   Where is the *Mother West Wind* mailing? This isn't a country club.

FIGURE 4–3

DONALD KENT, MANAGER OF PUBLICITY AND ADVERTISING

Mr. Kent is a graduate of Carlton College in Minnesota and has a M.B.A. from the Wharton School in Philadelphia. He is 43 and a family man—basically easy going and on the side a water-color painter and a player of Bach on the classical guitar. When he first came with Rockwell-Hayes seven years ago, he had several hassles with Miss Warinner—losing each time. Since then he has reluctantly, but obligingly, yielded to her demands—such as they have been. His department has ten employees, compared to only four in the Juvenile Department.

ALICE BOND, DIRECTOR OF PERSONNEL

Mrs. Bond is the newest salaried employee at Rockwell-Hayes, coming over from the personnel department of a downtown city bank four months ago. Though married for 22 years, she has never had any children and has worked all her life in the personnel area. Her husband is a successful stockbroker, and the two of them live in a large apartment on Central Park West, where they entertain often and lavishly. Mrs. Bond is a warm and sympathetic person, and it is generally acknowledged that she was hired in an effort to ease the tensions that have become increasingly unpleasant at Rockwell-Hayes in recent years. Miss Warinner appears fiercely jealous of her. Most of the younger girls like her; those she knows she calls by their first name, causing Miss Warinner to dub her "the Rockwell-Hayes mother figure."

EDIE CRAFT, PROMOTION ASSISTANT, PUBLICITY AND ADVERTISING DEPARTMENT

Miss Craft is 22 and is currently on a leave of absence after three years at Sarah Lawrence College. When she was hired, she expressed a desire to return to Rockwell-Hayes after her graduation, explaining that she was taking the year off now "to see what the real world is like." She is industrious, attractive, and personable—getting along well with the others in her department, as well as her immediate superior, Mr. Kent. Her duties consist mainly of preparing publicity mailings for Rockwell-Hayes' new books—mailings she sends to publishers' journals, libraries, and so on.

ANN GORDON, PUBLICITY ASSISTANT, JUVENILE DEPARTMENT

Miss Gordon is 24 and a graduate of Middlebury College in Vermont. She is not happy working at Rockwell-Hayes because, as she puts it, "there's nothing to do." Seldom does she have enough work during the day to keep her busy, so she spends her "free" time doodling and sketching pen and ink drawings for possible use in forthcoming juvenile publications. Her job is supposed to be roughly equivalent to that of a promotion assistant in the Publicity and Advertising Department, and she does get occasional books to send out and lists to prepare. She plans to leave Rockwell-Hayes in June and go to Ireland. She has been with the company three years.

THE SITUATION

As Mrs. Bond looks over the turnover figures for the Publicity Department, she finds the following:

1. In the last six months, three promotion assistants have left Rockwell-Hayes for other positions.
2. In the preceding three years, seven promotion assistants have left Rockwell-Hayes for other positions.

Word-of-mouth usually attributes these departures (all have been young college graduates) to marriage or poor pay. Actually, only three of the ten girls have married and only two left for better pay opportunities. Several times since she has been with Rockwell-Hayes, Mr. Kent has come to Mrs. Bond asking if something couldn't be done about the rapid turnover of his promotion assistants. This turnover, he feels, has been hampering the effectiveness of his department; he cannot, however, put his finger on any specific reason the girls are leaving his department with such regularity; pay is proportionally equal to that of other jobs of the same level in the company, and the work he assigns his people is demanding but not taxing. Mr. Kent has intimated several times that the fault lies with Mrs. Bond's predecessor, who was not careful about the girls who were hired.

While she was pondering this situation, Edie Craft, one of the promotion assistants, came into Mrs. Bond's office, obviously in a lather.

"I'm quitting this place right here and now!" she blurted out. "It's all fine and well, so long as I just do my regular P. and A. work that Mr. Kent gives me—but I just can't handle Miss Warinner's lists too! Why, she's over in the P. and A. office, or calling one of us up at least twice a day. 'Do this . . . Do that . . . Oh, forget about Mr. Kent's work; there's plenty of time for that.' And when I go to Mr. Kent, he just shrugs his shoulders and says he's sorry, but he just can't help it. I've been to Mr. Kent three times in the last two weeks, and I finally got him to speak to Miss Warinner about giving this work to Miss Gordon. That's where it belongs! Obviously! But oh, no, Miss Gordon is terribly busy—busy, my foot; she's over there sketching rabbits. And rabbits are Art Department work. I happen to know for a fact that Miss Gordon is bored to tears. Poor, dear Miss Gordon!! I tell you, I've had enough."

Mrs. Bond succeeded in quieting Miss Craft and persuaded her not to leave for the time being. Meanwhile, she was trying to figure out what her next step would be; she knew that the president and managing editor would not want to be bothered by this problem. She would have to handle it herself.

CASE DISCUSSION QUESTIONS
The Rockwell-Hayes Company Case

1. You have been retained as a consultant to Rockwell-Hayes. The president tells you he has reserved one enrollment for one of his three people for a sensitivity laboratory. He asks whether you would recommend one of the people in the case to attend. Which one would you choose? Bond? Warinner? Kent? Ann? Edie?

2. Why did you choose that person?

3. Is there anyone who should not be permitted to attend?

4. Explain your reasoning.

Training by Objectives— Using a Systems Approach to Training

ALTHOUGH it is apparent that an economic approach to training is timely, simply changing the emphasis of the training effort does not comprise a permanent solution to the training of management and administrators. More importantly, the nature of training should be so devised that it has sensing devices and control procedures that keep it constantly attuned to the vital and prevents its deviating from the important into the trivial—or even into the harmful. This deviation has been a costly practice in the past and could well continue into the future unless new approaches to the administration of training are devised. Such is the intention of a systems approach to training—training by objectives. It is an aggressive strategy of administration through which the training administrator not only gets his day-to-day work done efficiently but also responds to problems quickly and introduces the new. In addition to these two necessary demands of training function, the training department becomes an agent of change in the organization through innovation. Part II describes what a system is, the varieties of systems, and how the cybernetic system is especially suitable for training systems. How this system can be used to define needs, prepare outlines and materials, and evaluate training make up this part.

5 | A Systems Approach to Training

Clearly then, demonstrative knowledge is
knowledge about essential attributes, and
develops from premises about such attributes.

— ARISTOTLE

MAN is constantly in touch with systems. The light on your page is the output of a system. The *inputs* in some remote power-generating station were coal, water power, or atomic energy. The *process* was that of power generation and transmission. The *output* was light. These three ingredients comprise most of the systems we deal with: inputs, processes, and outputs. There is much to be said for adopting a systems approach to the job of the training director.

The system concept is primarily a way of thinking about the job of managing.

So states one leading text in the field.[1] It provides a framework for the solution to perplexing problems: what to train for, where to begin the process of training, what should the process accomplish, how to evaluate results. Such a system has many advantages. For one thing it starts at the beginning, moves to the middle, and proceeds to the end and

[1] R. Johnson, F. E. Kast, and J. E. Rosenzweig, *The Theory of Management of Systems* (New York: McGraw-Hill, 1963).

73

then evaluates how well it did. If a system is to be workable it should operate as part of a larger system, should permit subsystems, and perhaps equally important should make use of the experience and knowledge already being used.

Can Training be Systematized?

Living in a maze of systems as we are, the first step in making a training system is to clarify what a *system* is. We live in a solar system, an economic system, a political system, and a social system. Our trainees live inside bodies that are complex systems that include at least ten major systems: the circulatory, digestive, reproductive, endocrine, nervous, excretory, respiratory, skeletal, muscular, and integumentary systems. We go to work on transportation systems, get paid on a salary system, and talk to each other over a telephone system. System provides an integrated plan for the whole that goes from one place to another in regular fashion and by which progress and achievement can be measured.

Eight Kinds of Training Systems

By applying the systems concept to training we can classify the various kinds of training efforts that are extant and judge whether or not we are effective in our profession.[2] Eight systems often found in training departments can be described.

STATIC SYSTEMS OF TRAINING

The first system found in training is that of static structure. This is the geography and anatomy of the training department and the resources it calls on to train people. It consists of a chart on a wall. Geometric squares are drawn representative of a training director; perhaps some major staff department heads such as a supervisory trainer, sales trainer, apprentice trainer, executive developer, clerical trainer, and similar positions. It is usually pictured in an organization chart and in well-developed departments may include manuals and job descriptions. In some firms its geometric forms may include customer education and even tuition refund or college relations staff heads. Objectives and definitions are the input; classes and conferences are the process; and outputs consist of trained people (who have been through the process). This is the rudimentary level of system.

2 Kenneth Boulding, "General Systems Theory: The Skeleton of Science," *Management Science*, 2:3 (Apr. 1956), pp. 197–203.

The Clocklike System of Training

The next highest system of training is the "running out" of a program that has been "wound up" at the beginning of the season or semester. The plan is developed and has regular measuring points along the way, usually in the course outline. "We shall conduct ten hours of public speaking, ten hours of conference leadership, and ten hours of human relations" is a typical example. The inputs are a program and a budget. The clock runs its course, like the sun or the moon, until the budget is exhausted or the program is completed.

The Cybernetic System of Training

This is perhaps the most common form of system in use in advanced training departments.[3] It presumes that the needs will be identified in the organization, that the training processes will meet the needs, and that evaluation will measure the effect. This is a plan for restoring organization performance to ideal levels through changing behavior that requires modifying. Pictured schematically, it looks something like Fig. 5–1. Perhaps the most pervasive system, this one deserves a longer

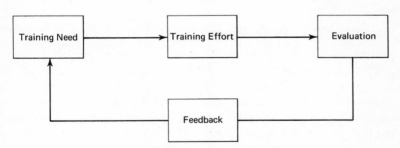

FIGURE 5–1 Cybernetic System of Training

look. We shall take such a look later on. It is at the level of the cybernetic system that complexity in planning and execution of training occur. The trainer must determine needs by defining what organizational needs for improved behavior are and array his courses and other educational efforts in such a way that the training program's results will support the organization that produces the need and that the behavior taught in the training course will be maintained back on the job.

[3] Norbert Weiner, *The Human Use of Human Beings* (Boston: Houghton Mifflin, 1954).

THE CELL SYSTEM OF TRAINING

Under such a system the training department itself as an organization is sustained on a self-maintaining basis. Its function as a supporter of organizational behavior is sufficiently clarified to itself and the organization that it often is able to charge back full costs on a fee basis to the parent organization. An example of such a cellular system would be the General Motors Institute, which charges the divisions for all costs of training, confident that it can sustain its own existence by providing needed training to the line departments. The same line departments will transfer funds into the training budget on a per-trainee basis to support the training effort. The Training Department of the University of Michigan's nonacademic departments is based on this level of system. Each department may enroll as many persons as it wishes in training department courses but must pay a per capita enrollment fee. The only financial support of training comes from the operating budgets of the departments whose people are trained. Thus the training department becomes a cell unit of the organization. It will do little experimental training beyond the amount the organization will "buy." If the organization is itself experimental, it will accept innovation by the training department.

THE PLANT SYSTEM OF TRAINING

Still another system that might be used to describe training departments and the training function is to analyze it to a central stem with branches and twigs. It is susceptible to having its branches (particular sections such as sales training; factory training; supervisory, executive, or apprentice training) truncated or new branches grafted on. It is also subject to having the entire plant wither and die, such as happens to many training departments when the economic or managerial climate fails to sustain the plant. The plant obtains its sustenance from roots established in a more basic foundation (the firm or the institution), and when this environment is altered drastically (a depression or new management that is not sympathetic to training), it may die. Yet the seeds it has generated often are the roots of self-renewal and a new plant springs into being after the environment once more provides sustaining fuels and energy for it.

Small companies, or other autocratically run organizations, are often hostile environments for training and fail to sustain a healthy training plant. In other cases the fluctuations in plant health result from excessive growth for the environment in which it grows. In some instances it has been known to have grown too rapidly until it outstripped the ability of the environment to nourish it, and it may temporarily or even permanently wither, either in all its branches (leaving only a dormant trunk) or in its entirety. Empire-builders in training should understand the dangers in their overstaffing, as depicted in this analogue.

TRAINING AS AN ORGANISM

A still different and perhaps higher level system that is analogous to many training departments is that of the organism such as animal or man.[4] Such a department has these characteristics:

1. It obtains and uses information through a brain. It has a series of information receptors located at its extremities. These receptors are providers of information to the central center or brain, which reflects messages back to the effectors or the striped muscles. Such a department in practice often relies heavily on advisory groups, research into training needs, and plenty of observation about the influences that surround it.
2. The training department that functions at the organismic level is probably more self-aware than lesser levels of system. It is more apt to work at symbolic levels and treats with its information symbolically. It communicates through behavior that results in an exchange of meaning. It is self-conscious in the better sense of the expression and is more apt to conduct evaluations of its effectiveness than lesser system.

In practice the training department that functions at this level is closely tied to personnel research and to information channels in the firm (such as profit and loss statements) and has orderly methods for defining training needs and measuring the impact of its own behavior on others around it. In some instances this is demonstrated in evaluations that seek out the acceptance and popularity of its programs among those it contacts. At its worst it becomes so self-conscious that it turns its major efforts toward maintaining its image through presenting sophisticated forms of executive and managerial entertainment for "something new." Its self-consciousness leads to gimmickry rather than service.

TRAINING DEPARTMENT AS SOCIAL ORGANIZATION

Industrial training is not conducted by such primary and personal organizations as the family, the tribe, or the neighborhood. As organizations go, the training department could be classified as a *secondary* kind

---

[4] Ludwig Bertalanffy, "General System Theory: A New Approach to Unity of Science," *Human Biology*, 23 (Dec. 1951), pp. 302–312.

of social organization, concerned with complex relationships and numerous contact points.

1. It is similar to other specialized groups that have risen to perform special economic functions demanded by the ecology of modern industrial society.
2. The groups with which it associates are often large in numbers of members, which are also widely distributed geographically. The large oil company training department may even have its own international relations program.
3. Large size and geographic spread means that their unity does not depend on personal sentiment but on the impersonal idea that the group has a life of its own apart from the individual persons comprising it. The plant training manager in Chicago may be nothing more than a name, having nothing beyond a status and function in the total training activity for those in corporate staff in New York.
4. Social groups of this nature are real but not too stable. Segments of the organization develop special interests.
5. To prevent such tendencies toward disorganization from gaining an upper hand, organizations maintain discipline through reports, policy statements, and the like. They may supplement this with persuasive communications, conferences, information bulletins, posters, and other kinds of personalized but mass appeals. In so doing they try to supplement organization discipline with voluntary self-control on the part of the members.
6. As a social organization the training department is not independent but relies on cooperation and coordination with other parts of the total organization to find acceptance of its legitimate function.
7. This coordination with other groups cannot be completely achieved because others may be competing with it for space, budget, and the attention of trainees and of top management. Many training departments have a hearty sense of competition with accounting, industrial engineering, labor relations, or the public relations department, for example.

Training as a Social Movement

Not as often found as in the past, some training departments have the nature of a social change movement. The social change that seems to have pervaded training most is that of achieving "industrial democracy." Its objectives seem to be the achievement of reforms within the organization through a kind of indoctrination. Faced with real or apparent opposition it may join hands with other trainers faced with similar opposition from line managers who resist the true faith and form a *sect*. This is close to a religious form of organization that is at war with the existing mores. It seeks to generate a state of mind and establish a moral code different from that of the world about it—based on some ultimate authority such as behavioral science. To achieve this it may set itself off in contrast with the rest of the world.

Because it is intolerant of infidels (autocrats) it often adopts distinct differences in speech (words such as *interaction* and *perceive*).

At this point, if affinity to religious sects is a close one, it will often slip the bounds of economic origins and make candid admissions of its sectarian nature. In such a posture toward the rest of the organization it may find itself in jeopardy when the economic winds blow adversely on the parent firm that sustains it.

Which One to Adopt

For the insightful trainer or training director, it is no small matter of passing interest that he see clearly which system best describes his own department. Training objectives, training content, training methods, and evaluation of training all follow the system that is being used, whether consciously shaped or unconsciously drifted into. As a simple test, try the chart in Fig. 5–2 on your own training department. The

Which System Best Describes Your Training Department? Rank 1, 2, 3, 4, etc.
(Refer to the text for detailed explanation)

	How You Place Your Department	How Others Place Your Department
1. Static System		
2. Clocklike		
3. Cybernetic		
4. A Cell		
5. A Plant		
6. An Organism		
7. A Social Organization		
8. A Social Movement		

FIGURE 5–2

eight major systems explained above are listed in Fig. 5–2. Take a pencil and place a rank-order position beside the three or four that appear to best describe your department. You will want to rank several of them because no real-life training department will operate wholly according to a single system described here but in all likelihood will be a combination of two or more.

Although your concept of your department may be perfectly accurate, you might also find it instructive to let some others tell you how they see your department (use the second column). To obtain comparable opinions it may be necessary to limit yourself to those who will take time to read the respective descriptions. This, of course, biases your data collection to those people who are sufficiently interested in going that far.

Finally you are in a better position to ascertain whether or not the actuality resembles what you would like.

Cybernetic Systems—The Modern Approach

Current training literature reveals that more and more attention is being paid to "systems." In almost every instance they are cybernetic systems. Is this the most appropriate system? In many respects it meets the needs of behavioral technology. On the other hand there may be temporary instances in which one system may have some distinctive uses that make it superior to all other forms. Analogies can help define and clarify your present condition.

Perhaps the most persuasive reason for adhering to a cybernetic system of organizing and managing training is the very popularity of the cybernetic concept. It is a communication theory that treats organisms and organizations as being very much alike—both can display behavior.[5] Because the subjects of the training department's efforts are organisms (employees), it seems to be sensible to treat the training process as a feedback or cybernetic process that is occurring to an organism. This paves the way to expanding your logic to presume that the training department itself is a cybernetic system.

Perhaps the easiest to understand illustration of the cybernetic system is the home thermostat, which controls the temperature of the room, at least that part of it where the thermostat is situated. The inputs are gas, oil, or electricity. The process is what goes on inside the furnace, which converts energy into heat and pushes it up the pipes or ducts. The output is British thermal units of heat measured by the thermostat as degrees of temperature. The thermostat simultaneously measures the heat in degrees and compares it with a predetermined level set by the householder. When the heat exceeds that temperature by a slight amount, it sends a message back to the control point and turns off the inputs. When the furnace is not operating and the

5 Kenneth Boulding, *The Skills of the Economist* (Cleveland: H. Allen, 1958).

temperature is discovered by the thermostat to have dropped below the preset level, it sends a message to the switch to control the inputs, and the inputs begin to flow again. This switching off and on is sometimes called homeostasis. The result is not wide fluctuation or perfect stability. It is control.[6]

The cybernetic system does not automatically ensure successful training, however. As a closed loop it merely assures the trainer that he is achieving the things he set out to do. If his goal is to run successful programs, he can do so by defining success in specific and measurable terms. He might desire that the programs be interesting to those attending. His inputs will be speakers, materials, and outlines. His process is a course with topflight instructors, lots of gimmicks, and enough novelty to keep the class intrigued. To measure his output he passes out questionnaires seeking their opinion. If they "liked" the course he achieved his objectives.

On the other hand the cybernetic system, combined with a business-like definition of the behavior change sought, provides him with a thermostat to assure the achievement of the training objectives. He is controlling the growth or behavior change of the trainee. The great danger in using such a closed-loop system is that as long as it remains a closed loop it is incapable of learning anything. Sadly, training departments have often been mechanical cybernetic closed loops, as devoid of information theory as they were of learning theory. The remedy for such isolation of training from real life, or the business purposes of the organization that supports them, requires the addition of modification of the trainer's values. In more detailed form, the earlier diagram (Fig. 5–1) of a cybernetic system is shown in Fig. 5–3. We complicate this in training by virtue of having control over only one of the com-

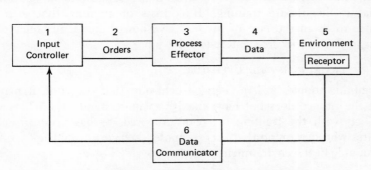

FIGURE 5–3 Cybernetic System Plus Trainer's Values

[6] Donald G. Malcolm, "System Simulation," *Journal of Industrial Engineering*, 9 (May–June 1958), pp. 177–87.

munication loops that affect the trainee. His boss, the company policies, his peers, his subordinates (especially if they belong to a union), the ropes of the organization, and other procedures such as the pay plans, the promotion system, and other "order communicators" push and shove the effector into a certain posture toward his job and behavior on it. The problem with training is that it often permits itself to be caught in the position of being the lowest-pulse communicator.

In operating terms, where the trainee system conflicts with the rest of the systems that are communicating (say, the boss) with the trainee on the job, the training will lose out. If, following the teachings of the trainer, he misses out on a raise or a promotion, then the future inputs of the trainer are overridden by other order communicators. What does this imply for training systems? Following the scheme shown in Fig. 5–3, we might conclude these things about training systems of the cybernetic model.

THE CONTROLLER AND ITS INPUTS

When the training department is to issue proposed instructions (actually they may not be orders but only suggested behavior) they should reflect information received from the environment itself as well as narrow bits of data received from the trainees at the end of the class. The trainer should be reading messages from the shop or office environment and the organization and its power sources as well as from its little "rating cards" from trainees.

TRAINING MATERIALS HAVE MUCH IN COMMON WITH ORDERS

To the trainee who is tacitly directed (or even openly ordered) to attend, the materials he receives have much of the coloration of directives. They will usually be so received if they appear to be *legitimate*. What is illegitimate training? It consists of training that asks the trainee to fly in the face of his boss's wishes or company policy or to go against his own career interests in his job.

THE TRAINING IS THE EFFECTOR

Training should lead to changed behavior. If it does not, it may be that the trainee does not have the IQ to understand, has a boss who conflicts with the training behavior proposed, or has peers or subordinates who determine that such proposed behavior would not work or be suitable in the environment.

THE DATA COMMUNICATION

What the training intends to achieve is important only in regard to what the trainees receive. The data that go to the receptor (the trainee) may not be what the trainer put into the system at all. For example, we find the trainer teaching "autocratic behavior is wrong." What the trainee learns is "My boss is not a very good boss; he should be here instead of me."

THE RECEPTOR WORKS IN AN ENVIRONMENT

This means that the trainees are reading from numerous sources of inputs at once. The environment, including the organization culture, the organization climate, and the boss are all sending data to him. If training is consistent and congruent with the other messages, it amplifies and accelerates behavior change. If it is incongruent or inconsistent with environment, it may lose out and simply confuse the trainee (receptor).

Summary

In the management of training we undoubtedly operate by some system or another. In being systematic we can be conscious of what we are doing and what the effects of different kinds of training effort might be. The cybernetic system has numerous advantages and points up what experienced trainers have realized for a long time.

1. For training to be effective, it should start from the top down, or, at least, have the endorsement or permission of the superiors of the trainees. Without such endorsement the training may be wasted or harmful. Where active opposition to the training behavior taught exists, the training will lose out.[7]
2. The identification of training needs consists of a trainer briefing himself thoroughly on the nature and intensity of other behavior change messages that are bombarding the trainee on the job.[8] Where he sees conflict, the trainer must either change that environment and its messages or forego the training as being harmful.

[7] G. S. Odiorne, "Supervisor-Subordinate Relations: The Last Systems Frontier," *Systems and Procedures Journal* (May 1965).

[8] Stanford L. Optner, *Systems Analysis for Business Management* (Englewood Cliffs, N.J.: Prentice-Hall, 1960).

THE SMELTZER CHEMICAL COMPANY

The Hoffman plant of the Smeltzer Chemical Company has 670 hourly paid workers and 130 salaried supervisory, clerical, technical, and staff employees. It is located in a town of some 45,000 people close to a large eastern city. This plant, which produces a variety of organic, inorganic, and plastic chemicals in some 20 independent departments, plus 6 service departments, is one of 20 domestic plants of the Smeltzer Chemical Company, which has a total employment of over 25,000 employees.

The Hoffman plant Personnel Department, which is composed of a personnel manager, medical director, safety engineer, nurse, and three clerical people, one of whom handles all pension, sick leave, and group insurance matters, reports directly to the plant manager. This department has been responsible for labor relations, and the plant has had a union for over 10 years. It is an industrial, plant-wide union of chemical workers (ICWU, AFL-CIO). The last strike occurred in 1948 and there was a walkout for a period of four hours one day in 1949.

The plant has seen some "bad times" in the past 10 years and has been, for the last three years, on an economic upswing as to profitability and return on investment. It is now, basically, a prosperous operation.

It was into this setting that Paul Schuler, a consultant, came on December 12 to talk with George Carlisle, the personnel manager of the Hoffman plant. The following conversation about training took place:

GEORGE: First, let me fill you in on what we have done. Our management development program included training for all supervisors down through and including foremen in such courses as Work Simplification, Human Relations, Rapid Reading, The Techniques of Performance Appraisal and Interviewing, and Conference Leadership. There have also been special courses in instrumentation for production supervisors, and also instruction on the cost structure conducted by the Accounting Department. Trips to other plants in the company have been used considerably as a training device. Approximately 12 supervisors per year have been sent to AMA conferences. In addition, two years ago we had a series of monthly round table meetings for all super-

The Smeltzer Chemical Company, Personnel 439. The case was prepared by Professor Alva F. Kindall of the Harvard University Graduate School of Business Administration as the basis for class discussion rather than to illustrate either effective or ineffective administration. Copyright © 1957 by the President and Fellows of Harvard College. Used by specific permission.

visory personnel including foremen in groups of approximately 15–20, set up in such a way that one plant general superintendent was the leader of each conference and there were no superior-subordinate combinations in any of the conferences. These conferences discussed various problems and always included a ten-minute information session. In the past few months we have done a lot of thinking about management development and would like to find out if any additional training is needed, and if so, what kind.

PAUL: That sounds like a good idea to me. How are you going to do it?

GEORGE: We thought maybe you could talk to the foremen. If you explained to them that anything they say will be held in confidence they might be more free with you in expressing their opinions than they would with a member of management.

PAUL: You are probably right there. What sort of things did you think we might discuss?

GEORGE: We don't have a list of questions yet but we would like to get information about these eight general areas: (a) What is the foreman's authority and how does he use it in dealing with his men. (b) Selection and training of men. (c) Scheduling of work. (d) What he dislikes about his job. (e) His relationship with his immediate superior. (f) His own selection and training. (g) How he works with others in the plant. (h) His feeling about top management and their policies.

PAUL: That looks like a good program. Why don't we make up some questions that will pertain to each of these next week. How about Tuesday, the 17th, at 2:00 P.M.?

GEORGE: Fine. See you then.

On December 17, George and Paul met to work up a list of questions.

QUESTIONS ASKED FOREMEN

A. *What is the foremen's authority and how does he use it in dealing with his men?*

1. If you caught a man going out the gate with some lead, what would you do?

   (a) For what actions can you fire a man?

2. If one of your men came to you today and asked for tomorrow off to go to a wedding, what would you do?

3. If a man had been 10 minutes late three days in a row and today he walked by your office 20 minutes late, what would you do?

4. Assuming your man has a bench or area to keep clean and he has left it messy, what would you do?

5. How do you go about hiring people for your department?

6. If you are sitting in your office and an operator comes in and says, "I'm not going to operate until you get that leaky caustic fill pipe fixed," what would you do?

7. Do you think praise is a good tool to use?

8. What is the usual procedure for handling grievances? Who do the men come to first in your department?

9. How would you rate the morale in your department? Why? What do you think you could do or have done to improve it?

B. *Selection and training of men*

How do you go about hiring people for your department?

10. Say I am a new employee who is going to work for you. What would you do to train me?

C. *Scheduling of work*

11. How far in advance do you try to schedule your work? Anything ever make this difficult? Do you order your own raw materials?

D. *What he dislikes about his job*

12. Any parts of your job you consider more important than others? Any parts of your job you dislike? Anything that makes it hard for you to do the kind of job you would like to do?

E. *His relationship with his immediate superior*

13. Is there any way you can tell how "you are doing" in the eyes of those above you? Do you like this method?

14. We mentioned praise as a tool—your boss ever use it?

15. If your boss does something or has an idea you don't like, would you tell him?

16. If your boss said, "I want you to build a case against so and so, so we can fire him," what would be your reaction?

F. *His selection and training*

17. How were you promoted? "They" ever tell you why? What type of training did you get?

18. Did you attend the conferences this summer on employee attitudes? Do you remember any of the attitudes people decided they would like employees to have?

G. *How he works with others in the plant*

19. If you needed two pipers, (a) nonemergency and (b) emergency, how would you go about getting them?

20. How do you find out what's going on in the plant?

21. What do the other foremen gripe about most?

H. *His feelings about top management and their policies*

22. What is your opinion of the present safety program?

23. If you were personnel manager, what is the first thing you would do?

24. Are we "kow-towing" to the customer too much?

25. What effect would there be on your department, or work load, or the plant, if the personnel department were eliminated?

When these questions had been decided on, 1½-hour meetings were scheduled with 17 of the plant's 30 foremen.

The interviews actually took about 1½ hours each. First, Paul would make sure that the man being interviewed knew exactly why the interview was being conducted and how the results would be compiled. After this initial assurance that the conversation would be confidential, most of the men answered the questions very freely.

When the interviews were completed, Paul prepared a report that he presented to George on January 4. Paul explained that his report included a brief overall summary of findings, along with typical answers by the foremen to the questions, without revealing any names. George seemed pleased with the report and said he believed it would provide a good basis for developing an improved training program.

PAUL SCHULER'S REPORT

Because the Hoffman plant of the Smeltzer Chemical Company has had no formal training program during the past several years and plant management wanted to determine the advisability of reinstituting such a program, I was asked to make a survey to determine how plant foremen felt about this matter.

A series of questions were prepared by George Carlisle and me, the answers to which we hoped would reveal any areas in which training should be given.

I conducted 17 "off the record" 1½-hour interviews with 17 of the 30 foremen to present these questions to them. In general, their answers indicate that there is a lack of understanding as to what the foremen's authority is with respect to discipline. I was told that foremen do have the right to fire anyone caught stealing but that a better procedure would be to suspend the man pending investigation. However, 12 said they can't fire anyone; 6 said they could suspend the man if he was a member of their department; 6 said they would advise the employee's boss that the man be suspended; and I said he could fire the man. Many remarked, "I'd like to fire him, but by the time you get witnesses and build up a case on the guy, it is hardly worth it." In my opinion training in this area is needed.

On the whole I believe the foremen do an excellent job in dealing with their men. In practically every instance I got the reply, "First I'd find out why" or "Get the facts" before I would take any action in the situations I presented. Their interest and understanding was illustrated even more by the fact that all said they made it a point to tell a man they appreciated his efforts when he had done an exceptional job. They also stated that they listen carefully to the men's gripes and suggestions and give them serious consideration.

When asked why they thought their department had such good morale, they mentioned, "I treat employees like I'd like to be treated myself" and "I try to be fair—but not necessarily run a popularity contest." To me these all indicate good human relations or an "understanding foreman" and they are to be commended.

Furthermore, I believe that the department superintendent should be commended because 15 out of the 17 questioned replied that they would not hesitate to tell their boss if they thought he had a "bum idea" or was doing something wrong. This indicates to me a wholesome relationship and not one built on the idea "I'm your boss and what I say goes."

However, I would look into the problem of how the department superintendent treats the foreman in other respects. Even though 10 of the 17 said the boss did tell them he appreciated it when they had done a good job, even those that more or less voted yes hesitated a minute before saying anything. To me, this might mean that because they liked their boss they were trying to cover up for him. Therefore, I would look into this aspect of the problem.

In regard to their own selection and training, most stated they were just told "We think you can do the job," and "How would you like to go on salary?" When they were sent to a new department that was not familiar to them, no one told them what to do. Many remarked that they would have appreciated some training at this time. This applies not only to those promoted to foreman 15 years ago but those promoted in the past 2–3 years.

It was interesting that when asked "How do you find out what's going on in the plant?" 9 of the 17 mentioned first the foremen's locker room. The plant manager's letter, which is sent out every two weeks, was looked on as very informative by only two of the men, and the rest regarded it more or less as a means of making official the rumors they had heard two weeks ago.

When questioned about what they would do if they were top management, the two most common answers were "Practice what they preach about being interested in people and getting to know them" and, second, "Have closer supervision over the men" and "Put the time clocks back in." One man put it very well when he said, "The thing stolen most in this plant is time."

I believe the best way to present the foremen's reactions to training is to list some typical replies to the questions asked.

EXAMPLES OF TYPICAL ANSWERS BY FOREMEN

1. If you caught a man going out the gate with some lead, what would you do?

Can't fire. Just recommend. Would tell the man's boss and the Personnel Department.

Have to judge on merits. Would suspend and tell his boss.

Can't fire anyone. Best he could do would be to recommend to his boss.

If own man, could suspend temporarily. But it is up to personnel to decide.

Can't fire. Just recommend to superior. As to lead, if not his own, contact the man's boss who would contact personnel.

Go to shop steward first. Then personnel manager. Don't have power to fire.

If not his department, wouldn't fire. Call man's boss. Let him decide. If own man could fire, but would just suspend.

Call up watchman and get in touch with personnel. If after hours, find someone whose jurisdiction man is under, because he can't do anything. He remarked, "Don't seek authority to fire because it is so hard to fire because of union."

Fire on the spot. Get hold of police. But probably couldn't do it, so just suspend.

Immediate reaction would be to fire. If one of own, could advise to fire. If not, just tell man's boss.

3. If a man had been 10 minutes late for three days in a row and today he walked by your office 20 minutes late, what would you do?

Call in at once and find out why. Could be sickness at home.

By the second day, call to the man's attention. Find out why.

Speak to man on the second day. Dock him if late second day.

Find out why. If necessary to continue, maybe some arrangement can be made.

Dock one-half hour. If it keeps up, suspend him. If a good excuse, will explain beforehand.

Dock him.

Would do something the second day.

Ask why late, dock him, tell him to get squared away.

Since shift man, do nothing. Wait until man he is to relieve gripes.

First day just call to his attention. Second day, dock him.

5. How do you go about hiring people for your department?

    (a) If you had the chance to interview a person before he worked for you, what would you want to know about him?

        All—Nothing to say about who works in my department.

        11—Wish to know man's past experience.

        2—Why he quit last job.

        3—His education.

        4—His intelligence.

        2—Ability.

        2—Physical appearance.

        4—Family life.

        3—Attitudes.

        2—Honesty.

        1—Hobby.

All stated that they had nothing to say about who works in their department. They stated that a job opening is posted and the senior man gets the job if he passes a short test. They did say they can send a man back to his old job within a certain period. When I asked the length of the period, I received answers ranging from 10 to 60 days.

I did not ask in detail how they could determine the qualities of the man they were interviewing.

6. If you are sitting in your office and an operator comes in and says, "I'm not going to operate until you get that leaking caustic fill pipe fixed," what would you do?

Check to see if it is as bad as he says. If bad, thank man for bringing it to your attention, and shut down until fixed.

Listen to him. Check it. If not bad, explain, but rope it off and check with safety engineer. If bad shut down.

Call area foreman. If you can't get it fixed, tell your supervisor you have to shut down.

Check. If bad, shut down. If not, explain that it is OK. If necessary, call area engineer.

Put in emergency job order. Don't operate until it gets fixed.

Do not ask to operate. Call boilermakers and get it fixed.

See if it can be operated. Explain why. Call safety and thank the man for bringing it to your attention.

Give man credit for being safety minded. Look over the situation. If it is bad and can't get it fixed, shut down.

7. Do you think praise is a good tool to use?

They all answered "yes" to this question. Some said, "A pat on the back never hurt anyone" or "I always make it a point to tell a man when he does a good job and even have my boss tell him too."

8. What is the usual procedure for handling grievances? Who do the men come to first in your department?

7—Men would come to me first.

6—Men would go to shop steward first.

3—It's about 50:50 as to whom they go to first.

One interesting comment was "They come to me first. You'll find some departments where they go to the shop steward first, but that's because the foreman isn't sympathetic."

9. How would you rate the morale in your department? Why? What do you think you could do or have done to improve it?

Good—because they know where they stand and I listen to their ideas and see if they are worth using.

Good—because all work together and speak to each other. I try to treat them right. If they do a good day's work I tell them.

Good—try to keep equipment in good repair, keep place clean, and if we hear of any gripes, go to the man before he comes to me. Show interest in men.

Excellent—because they know if they get stuck I'll help them and treat them as I like to be treated myself. Also try to go to all their social activities.

Very good—I lay cards on the table. If man knows your opinion whether good or bad, it helps.

10. Say I am a new employee who is going to work for you. What would you do to train me?

Here the procedure was much the same. They all recognized the need to put the man at ease and tried to do this by talking to the man in their office for an hour or so, explaining the rules, where things were, by introducing the man to the members of the department and by showing him the plant. The actual training was done by the "lead man" or the most experienced operator. The new man first just watched and asked questions of the operator or foreman. Then, after a couple of days he was allowed to run the process with the operator watching. After the man, operator, and foreman thought he was ready, he was allowed to do the job alone.

12. Any parts of your job you dislike?

Dislike book work.

Dislike time cards. Would like more rules so actions by foremen would be more standard.

Dislike time cards. Like job.

Book work heavy. Also the fact that management is not even courteous enough to suggest that foremen take a day off after working 36 straight hours.

Schedules get to be a pain, but the big thing is not being able to get the bosses to OK minor things up to $200. That would help make the job easier for me or improve looks of department itself.

13. Is there any way you can tell how "you are doing" in the eyes of those above you? Do you like this method?

Good question. Bone of contention. They say we get a typed copy but never have. Have them every year. Boss tells what he thinks is good and bad. We get a chance to answer and do some. Done by supervisors. Would like to know what others above my supervisor think about me.

Done annually. Good and bad things told and we reply. Like it so much I started it with my men.

Two times a year. Used to be done by superintendent. He delegated it to assistant. Like to know how boys further up feel though.

Like to know once a year. Been two years for him. Department supervisor should do it, but gave to his assistant who is not doing it. Like to know how those on up feel.

Too few and far between. Been about two years since had one. Do have a check list. He tells you and you have a chance to reply. Like it.

Once a year. But has been two years since done. "Just copy last year's anyway." Immediate boss to do it, but he doesn't.

14. We mentioned praise as a tool—your boss ever use it?

Ten of the 17 said, "Oh, yes, he does." But there is an indication from the other answers I received that some of the supervisors do not use this tool as much as they could. For example, one man said, "Once before I retire I would like to have him tell me I've done a good job." Another said, "Boss did it once. Like to have him do it again before I quit." I also noted that four others hesitated and hedged their answers by saying in essence, "He doesn't come out and say anything, but he accepts my ideas," or "He shows it in other ways."

16. If your boss said, "I want you to build a case against so and so so we can fire him," what would be your reaction?

Would go along with boss. He should know what he wants.

Would if ordered. But would scream bloody murder if I thought it was for personal reasons.

No. If I thought the guy was poor, I would give him a warning and tell him I was watching him.

Boss wouldn't do that. And I wouldn't go along if he did. I know more about my men than he does.

Wouldn't go along and can't imagine it happening.

Would go along if thought it was justified. Would tell everything I put in the record to the man.

If boss is right, OK. But don't think it should be done.

Wouldn't do it.

17. How were you promoted? "They" ever tell you why? What type of training did you get?

Was a laborer and subforeman. Had a good foreman and supervisor, but was never told why was selected. Also was never trained. Made a lot of mistakes in handling the men.

Was a lead man, very happy as such, hated to leave old department. Never told why I was selected, but people came to me when lead man away. Had no formal training.

Was assistant. When foreman died, took over. But never told why selected, and had no training, just hard work.

Was told I have been doing a good job. Think I was picked because I had shown initiative in working hourly men. Never told other than that. Was given job description, however.

Never was told why I was given job. Foreman stayed with me five days and after that did not have a supervisor, so learned job the hard way.

Have to keep nose clean, do good work and have a sponsor. No one told me much of anything when I took the job. Was told, "Don't get a swelled head."

Just told me they had watched me. I did a good job. Had no training but picked up stuff since then. As to training, would like to be sent other places. Also there are a lot of things would like to know about. Don't know how to find out about them.

Was a subforeman of a different building. No breaking in at all. Would have liked more. Man at disadvantage. Didn't know process. Never got enough training.

The old foreman came back now and then from his new department to help me. Also department supervisor was very patient. Made a lot of mistakes. At the time would have liked more training.

20. How do you find out what is going on in the rest of the plant?

Locker room. If really want to know, just visit department.

Letters from plant manager help. Keep in file if they are good. Have a copy made to put on bulletin board.

Plant bulletin. But employees get information first.

Letters by plant manager. But not interested in other parts of the plant.

Locker room. Plant manager's letter, which just makes rumors official.

Grapevine. Letter just makes rumors official.

23. If you were personnel manager, what is the first thing you would do?

When he gives foreman okay to do something, he should stand behind him.

Fewer grievance meetings.

Get tougher with union and stand behind foremen.

Get out into plant more and take more interest in the men.

Tougher with union.

Be available more. At least return calls.

Quit pussy-footing with union.

Be more strict.

25. What effect would there be on your department, or work load, or the plant, if the personnel department were eliminated?

What would union do? What about contracts?

Have to take over welfare, insurance, sickness obligations, a lot of extra work.

Have to handle grievances.

Handle all labor problems. You know, I don't know what they do.

Handle grievances.

Who will hold union's hand?

Have to have some system to deal with union. Handle safety programs and social activities. Reviews of men, medical records, payrolls.

Good question. Have to take care of safety, all kinds of insurance, care of labor relations, assign people, hire and fire. Really not necessary.

Make job harder. Have details like insurance and safety. Doctor to take care of.

No effect at all really.

Have to make a lot of decisions on labor relations. Don't have to now and have to be very careful about setting precedents.

CASE DISCUSSION QUESTIONS
The Smeltzer Chemical Company Case

1. How valuable is the Schuler study?

2. How might he have improved it?

3. What should be done now, given the facts as they exist? How?

6 Training by Objectives —A Cybernetic System

Pursue your purpose, if indeed you think
there's wisdom in it.
                    —SOPHOCLES

TRAINING expense apparently makes line managers uneasy. Money spent for production is tangible, visible, and apparently related to measurable output. Money spent in research is more uncertain but still has an air of practicality about it.

Training money, however, often seems to be considered an item of luxury expense, to be engaged in only when profit levels are high or the costs are being borne mainly by its tax deductibility as an expense.

Yet, there are organizations where training is considered to be a normal productive expenditure, and such organizations must be numbered among the most successful. The military has always considered training one of the four major management functions. The training staff and the officer in charge are among the leading functions of the command. General Motors, the number one manufacturing firm, and Bell Telephone, the leading utility and the number two corporation, have always spent considerable time and effort in improving the skills of their people. The average employee and supervisor in the Bell Telephone Company, for example, spends an average of 20 per cent of his time in training, according to one estimate. The typical General Motors manager spends approximately the same amount of time in training.

Not only are these two firms not typical, but they are unique. In one way they are unique because they are extremely successful as firms, and in another way they are unique because they devote so much of their resources to training. It could be argued either way which is cause and which is effect, that is, whether it trains because it can afford to, or whether it can afford to because it trains. Undoubtedly training costs money. It costs money in trainers' time, in staff, in facilities, and in trainee time. A compromise explanation would be that the two reinforce one another, and the successful company can accelerate its rate of success by training.

An alternative explanation could be made that looks in another direction. Rather than asking whether the training makes the profit or the profit supports the training, we might ask is there another explanation that would differ from both? Perhaps the best explanation lies in the kind of managerial system that governs both of the two illustrative examples, as well as others that are extensive and success users of training.

That system is the managerial system of management by objectives. In its briefest form it is a system in which the first step of management is the clarification of corporate objectives and the breaking down of all subordinate activity into logical subdivisions that contribute to the major objectives.

Training thus becomes a means by which corporate objectives are attained—but only one of many such means.

The System of Management by Objectives

The major details of management by objectives have been spelled out in greater detail in other places. The term is grammatically awkward, and can be considered sensible only when it is considered as grammatically akin to navigational terms. Navigation by the stars, the sun, or some other fixed point of reference indicates the steady reference point around which the ship's captain and all the crew govern their activity. Management by objectives by analogy suggests that the first step in movement in the organization is a definition of the objectives of the organization, and other activities are governed by their contribution to this central focal point. If the firm's objective is profit, then other activities are geared toward this objective—in making contributions directly or indirectly but always measured by ultimate contribution to the objective. If the objective is philanthropy, the activity changes; if it is national defense, health education, welfare, or labor peace, the pur-

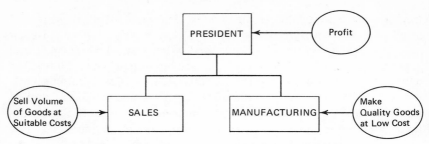

FIGURE 6–1   Major Objectives of Functional Chiefs of Department

poses of subordinate organizational units are measured by their contributions to those central navigational objectives.

In addition to the objectives, a principle of summarization must also be applied. The cumulative efforts of all subordinate units are contributory objectives. The summarization of efforts of subordinate units adds up to results. The *effectiveness* of the results is measured against the objectives that were sought when the effort was committed.

The central objective of the chief executive is broken down into activities by means of which he chooses to move toward the goal. Although these subordinate activities are means to the top man, for the subordinate to whom they are delegated, each activity becomes an objective. As shown in Fig. 6–1, the objective of the company president is profit, which he intends to achieve by making and selling a product. Although vastly oversimplified, this figure illustrates the summarization principle by which organization objectives break down into activities and in turn become objectives for the responsible subordinate. The president alone has total responsibility for profit. To him, selling and manufacturing are means. For the vice presidents of sales and manufacturing, however, their area of responsibility is their primary objective —the major vehicle through which they may contribute to the objectives of the senior executive from whom they have received their delegated responsibility and powers.[1]

Training by Objectives

Under such a managerial system training assumes the part of contributory activity. It acquires its objectives from the definition of

[1] For more detailed explanations of the management by objectives approach to managing, read G. S. Odiorne, *Management by Objectives—A System of Managerial Leadership* (New York: Pitman, 1965). This is a systems approach. For explanations of the philosophy of management by objectives, one might read the excellent works by Schleh, Drucker, and Hughes.

corporate or organizational objectives, and must be considered a subordinate activity of the head of the organizational unit. If, in fact, the training director usually reports to the industrial relations chief, this is merely an accidental mistake that grows out of the attempt to cut the number of major subordinates who report to the chief. In the military this error in assignment is avoided by making the G-4 (Plans and Training) a major staff chief reporting to the commander or his chief of staff. The end effect of training being subordinate to the industrial relations manager is usually his being preoccupied with the perfectly logical task of helping his boss succeed, even where the potentials for the firm's major objectives are vastly greater.

Yet the knowledge that training has a major contribution to make does not mean that being located in the industrial relations department—even the type that spends its time fire-fighting union rumbles —is an insuperable handicap.

1. It requires a strong orientation to organizational purposes other than the parochial interest of training or of industrial relations.
2. It demands feeder lines into and from the major organizational units that have been created and that work under the structures of objectives contributory to the major organization objectives.
3. Its activities are managed in a systematic fashion. The activities themselves are governed by their compliance with guidelines agreed on in advance. It is forward-looking rather than retrospective, and the scope of its planning matches or exceeds the scope of planning of the entire organization and its objectives.
4. It operates to achieve results (produce outputs). The results are chosen before the activity is planned, and the activity is planned before the resources are put in or released. Three major ingredients comprise the training system where training is being managed by objectives. Treating all three of the ingredients as a whole, we note (see Fig. 6–2) that training managed by objective begins (a) with a

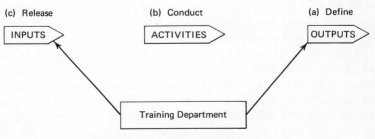

FIGURE 6–2 Basic System of Training

definition of outputs or *results* that will occur as a result of training taking place. Following this definition of results, the actual training effort, (b) activity, is planned and carried on. This calls for certain resources, (c) inputs—budgets, staff time, facilities—to be devoted to the training.

5. To avoid the pitfalls of gimmickry, of activity for activity's sake, of imitative activity, or of program administration, training by objectives requires that *context* be defined. Out of this context, which is the organizational frame of reference within which training must function, come regular programs, *problems* that can be solved by the change of behavior of members of the organization or innovations. The identification of behavior change required leads to a choice of activities, methods, techniques, and skills, which includes activities of trainers and a feedback to the trainees in their new behavior. The final outcome of training is the changed behavior of individuals, groups, and the organization itself, which makes it more effective in its own search for objectives.

6. The nature of behavior-changing activity means that training becomes a subsystem of the personnel systems of the company. Behavior change may be achieved by means other than training. It may be brought about by changing the environmental forces shaping behavior, it may be achieved by policies and procedures such as salary policies, or it may be achieved by the behavior of others whose opinion or actions affect the subject himself. Finally, it may be brought about by a conscious developmental effort, in which the individual undergoes certain artificial, simulated kinds of experiences during which he receives feedback of success for some kinds of behavior or of failure for others. This feedback of success or failure is the nub of the learning process and of training itself.

Training Policy and Training Systems

Policy is commonly defined as a "guide to action." Static approaches to policy often treat policy as a triangular scheme that begins with objectives and out of which come certain policies. These policies are the basis for procedures, which in turn produces and guides rules and regulations. This is pictured in Fig 6–3.

The system approach to policy starts at the same place but assumes that fixed procedures and regulations may stultify. Therefore the systems approach moves in a different fashion. It starts with objectives and ends with results achieved, and a linking of the two by a feedback adjustment mechanism. The system approach is more dynamic and relates to the situation as it exists rather than by unreasoning adherence to the old saw "there's no reason for it, it's just policy."

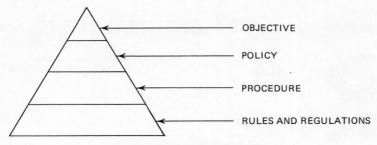

FIGURE 6–3   The Pyramid of Policy

The systems approach to policy (see Fig. 6–4) starts with objectives but proceeds through the respective stages of studying context, finding organization problems that can be solved by training, developing optional solutions, and taking the one that best meets the criteria of economic solution.

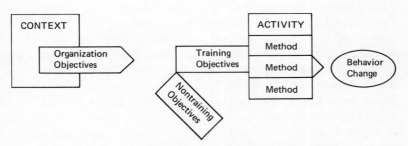

FIGURE 6–4   A Systems Model for Management Training

This approach to training policy shapes the existing elements in new forms, without requiring that all the elements now used in training be scrapped or amended. They are simply managed differently, managed in a way that enhances their effectiveness.

Yet systems are more complex than this, and perhaps a look at the ways system can work in training would be suitable at this point. The system approach to training—a cybernetic system—as we shall present it in this book, is *training by objectives*.

Guides for Construction of Trainer's Objective Statements

When the training manager or members of his staff prepare to establish training objectives, they will find that a convenient kind of classification system of preparation of objectives statements for training can simplify their preparation of such statements.

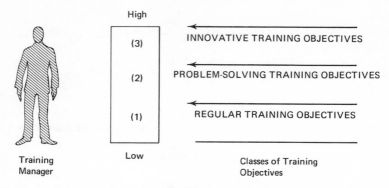

FIGURE 6–5   A Hierarchy of Training Objectives

As shown in Fig. 6–5, three classes of objectives comprise an ascending scale of excellence in training administration.

1. The minimum requirement for training departments is that they should conduct the *regular* recurring or routine kind of objectives in training. These might include such training objectives as induction training for employees, foreman training for new foremen, new product training for salesmen, or sales system training for new retail employees. These objectives should be based on realistic figures drawn from history (the same quarter last year, for example) and should provide for such trade-off objectives as measures of numbers of trainees, hours of training, cost per trainee, time required for trainee to come up to standard levels of performance, and similar statistical indications of performance for the training department. These should be reality-based and should include a range of possible outcomes including the highest and lowest possible outcomes permissible, plus a reality base from history. Such data establish a general base for administration of training and comprise the minimum standards of performance for the training manager.

   The training manager who performs all his regular objectives within past limits is entitled to the same job for the same pay for another year. Excellence for a manager of training is performing problem-solving training or introducing innovative forms of training.

2. The second category, and one that comprises the major kind of goals for trainers, is *problem-solving objectives*. The training department that is finding and solving human behavior problems through applied training skills is worth more than the training department

that merely performs last year's courses as before. This is a never-ending process, for this year's problem analysis and course designed to alleviate the problem becomes next year's standard or recurring course in many instances.

The manager of training who sees problems that really exist and who solves them through training is of a higher level of excellence. This area of training is often the major point of emphasis in the system approach to training.

3. *Innovative goals* comprise the highest level of excellence for the training manager and his staff. Innovation can take the form of objectives of special training projects that have as their purpose the achievements of breakthrough to new higher levels of excellence through added kinds of behavior and new techniques to improve the quality or cut the cost of training or assure that the effects of training can be more certainly achieved.

Innovation goes beyond problem solving, for it assumes higher levels of achievement than problem solving that often does nothing more than restore the status quo through eradicating causes of deviations from norms.

The difference between problem solving and innovation in training can be illustrated by the following case. The training manager, in addition to conducting regular courses, discovers that because of new orders and new products quality control is slipping in a plant. He conducts a new course in statistical quality control for all operating managers. The quality of the product is improved; that is, it is restored to previously former high levels. The problem is solved.

In another plant the submission rate of new ideas to the suggestion plan has reached a new level. The training manager, desiring to see it go even higher in order that even greater breakthrough to high levels of creative suggestion can be reached, plans and presents a work simplification course that teaches systematic skills in innovative behavior to managers and operators. As a result the plant moves beyond the highest expectation of anyone involved. The added earnings are a result of sharpening the creative behavior of many people and are based on some new forms of training.

Nobody had decided that a problem existed; in fact, they were well satisfied that the suggestion system performance of the people was excellent. Yet the trainer saw an opportunity to exploit the latent creativity of the people and moved the organization performance to higher levels than imagined feasible. This would illustrate an innovative goal.

Innovation might also include new forms of training technique to improve existing programs, even when the present programs seemed to be working quite satisfactorily. Some examples of this would include such objectives as the following:

1. Preparation of an instructor briefing guide.
2. The application of video tape to conference leader skill training.
3. The use of programmed texts in retail clerical training where it had not been used before.
4. Simplification and increased effectiveness of supervisory chalk talks on selling unwanted jobs to cut the time needed.
5. Reducing the paperwork without losing essential control in the tuition refund plan for employee outside courses.

THE GOAL-SETTING PROCEDURE

About one quarter before the beginning of a new training year every staff member of the training department is required to set forth his objectives, using the three major categories involved. These objectives are discussed individually with the manager of the training department, and the training plan for the year is fixed in almost final form. The training staff then meets a couple of weeks prior to the beginning of the budget or training year, and each staff member presents his training plans for the coming year. Jurisdictional conflicts are discussed, and areas of possible collaboration on objectives are discussed. See Fig. 6–6.

The first step is a dialogue confirmed by a memo (1) between the manager of training and his departmental members. This dialogue and memo comprise a commitment by each staff member to deliver on his regular goals and to try to solve certain problems and hoped-for

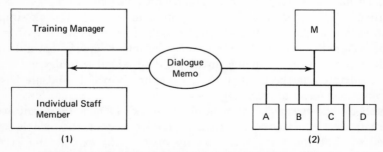

FIGURE 6–6 The Commitment Stages in Setting Training Objectives

innovations. (2) The staff meeting is the final commitment of all members of the team to their plan for the year.

THE FOLLOW-UP

Clearly stated objectives comprise the basis for regular review during the year. Perhaps quarterly staff meetings with reports of results achieved against objective stated, with reasons for exceptions, will serve to keep progress moving. At the end of the year the goal-setting process is repeated, except that last year's plans are reviewed, differences in achievement from stated goals are discussed, and the new goals for the forthcoming year are once more presented and discussed.

The achievement of results against objectives comprises the review and follow-up process. Because they are in writing there should be no disagreement as to the content of the objectives. If conditions change during the year, reopening discussion confirmed by change memos are permissible if mutually agreed on. These can be covered in quarterly review sessions as well as individual discussions between the manager and staff.

The staff member should also feel perfectly free to discuss the possibility of knocking out inappropriate goals when conditions change during the year in such a way that goals that looked sensible at the start prove no longer sensible or feasible. The purpose is not to set up a punishment system but to gain commitment system for every staff member. The training manager summarizes the goals and these comprise his commitment to his boss.

Despite the nonpunitive nature of goals, they can be used for performance appraisal of staff members and for such purposes as raises, promotions, coaching, self-development, and the training of trainers. It also provides some insights for the manager into which trainer can best complete the tough new jobs and is a form or organization planning, managerial control, and departmental planning. It also has numerous motivational effects on staff performance and includes the major communications vehicle for departmental operation.

Classifying Training Needs According to Objectives

It should be noted here that much prior discussion of training needs has centered around problem-solving goals. Although it is true that training should solve problems, it is also true that this does not satisfy the total requirements of training departments. The term *training need* has been treated in the literature in the past as being a single unified item of concern. Usually this has been limited to problem solving.

Problem-solving objectives merely restore normality, and training should do more than merely solve problems. It should serve as a change agent to improve the already satisfactory, to make breakthroughs to newer levels of performance, and to have improving and innovating effects in the organization through enlarging and altering the behavior of people in the organization.

Thus the use of the term *training need* should be dropped and the term *training objective* substituted for it. These training objectives or goals[2] are statements of the behavior change hoped for as a result of training.

Thus training needs—or objectives—should be classified into three major categories at the time choices and decisions are being made about activities being planned and resources being allocated. These three as outlined here include:

1. Regular training objectives.
2. Problem-solving training objectives.
3. Innovative or change-making training objectives.

All such goals and objectives are not isolated from the real world but are a product of an environment or context. Identifying and analyzing this context becomes the first step in identifying training objectives.

---

[2] The words *goal* and *objective* are treated as synonymous here.

THE FIVE-YEAR DEVELOPMENT PLAN CASE

Countrywide Foods had for many years been a centralized organization with functional heads of manufacturing, sales, research, and so on. In the 1940's it changed this organization form to a decentralized one, with six major product divisions, each with its own general manager and each having a complete operating organization. The corporate staff department provided support and advice to the respective divisions.

Following the decentralization, there was a natural amount of difficulty that seems to attend such a drastic shift in organization, or at least it seemed natural to the officers, although many individuals in the line organization felt that it was more than ordinary.

In 1952 the executive board of the company decided that some training and management development, planned in the corporate personnel administration department and conducted across all divisions and departments, would be beneficial in making decentralization work better. A study was conducted, and interviews with general managers in field offices, plants, and corporate staff departments were held. As a result, the conclusion that seemed to present itself most forcibly was that improved human relations and understanding of management principles would be of great benefit to the whole firm and make the new organization function more smoothly.

The president, a student of management practices, felt that the underlying theory of decentralization was to force decision making to the lowest possible level in the organization and that the term used in the American Brake Shoe Co., known as *Bottom-Up Management,* would sum up his thinking on the philosophy required.

Accordingly, the staff prepared a conference series to be conducted as follows:

1. Each location would appoint a conference leader who would be sent to the home office for one-week training course, where he would learn conference leadership techniques plus the content of the materials to be presented.
2. Following the home office course, the local conference leader would return home and arrange and lead a series in his own location. A list of the conferences conducted that year and each year for five years following is shown in Exhibit I.

Exhibit I. Management Development Conferences (1954–1959 Inclusive)

YEAR		PARTICI-PANTS	LEAD-ERS	NUMBER OF SESSIONS
1954–1955	Bottom-Up Management in Countrywide Foods	240	13	7
	Why People Do What They Do			
	Motivating People in Business			
	Making Meetings More Effective			
	Making the Most Out of Talks with Our People			
	Using Planned Conversations to Affect People in Business			
1955–1956	Building Men Through Coaching	1075	67	7
	The Art of Delegating			
	The Importance of Communication and Consulting			
	Obstacles and Pathways to Mutual Understanding			
	Letting the Man Know How He Is Doing			
	Handling Problem Situations			
	Overview of the Manager-Man Relationship			
1956–1957	The Incident Process comprised the entire year's program (human relations problems)	1407	79	7
1957–1958	New Management Concepts	1441	74	5 plus workshops
	The Planning Function			
	The Organization Function			
	The Action Function			
	The Controllable Function			
1958–1959	Bottom-Up Management—What It Is and What It Isn't	1356	88	9
	The Action Side of Management			
	Various Ways of Inducing Action			
	Changing Poor Work Habits to Good			
	14,000 Brains and How to Use Them			
	Authority and Responsibility			
	Recognition—Praise and Reward			
	Utilizing Our Manpower			
	Decision Making			

At the end of five years of such training, the director of personnel asked that the members of each group complete a questionnaire showing their reactions. Based on these results, the approach for the sixth year would be decided and recommendations to the executive group made. These questionnaires were routed to the director of personnel research for analysis. His analysis follows:

Exhibit II.
Analysis of Comments Offered by Participants in the 1958–1959 Management Improvement Program

Memo: to Vice President, Personnel—Countrywide Foods

From: Director of Personnel Research

Subject: *Management Development Conferences 1954–1959 Inclusive*

The following are some of the facts and opinions emerging from the questionnaires pertaining to the management improvement program. The analysis was done on the basis of 454 returned questionnaires.

Another batch of questionnaires were given us after these results were computed—they were for the plants and had been in the possession of the plant training manager. The total of that group was 187 plant supervisors and 74 plant staff.

1. Sales groups showed the lowest attendance this year, but it was still very good.

   89 per cent of those questioned in sales attended five or more sessions.

   96 per cent or more of other groups attended five or more sessions.

It should be noted that of the 1,400 or more who were originally invited, questionnaires were received from only about one third—so attendance was probably much poorer than would show up by this information.

2. 20 per cent were at the meeting this year for the first time.

   68 per cent had attended for three years or more.

3. 72 per cent said this year's sessions were better than last year's.

   38 per cent said this year's sessions were better than all previous sessions.

Of those who had attended four and five years,

   40 per cent of office staff said this year better than all years.

   66 per cent of sales management said this year better than all years.

   34 per cent of technical supervisors said this year better than all years.

On the other hand, only

   6 per cent of total said it was worse than 1957–1958, and

   1 per cent of total said it was worse than all other years, these being in "office."

4. The two "most helpful" meetings were found to be session 2 and session 9:

   #2 Make Things Happen—16 per cent

   #9 Decision Making—19 per cent

The three next "most helpful" meetings were

   #4 Changing Poor Work Habits—13 per cent

   #8 Utilizing Manpower—11 per cent

   #3 Inducing Action—11 per cent

The one with the lowest "most helpful" response was

   #1 Professionalization in Management—5 per cent

For the office staff the highest rated session was

   #9 Decision Making, with 45 responses

For Sales Management the highest rated session was

   #2 Making Things Happen, with 29 responses.

For Technical group the highest rated was

   #9 Decision Making, with 15 responses, and

#2 Making Things Happen, with 14 responses.

The sessions this past year that received the highest number of "least helpful" votes were

#1 Professionalism in Management—14 per cent

#4 Changing Work Habits—12 per cent

#5 14,000 Brains—14 per cent

#6 Authority & Responsibility—16 per cent

#7 Utilizing Employees Better—13 per cent

It is noted that the responses here were more consistent among the least liked than they were among the most liked.

5. Seventy-two per cent of the respondents indicated their leaders were well prepared. (It should be noted here that most of the questionnaires were returned directly to the leader when completed.)

6. Additional topics suggested for future conferences were

Company Information	11 per cent of total N
Decision Making	7 per cent
Human Relations	6 per cent
Communications	5 per cent
Labor Relations	4 per cent (mostly plant or technical)

Fifty-five per cent of the blanks had suggestions as to additional topics. Although the largest number of suggested topics came from the office (actual was 86), the participation of the groups was as follows (by per cent of blanks received):

Sales Nonmanagement	93 per cent
Sales Management	61 per cent
Technical	58 per cent
Other	57 per cent
Plant Staff	56 per cent
Office	44 per cent
Plant Supervision	43 per cent

7. In addition to making suggestions about courses that could be added, there were about 19 per cent of the blanks that had suggestions of a more general nature for improvement that might be made in the handling of the course. These additional suggestions were distributed as follows:

Plant Supervision	1
Plant Staff	3
Office Staff	45
Sales Management	17
Technical Supervision	10
Sales	4
Other	8

Below are some of the more interesting of these suggestions:

The use of case study in one form or another came from 41 per cent.

More personal appearances of other company personnel or the use of some professional leaders mentioned by several.

Having more specialized programs—that is, sessions more directly related to the job skills and interests was mentioned in various ways by several.

Other suggestions on which only about one or two comments were found are illustrated by

(a) Have rotation of conference participants so that there can be more exchange of ideas.

(b) Have two levels of classes—one for those who have gone through previous conferences and one for those who haven't.

(c) Have sessions in evening, in conjunction with dinner.

(d) Foster the attitude that attendance is desirable for the values gained and that it is not merely a requirement.

8. Recommend that some serious consideration be given this year to "getting away from" the approach to modern and professional management as such and to come closer to what might almost be likened to an "advanced orientation" course. The course could still be put together in such a way as to weave in much of the prevailing company management thinking and procedure.

The idea that has been expressed that there be two or three different concurrent series for different segments of the company would give some satisfaction to those who want more specific application of the course. Because the predominant interest of the respondents seems to be for more information about the company as such, each series should be put together so groups could get information they need in their assignments.

The preponderance of requests for more case histories would not be as important in this kind of program. Although case studies have been highly advised by the questionnaire results, this is interpreted as important primarily in terms of the subject matter. If it is to be on how the company operates—its history, policy, procedures and objectives—the case study is not so valuable as where management concepts are being studied in the abstract.

Exhibits I and II outline some of the specific details and statistics on the Management Development Conference Programs from 1954 to 1959 inclusive. Exhibit I indicates by year the topics of each of these, the number of participants, the number of leaders trained and the number of sessions held each year. A session in each of these locations was generally a two-hour meeting held either during working hours, half on working hours and half on the employees' time, and in some instances on the employees' time. In each case the material presented to the leaders and which they in turn led in their individual sessions was uniform for all persons listed as participants. The general objective of this was to make clear what Countrywide policy was on management and to clarify and expound what was required of a manager in a divisionalized company. Exhibit II is the result of a survey made of the 1,356 participants this year and shows in summary form what their opinions were.

CASE DISCUSSION QUESTIONS

The Five-Year Development Plan Case

1. In the light of the objectives set for the management development conferences, how suitable was the plan?

2. If you were responsible for recommending a training program for the following year, what would you propose as a major outline?

(a) Would you continue a company-wide program, or would you develop several programs for different functional areas of the business?

(b) How much would you leave to local discretion and to what extent would you centralize and impose uniformity?

(c) What major theme and what specific topics would you suggest?

7 Context—The First Step in Defining Training Objectives

Man is a creative animal, doomed to strive
consciously toward a goal.
— F. DOSTOEVSKI

BEHAVIORAL technology is concerned with all the influences that affect the behavior of people at work and that shape it to a predetermined pattern. Unlike some of the earlier approaches that assume that training is a rather private relationship of a teacher and a pupil—sort of Mark Hopkins and student on a log—it presumes that training should change behavior on the job. Thus the first step in training becomes identifying the training needs, and the first step in identifying training needs lies in describing the context.

Let us suppose that Mr. Smith, office manager, is sent to a training course, Work Simplification in the Office. The trainer has heard numerous horror tales from younger colleagues in purchasing, accounting, and other office departments about the waste and inefficiency in the paperwork system. He proposes a course in paperwork simplification to his boss, the personnel manager. Bemused with a new union organization drive, the personnel manager assents more to get the trainer out of his hair than for any other reason. The trainer organizes his materials, his instructional space, and his outlines, and begins the course. Twelve various office supervisors including Mr. Smith attend.

The course is well taught. It teaches the people attending the various stages in applying work simplification. This is pictured in Fig.

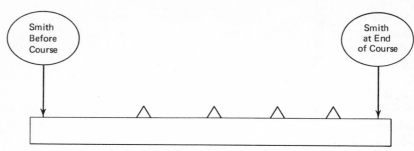

FIGURE 7–1   The Pre-Course Training Plan

7–1. Mr. Smith makes very satisfactory progress. He enters into the discussion and works the peg-board and flow-chart session with intelligence and friendly interest. He tells the instructor privately that this stuff is certainly needed, and he sees many uses for it in his area. The course progresses through the eight two-hour weekly sessions, conducted half on company time and half on the employee time.

At the end of the course a small evaluation card is passed out and the ratings are almost all very favorable. Many enthusiastic comments are noted on the space permitted for free responses.

Now Mr. Smith goes back to the job. This is pictured in Fig. 7–2. There he finds that there are some influences at work that can importantly shape his behavior there and can wipe out the things he learned—at least effectively prevent his applying them. For one thing his boss is very cool to the whole idea of changes and in some matters is downright scornful.

As you know, Smith, we have a systems department which set up these methods. The reason we have this department is to free chaps like you from the necessity of getting tied up in complex methods studies. If they aren't doing their job, I'll let them know. I guess you can find small ways of improving your personal efficiency, and that's what I had in mind when you went. But as for methods . . .

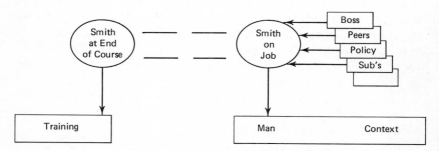

FIGURE 7–2   The Post-Course Effects of Training

Smith talks to some of the other office managers at lunch. One is especially vocal against any programs adding to his responsibility and making waves. The others eat in silence or are kindly tolerant. None expresses any enthusiasm. A few ask some questions that indicate clearly to Smith that they really need the course themselves, because they do not understand what he is talking about.

One by one the pressures on Smith *unteach* on the job the things he learned in the training class. As a result he files the course materials with the determination that someday he will find the climate better and will start applying it. Meanwhile it was certainly a thought-provoking course, and he will try to use some of the things he learned in handling his own in-basket, desk procedures, and routines. He revises his filing system, gets new route slips, and eliminates a report that nobody has been reading for years. After this he lapses back into the same pattern as in the past. How could such an outcome have been averted?

The Trainer as a Behavioral Technologist

The new orientation in training, toward behavioral technology, is a consequence of the systems approach to training. It requires some hard criteria for training and the management of the total behavior change environment. There are some requirements for the trainer if he is to tap the multiple advantages of the systems approach and apply behavioral technology to his training efforts.

1. He must fix in mind the definition of training as "Training means changing behavior back on the job."
2. He notes that behavior is "activity that can be seen, measured, observed, counted, photographed, or recorded."
3. The behavior change sought should be useful, germane, and possible of maintenance in the environment into which the man will work when the training is over.

This puts a new slant on the definition of training objectives. Traditional training objectives have been identified as the needs of the individual or group of individuals. Thus the psychology of individual differences, attitudes, motivation, and even personality have been considered to be the main ground for finding training needs.

Training systems start with the hard assumption that all training objectives are organizational needs.

Training departments being an organismic part of the company, agency, or institution means that they are oriented toward solving organization problems or introducing change *by means* of affecting individual behavior. The traditional dilemma of "How to uncover training needs" sometimes delved into such needs, and in the most flourishing and successful training departments the assumption has always been made along these lines. Yet hesitancy in defining training objectives as organization objectives has led to numerous diversions and waste in training.

Organization of Training Objectives Requires a Study of Context

Context in training means that the trainer must define the frame of reference within which his training is to occur. Out of this frame of reference will come definitions of problems, agreements that behavior change is needed, and acceptance of the behavior change after it has been effected by training. It also means that the actual means of behavior change may be accomplished by a wide range of different action. The place of context studies to the rest of the training activities can be pictured as shown in Fig. 7–3.

Within the context are problems that require solution or opportunities for improvement. Some of these training goals can be fulfilled by changing the system by which things are done. Some can be done by close supervision. Others can be done by "training" in the form of classes, coaching, counseling, and other means. The sequence of train-

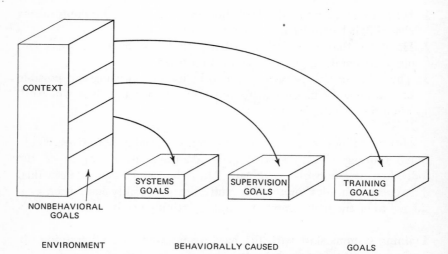

FIGURE 7–3 How Context Shapes Training Objectives

ing in the systems approach then follows a pattern that can be described as follows:

1. A study of the context is made and described.
2. Out of this come *goals* that exist. Finding good objectives alone will not assure satisfactory training, because the organization culture, organization climate, and the "ropes" of the organization have created the objective. These goals can then be classified into three major categories:
   (a) *Systems-based objectives.* The flow of work, the policies, and the way things are arranged encourage a kind of behavior that causes people's actions to vary from the desired way. To effect behavior change here calls for objectives in systems analysis and procedural change, not training.
   (b) *Supervisory failure.* When the system is adequate but because of ignorance or simple laxity the supervisory management does not check and correct the behavior of people to be sure that they are following the procedures, then training the workers will not be enough. This may be a problem of simple enforcement, or it may be that the unfavorable consequences for the worker or the supervisor lie in following the procedure. Safety procedures are often well prescribed, but the supervisor is faced with a choice of operating safely or getting out maximum production. If his pay, promotions, and general comfort on his job are higher when production is high and he feels no penalties for a nominal amount of accidents, then he will stress production and place safety in a lesser level of priority.
   (c) *Training objectives* are those that involve the behavior of people, caused by lack of knowledge, insufficient skills, wrong knowledge, or wrong information.

   In summary, training objectives are those that require behavior change from people; they cannot be solved by changing the system or tightening regular control over their behavior by supervision.

3. *Task Analysis.* After a problem has been clarified as a training problem, then a behavior change program can be developed. There are two ingredients here: (a) Describe the present behavior. (b) Describe the desired behavior in specific terms, as well as the consequences of that correct behavior. The difference is the training objective.
4. Next, apply the *skills of the trainer.* He prepares outlines, devises behavior change methods for the class that simulate the job

environment to which the man will return, arranges for feedback to take place while the new behavior is being practiced, and plans the outlines and procedures of the training effort.

At this point the trainer begins to show concern for his training techniques. He decides on the mixture of reading, lecture, role-playing, case study, in-basket, programmed instruction, film forum, problem-solving conference, chalk talk, demonstration, reading assignments, management game, or other methods of training.

The almost compulsive practice of trainers to see their activity as one of finding new techniques of presentation that are interesting, exciting, or novel is useless gimmickry unless he has started with context, identified objectives, and assured himself that he is dealing with a training objective through a task analysis.

5. *Evaluation of results of training* is the final stage in the training system. By this he measures whether or not the behavior change objective that he set out to achieve has actually occurred. There are several methods of doing this, and they will be discussed in Chapter 10.

We have reviewed quickly the whole system of training as it fits into the management system (management by objectives) for the firm or organization that the trainer serves. We have also looked at the subsystem of training itself. It is apparent that system approach calls for a context study of the whole organization before the training system becomes operational. How is this done?

Sizing Up Total Organizational Context

It is not an especially useful exercise to state that context must be studied or even to suggest that organization culture and climate must be assessed. What specific step does a trainer take in studying context? Some of the most useful context studies have been composed of the following elements:

1. A picture of the organizational relationships (charts).
2. Economic information about the firm or organization.
3. A list of major organization objectives.
4. A first draft of the organization's major problems or opportunities.

Because these obviously are not self-explanatory and need illustration and devices for clarification, let us look at each in some detail.

How to Study Organization Relationships in Your Parent Organization

The training department does not exist in a vacuum, nor does it operate on an island populated only by its own staff. The first step is that of sketching out the organization relationships.

Step 1. Defining Formal Organizational Relationships. The plant trainer works in a different organizational environment than does the divisional trainer or the corporate staff training specialist.

Take the case of Harry Smith, plant training manager for a large appliance firm. He reports to a manager of salaried personnel, who in turn reports to the plant industrial relations manager. The industrial relations manager reports to the plant manager, except for labor relations central staff, which has an open phone by which it coordinates the relations with unions (to prevent whip sawing and other union tactics from working). On the other hand, Smith has frequent direct contacts with the divisional training manager and receives memos, research reports, and policy statements from the corporate office as well. His bosses also receive these memos but have authority to modify them. Sketched out in organization form, omitting some of the other parts of the organization temporarily, we might see something as depicted in Fig. 7–4.

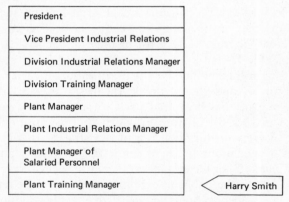

FIGURE 7–4 How Plant Training Context Appears

It is pretty obvious that Harry is subject to many more influences in shaping his program, identifying his objectives, and getting access to trainees and students than if he were in a different kind of organization. *His job is substantially different* and he should become very familiar with how each of these organizational units can alter, amend, wipe out, or accelerate his own objectives.

1. If Harry were training manager in a small single-plant firm and reported to the president, if there were no union, and if he sat in on management meetings, his objectives would be different from those of a training manager in a multiplant firm.

2. If Harry were *divisional* training manager, his objectives would be different and his ways of doing his job would be drastically different —more service-oriented and less operational.

3. If Harry were *corporate* manager of training, his objectives and working plans would be much different—higher level, more advisory, and less operational in scope.

4. If Harry were in sales training, the entire context of his training job would be different; in fact, if he were in industrial sales training, it might be unlike being in consumer sales or retail sales training.

5. If Harry were in government, the number of contexts would be just as wide as they might be in industry. He might run through the organizational structures of local installation, small independent unit, or staffer in one of the large monoliths in Washington where he reported to an assistant secretary.

Step 2. The evaluation of your organizational relationship, then, is done by sketching the organizational unit and its relationships with other parts of the parent organization. One then lists the five or six distinctive features in the organizational arrangement that make it different from other organizations you know. The old saying "our company is different" is true. Make a list of these differences. A typical list is shown in Table I.

Such a listing will be unique for the organization of each firm, department, or company and should define the basic leverage or operating guides the company has organized itself to achieve. It a good idea at this stage to make a list of ways in which the organization is a mess. At the core of every organization is a master strategy that the organization form is formed around. Try to define this strategic plan.

Step 3. *What Is Your Constituency?* A *constituency*—a word adopted from politicians—is the public or organizational unit to be served by the trainer. In large organizations where there may be divisions, departments, plants, regional offices, local offices, sometimes with a trainer in each, it becomes important for every trainer to clarify his relationships by spelling out—and obtaining agreement with somebody higher up— exactly what his area of concern should be. Take the case of a 'large manufacturer with several product divisions. It also has a corporate training director, divisional training managers, and plant or sales district training managers. There is also a national sales training manager and a variety of other training jobs, including customer service training and

Table I

Kind of Organization	Three Distinctive Organization Features That Distinguish It
Insurance company	Sources of income from investments and underwriting
	Sales (agency) plant is not under company control but works through brokers and independent agents
	Many specialized expert departments such as claims, actuarial, etc.
Large retail store	Essentially a buying and selling organization; buyers and merchandisers are dominant people
	Floor supervisors are apt to have dual management above them
	There are times of year when many part-time workers are employed and business is seasonal
Manufacturing plant	Based on three major manufacturing functions, stamping, assembling, and packaging, at high speeds
	Highly mechanized, and mechanical and craft skills are premium skills
	Cost considerations are very important
	Most managers are promoted from the ranks

corporate apprentice training. Simply an agreement with the Labor Department affects the whole company. To prevent a duplication, self-canceling activity, and overlap of responsibility among the various training entities, a clear definition of jurisdiction and constituency is needed, or the objectives of the various training groups will be wasted. A typical breakdown of such a definition might look, in simplified form, like Table II. It is pretty clear that Table II is not a complete job description or a definition of functions, authority, and responsibility in toto. It is one way, however, of clarifying the working constituency and of sharpening the context of the trainer.

Step 4. The "Product" of the Training Department. Still another useful instrument for the analysis of the trainer's organizational relations is to take a product line approach to studying organizational relations. In this approach we assume that the training department is a production department that makes and sells intangible softwares to a captive market. Because this product costs something, we should identify the contents of our product catalog and determine what the mix of various

Table II. Constituency Definiton

Level	Training Departments Constituency
Corporate training office	Trains trainers and training managers in all divisions and plants. Trains corporate-level officers and staff. Trains division general managers including choice of outside university executive programs.
Division training managers	Trains plant trainers, division manager's staff, and division executives. Also trains plant manager and division and regional sales managers.
Plant training manager	Trains superintendents, general foremen, foremen, foremen candidates, mechanical and apprentice employees, job instructor training, office and clerical supervision and employees. Arranges to send plant employees to outside schools, seminars, and the like.

products in that catalog are. Table III shows a classification system into three major categories of product. Across the top of the table are listed the criteria for classifying your training effort: type of organization, basis of your authority to act, size and kind of staff personnel employed, the general nature of your organization structure, and the major product generated and sold. Down the left margin are three major categories of organization types. You may find, for example, that you are a mixture of all three or that you are exclusively one (most unlikely).

A more detailed look at your organization might lead you into a specific definition by type of organization, whether advice, service, or operations. Types of training departments are as follows:

1. *Advice-oriented department.*
   (a) Responds to technical requests.
   (b) Conducts original research on training.
   (c) Keeps abreast of new techniques.
   (d) Solves long-run chronic problems.
   (e) Interprets company objectives for training.
   (f) Conducts, audits, and issues reports.
   (g) Trains trainers in new techniques.
   (h) Issues bulletins, reports, and instruction sheets.

Table III. How to Classify Your Training Organization

Type of Organization	Basis of Authority	Staffing	Organization Structure	Major Product Contribution
Advice-oriented	Technical know-how	Small expert group	By project	Policy recommendation New ideas Interpretation of policy Evaluation
	Acceptance by users			
Service-oriented	Technical know-how and skills Special facilities or equipment needed by users	Functional experts and technicians— Medium size	By type of service provided	Efficient service
Operations-oriented	Delegated jurisdiction Defined Constituency Special skills, authority, and responsibility	Matches line organization Large functional group	By departments controlled	Develops, conducts, and evaluates training programs

2. *Service-oriented department.*
   (a) Operates school physical facilities.
   (b) Operates testing facilities for personnel.
   (c) Runs test courses and pilot courses.
   (d) Gives technical service in training.
   (e) Does task analyses.
   (f) Trains staff trainers for others.
   (g) Staffs training jobs in plants.
   (h) Operates a library of books, films, and training materials.
   (i) Tests, stores, and maintains audiovisual equipment.
   (j) Designs, prepares, and stores visual aids.
   (k) Maintains list of avaliable courses and outside facilities.
   (l) Responds to special requests.

3. *Operations-oriented department.*
    (a) Confers with line on training needs.
    (b) Performs task analyses.
    (c) Develops outlines, curricula, and training plans.
    (d) Selects, briefs, and rehearses instructors.
    (e) Schedules, promotes, announces, and enrolls trainees.
    (f) Arranges facilities and aids.
    (g) Conducts classes, clinics, courses, and meetings.
    (h) Surveys acceptance of instruction.
    (i) Keeps records of trainees, classes, and activity.
    (j) Evaluates effect of training.

Such a checklist might be slightly different in your department but its use is great. To analyze to what extent your department is one of these three categories, try the following:

1. Place a check beside each of the listed functions that are performed by your department.
2. In the left margin next to those checked, note the per cent of total staff time available that is devoted to each. (The total could be in both hours and budget dollars.)
3. Compute subtotals by the three categories (advice, service, and operations). This will provide you with an index of where your training effort is being concentrated.

For example, take Harry Smith's department (plant):

	Per Cent of Manpower	Per Cent of Budget
1. Advice functions	0	0
2. Service functions	35	40
3. Operations	65	60
	100 per cent	100 per cent

As long as Harry is supported by division and corporate training departments this may be a perfectly suitable arrangement. The trend in corporate training departments is more toward the advice type. In those instances where they have tried to centralize through making corporate training perform all three, the weakest link has been in operations. The training loses touch with reality. As a general guide, advice should probably be corporate and service divisional, and the plant should be concentrated in service and control. This, of course, will not fit every company, and the mix must fit your own. More important than finding a formula that fits all, it is important in setting objectives so that you know (1) what kind of department you run and (2) whether you actually want to be that type.

Which type is best? The major point in such analysis is that context will shape the kind of training objectives that you find. Having decided for example that your plant training department should be operations- and service-oriented, you then find training objectives that suit such a context.

The closer training works to production or selling, the more likely is the probability that it will be operations- and service-centered.

To attempt to operate operations-type departments from a corporate headquarters is to invite delay, role conflict, and bad communication. The product catalogue at the corporate level should stress advice as its product. The influence of the training function is thus enhanced, and the quality of other training in the company is likewise improved. A trainer's long-run weight and importance is raised because his advice is followed, whereas its lower level operations actions are often resisted.

In those departments where these three functional types of organization have been clearly spelled out and consciously chosen, the quality of the training done is superior that in those companies where it is left unclarified or where it varies from week to week.

Step 5. A final device that will assist in clarifying your organizational relations is a simple sketching of the kinds of other services you use and the kinds of people you serve in any of several ways. There are many who serve us—the typing pool, the employment department, the accounting department, traffic and transportation, the art department in marketing, the duplicating department, addressograph department, company library, janitorial staff, and the like. There are also many departments that we serve. We provide in return information, advice and service to other sections of the industrial relations departments. In Fig. 7–5 we see a diagram in which we can sketch these relationships. Although the diagram includes space for only a few relationships, it illustrates the principle. In practice you may wish simply to list them in two parallel columns. In one firm the drawing up of a roster of organizations served achieved two benefits:

1. It pointed up the absence of certain organizations who might have been served but were not. A conscious program of discovering reasons for this failure to sell the services available was undertaken and the blocks eliminated. The controller's department, it seemed, never

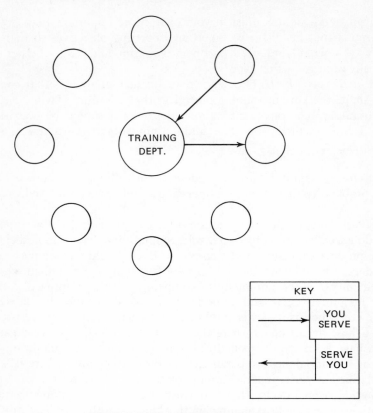

FIGURE 7–5   Mutual Exchange of Services

trained anyone. By chatting with the controller about the causes and outlining the ways in which accountants might be professionally developed, the training manager was able to provide useful and practical services for this important group.

I pointed out to him that 10 per cent of all income in the large CPA firms is devoted to training of staff and that this is a beneficial process in staff performance and also makes the CPA firms more attractive to college recruits than industrial accounting jobs.

2. It points up areas where service is being received and may focus attention on ways in which this service can be improved.

ECONOMIC INFORMATION ABOUT THE ORGANIZATION

Many trainers in their excessive interest in individual psychology omit an overriding dimension of their organization, its economic or monetary base. Even nonprofit institutions and government agencies are importantly shaped by economics. In this stage the financing of training, the emphasis on training, and the possibilities for certain kinds of training activities will be shaped by the funds available and the possibilities of improving the economic dimension of the firm through behavior change.

A context study calls for a listing of the major economic facts of the organization. A sample, by no means complete, is shown in Table IV for different kinds of economic climate.

Table IV

Type of Organization	Major Economic Facts
Government agency	Program budgeting now required by the Bureau of the Budget calls for five-year plans and one-year commitments in budget planning.
	Programs are subject to sudden cutbacks and changes in direction.
	Numerous approvals are required to spend funds and are difficult to obtain changes in budgets after they are established.
	Funds are a function of political decisions rather than real need in some respect.
Consumer marketing department	Funds for training are easiest to get when they promise to produce higher sales volume.
	There is far less concern over cost reduction and expense control than in manufacturing.
	Research and analysis funds are increasingly available.
	Premium is placed on new ideas, innovation, and growth plans.

What are the dominant economic facts in your organization? You might be required to answer some of the following questions to discover the economic aspect of your context in training:

1. Are you working in a high labor content or low labor content business? That is, do labor costs make up more than half of the total costs of doing business?
2. Are the profit levels in your business ordinarily high (above 6 per

cent) or low? How does your company stand with respect to industry averages? Last year's results?

3. Has your company undergone growth in sales? Is profit commensurate with that growth? Is your division growing faster or slower than the company? The industry?

4. Is your company under the control of outside influences in a way that affects wages, prices, and profits? Utilities, banks, insurance companies, and transportation companies would fall into this category. Companies working through dealers and distributors are influenced by private outsiders.

5. What are the major inputs in your business? People? Capital? Materials and supplies? In what per cent is each significant in economic terms?

6. What are the major outputs? Products? Hardware? Software? Service? What percentage of your total revenue comes from each?

7. Are you a family-owned firm? What is the family's attitude toward modern management practices? Toward training expenditures?

These and other questions should give you a better "fix" on what your own top management is thinking about and on the hub around which most top-management decisions are being made.

Major Organization Objectives

In every organization there are three categories of objectives that are being pursued. The context for your firm is probably best explained in terms of its objectives, its unfulfilled projects. These are not the objectives of the training department alone but are the objectives of the firm. These objectives are then subdivided into objectives for departments, plants, sales districts, and staff departments. The three categories of goals can be uncovered by the following kind of analysis (again partial and illustrative rather than complete):

1. What are some of the regular or routine things that the organization for which I am trainer must perform? Are there any tasks, functions, or responsibilities that recur constantly? Are there any that are indispensable?

2. What are the major problems that need solving? Are there things that have gone awry in recent months or years? What kinds of problems are the higher managers in my unit working on these days? Which ones take top priority with them?

3. What significance does innovation have in this business? Are there plans afoot to find tomorrow's breadwinner as well as making and selling today's breadwinner? What importance does research in

product, process, methods, markets, and personnel have in the organization?

In recent years more and more firms have moved toward the system of management—and management appraisal—known as management by objectives. In its simplest form it requires that every manager and subordinate manager sit down at the beginning of each year and define the objectives for the subordinate's job for that year. At the end of the year—as well as during it—the two use these objectives as guides to action and a standard for measuring results.

If your organization is being managed by objectives, the trainer should be probing with managers everywhere to get samplings of the kinds of objectives the line managers will be trying to achieve. This is not "collecting" objectives but conducting dialogues with managers that ask bluntly "What objectives have you established for this department this year, and how could training help in their achievement?"

One training director of my acquaintance has instructed his staff to talk to line managers in his plant on every occasion and to lead the discussion whenever possible to a discussion of that manager's objectives for the coming period of a year or less. This sensing of goals provides a better link to definition of training needs than any past method (job description, attitude surveys, interviews with managers about their felt needs, and the like).

This background information on context, which includes organizational form and organizational relations coupled with economic data and objectives of management, opens many new avenues to finding training needs.

The key to finding training and objectives is uncovering organizational objectives.

To make this definition most productive, a clear statement of organization is needed, and this requires some discipline in specifically stating them.

Thus if costs are at 100 and somebody wants them to be at 80, the objective is in the 20. Such a definition has numerous virtues in defining training objectives. It prevents us from getting all snarled up in causes and ruminative conjectures about who's to blame and allows us to get to what is really the heart of the objective.

Let us look at some examples to show how this tight definition of objectives would work in some business situations.

1. In a manufacturing plant the safety rate is measured by frequency and severity. The present frequency is 50 accidents per million man-hours. The management wishes it were lower. Under questioning they set a goal of 10 per million man-hours as desired frequency by the end of the year. The objective: the 40 per million man-hours. Subtract the desired from the actual. Result? The objective defined. Note that it requires three things to be precisely defined:
   (a) A statement of what exists now.
   (b) An objective with a time commitment.
   (c) The difference between the two.
2. A sales department finds that it has 4 per cent of the market in six states for its product. It studies the market and decides that it should have 10 per cent. What is the objective?
3. Quality control reports that the present reject rate on photon correlators is 30 per cent. How would you help the quality manager specify his objective?
4. The industrial relations manager states that "grievances are a headache in this plant. They are just too doggone high." How would you help him specify the grievance objective?

The great leakage in defining training objective in the past has frequently been the zeal we have shown for defining causes, symptoms, side effects, or general dissatisfaction as objectives. We cannot start solving the problem or introducing change until we have specified present and desired levels. We are then ready to start working on finding causes and then on classifying those causes as training or nontraining causes. Some common sources of organization problems where trainers might look are illustrated in Fig. 7–6.

The simplicity of this approach should not conceal its extreme use-

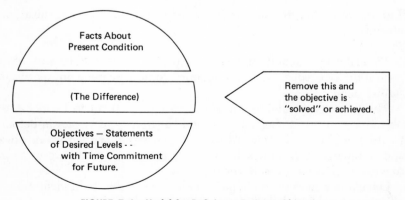

FIGURE 7–6   Model for Defining a Training Objective

fulness. As the systems experts have found, narrowing your definition of what an objective is makes subsequent steps—finding causes and alternative solutions and taking action—vastly more manageable.

1. It presumes that the objective belongs to the man who saw the present condition and set an objective to eliminate the difference.
2. It presumes that if you like what you already have (facts) then you do not have an objective.
3. It gives you some criteria for knowing when the objective is achieved and when you are making progress toward its solution.
4. It is a form of managing by objectives because it is the establishment of the objective that creates the problems or defines the innovation needed. If you do not have an objective, then you do not have a problem and change is not required.
5. It suggests avenues toward solution. If you do not know where you are going, then any road will get you there.
6. It defines the consequences that can be expected if a successful program of solution is tried.

These objectives are the definition of your training needs.

We should use spartan discipline (intellectual, of course) in limiting our definition of objectives. For one thing they permit us to evaluate training later by its organizational context and contribution.

An objective specifically defined is the best kind of training objective. It permits us to plunge into the details of identifying intervening causes and root causes with a compass to keep us from getting lost on the way. The old saw "A problem defined or a goal established is half solved" may seem a little optimistic as we press into the rest of our systems approach, but it will prove to be of great worth.

The distinctive feature of the systems approach suggested here is that it starts with the definition of the need by finding objectives within a context. The next step is to uncover causes, to classify them, and from this to work out training plans.

Is all this analysis needed to conduct a single training program? Clearly it is not. In managing training by objectives it should be done *once* and updated at least annually.

Cautious trainers will probably note that the definition of organization objectives really is not a complete basis for setting objectives for the training department for the year ahead. This is perfectly correct. For one thing the objective may not even be a training objective, and thus the training manager would be rather presumptuous if not foolish to make a commitment such as "We will cut costs of assembly 3 per cent during the coming year." If the costs went up, it might have been for reasons beyond his control or even despite the training effort. They went up 2 per cent instead of going down but would have gone up 5 per cent if the training had not been conducted. How then does the trainer define objectives for his department and himself and make commitments on effects that are under his control or influence?

To establish objectives that actually reflect the results of his own ingenuity, skill, and effort, the trainer takes the organizational objectives he has defined in his context studies and screens them for behavior change objectives that will lend themselves to training. This process is task analysis, the subject of Chapter 8.

THE ATLAS INSURANCE COMPANY CASE

BACKGROUND INFORMATION ABOUT THE ATLAS INSURANCE COMPANY

The Atlas Insurance Company is a medium-sized stock life company writing ordinary life, accident and health, and group policies. During the period from 1947 to 1955 the sales and earnings growth of the company had leveled off, after over 25 years of steady growth. Then, in 1955, the company Board of Directors brought in John Walker as president—primarily in order to work with the senior-management group to orient the company back to a pattern of expansion.

At the time Walker took office, the majority of the company's business was concentrated in the New England and Middle Atlantic States. One of Walker's first steps as president, and one that was effected without considerable debate among the company's top-level executives, was to decentralize, establishing regional offices in several cities. This change has already begun to pay dividends; sales are up, service has improved, and costs are fairly well in line.

The current organization of Atlas includes the following senior officers who report to the president: (1) the treasurer, responsible for all investment activities; (2) the agency vice president, in charge of all sales activities; (3) the vice president and actuary, responsible for actuarial, underwriting, and claim functions; and (4) the comptroller, responsible for accounting, expense control, and personnel.

At several recent meetings of the Board of Directors there were lengthy discussions of the pros and cons of entering the casualty and fire business. A majority of the board felt that there would be some competitive advantages to being able to offer all lines of insurance to their policyholders. It was felt that it would be better to consider purchasing a majority interest in a small casualty company than to start from scratch in these unfamiliar lines. The financial position of Atlas was such that funds were available for a purchase. It was decided to cautiously explore merger possibilities and Walker was instructed to be on the lookout for suitable casualty companies that might be for sale.

A few months later Walker attended a seminar given by the American Management Association in New York City. At the seminar he became acquainted with Axel Heyst, president of the Kurtz Automobile Insurance Company. Both men were interested in the marketing problems facing the insurance industry and decided to meet that evening to discuss the matter in more detail.

During this discussion, Walker got the first glints of a possibility that was soon to become a major concern for the Atlas Insurance Company. The two men were rambling over the status of their companies in general when Heyst happened to mention the fact that the majority holding of his company's stock was going on the block—probably in about a year.

When Walker heard this, he pursued the issue. The Kurtz Company, he learned, had been started in 1915 by Albert Kurtz, almost as a one-man operation. From there the story of the company could have been written by Horatio Alger, at least through World War II. Kurtz had died suddenly in August 1949. Three weeks later Kurtz's son, Paul, the heir-apparent to the presidency of the company, had suffered a stroke. This put him out of the office for 18 months, and when he returned, he did so, minus the drive that had characterized his previous work. The company limped through the following decade, undergoing a major organizational shuffle, diversifying its line to cover more of the casualty field, and experiencing a number of problems.

At a recent Board of Directors meeting, Paul Kurtz had announced that his family planned to relinquish its controlling interest in the company primarily because of his ill health and his sons' choices to enter other businesses. This announcement had come as a complete surprise to many of the board members and top-level executives of the company. Heyst, who had been with the Kurtz Company since 1920, remarked that he felt as though he had been working for a "sinking ship" for the last few months. At the age of 68, he had been thinking of retirement, though his health had been perfect to this point. Heyst joined the company as a personal friend of Albert Kurtz and had come to think of himself as almost part of the family enterprise.

He and Walker did not touch on the merger possibility at this time and their discussion veered back to more general topics of mutual interest.

On his return to the home office, Walker called several of his vice presidents together to discuss the Atlas Company's expansion plans. He did this with the express intent of bringing up the Kurtz Company as a merger possibility. In the meeting Walker outlined what Heyst had told him of the Kurtz Company's history and current status. He also went over various other bits of knowledge he had picked up about the Kurtz Company, from Heyst and his own general knowledge of the insurance industry.

The first response was favorable, with the exception of one officer who mentioned some losses taken by the Kurtz Company in recent years. Walker decided to bring up the Kurtz merger possibility at the next meeting of the Board of Directors. His timing was good because the next meeting started with a review of Atlas' results for the past year. The annual report showed encouraging gains on all fronts; the company was in a solid position and could well stand some expansion.

In presenting the Kurtz merger to the board, Walker followed essentially the same pattern he had used with his executives the previous week. He sketched the Kurtz Company, historically and in the present, went quickly over some recent financial figures, and then opened the meeting to discussion of the merger with emphasis on Atlas developing the casualty and fire business through a merger with Kurtz.

Again, the response was favorable. Although it was agreed that Kurtz had not been moving well during the last decade, the fault was placed with management problems, not with the intrinsic reputation of the firm itself. Kurtz was a good name to the public, which was, after all, quite unaware of the company's interior difficulties. Another favorable point was the geographical location of this company. Kurtz operated in fewer states than Atlas, but Atlas had a number of agents in the three states where Kurtz did business.

At the conclusion of the board meeting, it was decided that a detailed study of the Kurtz Company should be undertaken. To do this, Walker arranged with the top management of Kurtz to send a representative to spend several weeks at Kurtz to completely analyze the financial, marketing, underwriting, and general management of the Kurtz Company. Following is the report that was prepared about Kurtz for the Atlas Board of Directors.

REPORT ON THE KURTZ AUTOMOBILE
INSURANCE COMPANY

HISTORY: FINANCIAL AND ECONOMIC

The Kurtz Automobile Insurance Company was organized by Albert Kurtz on August 30, 1915. The initial Kurtz policies were of the typical all-or-none variety, with no optional coverages. They covered the assured for losses by fire and theft to the automobile not to exceed $1,500 and liability for property damage and personal injury not to exceed $5,000. The annual premium was $.25 per horsepower plus $1.00 for policy fee. During the first year of operation slightly over 13,000 of these policies were sold, and the company ran at a steady profit from that time to the early 1950's.

From 1946 to 1955 there was a rapid, almost booming, growth in sales volume, the high point being 1953, when the company wrote over $19 million worth of policies. During this period, however, the surplus did not increase enough to justify the increase in volume. In light of this the Best Company dropped the Kurtz Company's rating from "A" down to "B—," a turn that caused considerable alarm among the board of directors and executives.

In late 1953 the board of directors met and decided to institute a cutback in sales in order to place the company in a more sound financial and underwriting position. Actuarial reports had indicated that several parts of the territory were particularly poor risk areas; underwriting was tightened up and rate increases were obtained. In many cases agents with poor loss ratios were either dropped or strongly prodded. The company held special meetings with agents to acquaint them with the company's problems.

After several years' adjustment, the directors found this plan paying off the way they wished it to. Writings dropped from $19 million to $15.5 million, but the ratio of writings to surplus improved and the surplus rose from $2.234 million to $2.889 million, an increase of 22.7 per cent. This was primarily responsible for the Best Company's revising their rating to "B+" as of January 1961. President Axel Heyst feels confident that several more years of a similar increase will bring the rating back to the "A" level.

Another measure undertaken to help the Kurtz Company recover its position was a plan to diversify the company's writings. Prior to 1950, 97 per cent of the company's policies were limited to the automobile line. The state law under which the Kurtz Company was originally organized in 1919 was amended to permit the writing of forms of insurance other than automobile in 1941, mainly through the lobbying efforts of Albert Kurtz. But little had been done to take advantage of the change; the only significant innovation was a service station policy covering not only property damage and liability but also theft.

Shortly after Albert Kurtz' death, the company decided to take further advantage of the 1941 legislative change. It would be much to the company's advantage if it could enter the mass field. "Package Plans" were much more in demand than before, and they could, if carefully written, almost certainly increase the company's earnings. In view of this, they prepared a new series of policies in the casualty and fire fields. In 1953 the company was still writing 93 per cent automobile insurance and only 7 per cent other lines. In 1960, however, the automobile percentage had decreased to 81 per cent and the other lines had risen to 19 per cent. The breakdown is as follows:

Casualty		
Automobile	81.5	per cent
Workman's Compensation	7.4	
General Liability	3.1	
Burglary and Theft	.4	
Glass	.25	
Miscellaneous	.8	
Fire and Allied Lines		
Fire	2.4	
Extended Coverage	1.3	
Homeowners	2.6	
Marine	.25	
	100.00	per cent

Although this change has not greatly increased the company's overall earnings, the Kurtz Board of Directors felt that it put their firm in a more advantageous position. For one, it placed the local agent writing policies in a position to write more inclusive package plans; for another, the diversification made the company a little less dependent on the fluctuations of the automobile industry; and finally, in terms of a merger with Atlas, it provided a base for further diversification into several different lines.

With the exception of the 1953 cutback and the gradual diversification, company strategy has been fairly consistent, as have its earnings. It is not a big business, but it has been a reliable and fairly profitable organization. Several of the Kurtz executives feel that the Best Company has been unduly severe in their ratings, that the drop to "B—" exaggerated a slight decline in the company's effectiveness. Whatever the case, the increase in surplus does indicate that Kurtz is moving in the right direction.

Best's reports made the following statement concerning the company's underwriting: "The underwriting experience in 1960 was the most favorable registered during the past five years. The combined loss and expense ratio was 97.0 per cent. The statutory underwriting profit was $304,000. This gain coupled with returns from investments provided for the addition of nearly $540,000 to policyholders' surplus and special funds. Last year's good showing was attributable to revised and more rigid underwriting standards in not only the acceptance of new risks but in the renewal of outstanding policy contracts."

Exhibit I shows comparative annual statements for 1959 and 1960. Exhibit II shows financial and operating results for 1956 through 1960.

HISTORY: MANAGEMENT ORGANIZATION AND STRUCTURE

From its founding in 1915 until 1949, the company was run very much under a one-man regime—Albert Kurtz. His son, Paul, still recollects his father's "iron hand," which controlled not only the company but also much of the insurance legislature in the home state.

Early records show that Albert Kurtz prepared some of the state's early statutes authorizing the sale of automobile insurance. His close friend, Solomon Rout (who was the company's first president), introduced it in the legislature. To his death in 1949, Albert Kurtz was always in close touch with some important members of the legislature and the governor. As times changed, various amendments and bills were pushed through the legislature to accommodate the automobile and casualty insurance industry in the state, particularly the Kurtz Company.

Albert Kurtz's running of the company was, at first, an entirely personal affair. He started out as an individual, did his own bookkeeping and accounting, and also sold, underwrote, and processed claims. Slowly he began to recruit a body of salesmen from among already established agents,

EXHIBIT I. COMPARATIVE ANNUAL STATEMENTS

ASSETS	DEC. 31, 1959	DEC. 31, 1960	LIABILITIES	DEC. 31, 1959	DEC. 31, 1960
Bonds (amortized value):	$ 5,261,779	$ 6,482,050	Losses—adjacent expenses	$ 4,096,734	$ 4,196,276
Stocks (authorized value):	2,071,500	2,140,293	Expenses, taxes, etc.	35,489	18,500
Mortgages	1,086,343	1,087,313	Federal income taxes	95,761	103,150
Real estate	1,473,461	1,463,940	Unearned premiums	5,488,014	5,923,462
Cash	1,492,115	1,286,833	Reinsurance treaty funds	8,400	13,500
Premium balance	1,843,137	1,721,032	Other liabilities	472,942	368,211
Reinsurance recoverable	11,735	2,270	Excess stat. loss reserves	852,205	733,695
Accrued interest	37,490	55,509	Total liabilities:	$11,049,545	$11,356,794
Other assets	6,122	6,699	Guaranty Fund	200,000	200,000
			Net surplus	1,734,137	2,389,145
			Voluntary reserve	300,000	300,000
	$13,283,682	$14,245,939		$13,283,682	$14,245,939
			Policyholders' surplus	2,234,137	2,889,145

Exhibit II. Comparative Financial and Operating Exhibit (All figures are in thousands)

YEAR	TOTAL ADMITTED ASSETS	REPORTED POLICYHOLDERS' SURPLUS	NET PREMIUMS WRITTEN	UNDERWRITING PROFIT OR LOSS	NET INVESTMENT INCOME	OTHER INVESTMENT GAINS OR LOSSES*	FEDERAL TAXES INCURRED	DIVIDENDS DECLARED
1956	12,516	2,407	13,878	−254	279	−100	141	71
1957	12,544	2,456	14,437	162	264	−100	146	74
1958	13,329	2,856	15,347	−178	259	438	156	76
1959	13,284	2,234	15,862	35	272	39	161	83
1960	14,246	2,889	15,565	304	308	201	157	179

* Sales and appreciation.

barbers, storekeepers, lawyers, and several boys who had just completed school. In 1917 he moved his office from its original site (a suite of rooms over a drugstore two blocks from the capital building) to a whole floor above the First State and Savings Bank. Two years later, the Kurtz Company moved into its own office building.

The office staff grew from 1 clerk in 1915 to 13 clerks, 3 executives, 2 office boys, and a janitor in 1920. At present over 200 people are employed in the new $1.5 million home office built in 1955. Another 100 are employed in a regional office, first established as a permanent fixture in 1928. All in all, there are 350 employees with a total payroll of $1.72 million.

While Albert Kurtz ruled the company, he deliberately kept it a relatively small operation. He wanted a firm over which he could execute minute, solid, and efficient control, and the times were many when he called it "my company" or "the firm I founded." When size did become a threat, as it did in the late 1920's, Kurtz twice ordered cutbacks in writing, thus checking growth.

In 1927 Kurtz did set up what may be called the company's first organization structure on a formal basis. Solomon Rout, as company president, was really only a figurehead with no voice in company affairs save through his membership on the Board of Directors. The Kurtz Company's first organization chart is shown in Fig. 7-7, and details of the officers are as follows:

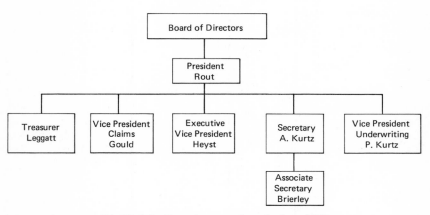

FIGURE 7–7   Kurtz Company Organization—1927

1. *Secretary:* Albert Kurtz (born 1874–died 1949). As Secretary, Albert Kurtz held the power in the company, directing and supervising every department and making all major decisions.
2. *Treasurer:* Mark Leggatt (born 1897). Leggatt came to the Kurtz Com-

pany as a CPA in 1922 and has handled as much of the firm's finances as Kurtz would allow him. This was never as much as Leggatt would have liked, and there were often times when he felt as though Kurtz was ignoring him. They were, however, consistently close friends.

3. *Vice President, Claims:* Charles Gould (born 1900). Gould was one of the Kurtz Company's original salesmen, a job he took up directly after graduating from college in 1918. Like Leggatt, Kurtz never gave him as much of a say as he would have liked. He sometimes felt as though he was being put to unnecessary menial and degrading tasks. There was a time when Kurtz contemplated dismissing him, but Gould has always been willing, efficient, and reliable.

4. *Executive Vice President:* Axel Heyst (born 1893). He came to the Kurtz Company in 1920 after varied work as a salesman and an agent (at which he was not a great success). He has been, almost from the time he was hired, Kurtz's right-hand man.

5. *Vice President, Underwriting:* Paul Kurtz (born 1898). Paul Kurtz was groomed for the insurance business, almost from the time he could talk. He has always lived in awe of his father's success, and some of the members of the company strongly felt he should get out on his own, where he would not be dominated by his father's personality.

6. *Associate Secretary:* James Brierley (born 1898). Brierley is a life-long friend of Paul Kurtz, and in 1920 he "married into the company." His wife, the former Laura Kurtz, often shows a strong interest in the family business, frequently pressuring him. Brierley is a competent business-man with an exuberant capacity for friendship. Albert Kurtz had felt his son-in-law was a definite asset to the company.

This was the organization of the Kurtz Company from 1927 to 1949 when Albert Kurtz quite unexpectedly died of a stroke. Until that time his health had been near perfect and, consequently, the company management had not done as much as it might have to prepare for the adjustment that his death necessarily demanded. Matters were complicated when, three weeks after his father's death, Paul Kurtz suffered a stroke that took him completely away from the company's office for almost 18 months. When he did return, Paul had to force himself to work at a slower pace, and it is generally agreed that he is not the same man he once was. Some even doubted the advisability of his return at all. Paul Kurtz now walks with a cane and has only partial use of his left arm.

The death of Albert Kurtz precipitated what amounted to a "power scuffle" among the top-line executives. Rout, as figurehead president, did little except tell the men "under" him to "go right ahead and do what you think is best for the company." Several months after Paul Kurtz's stroke, the Board of Directors met with the top-level executives and elected Heyst as president; Paul Kurtz was placed in his father's old position (secretary) on the basis of medical reports that indicated he would be able to return to work, and Brierley became the Kurtz Company's executive vice president. Rout was more than content to resign the presidency for these shifts, retiring entirely to a position on the company Board of Directors.

For two years the company went ahead on a near status quo basis, continuing Albert Kurtz's policies as he had established them before his death. The only significant change was a push for a greater quantity of writings, done without any great campaign because of the post-World War II boom. The diversification policy was put into slight effect also, though it gained hardly any momentum until the mid-1950's.

When Paul Kurtz returned actively in September 1951, a management pattern was established, a pattern that has plagued the operation of the Kurtz Company to the present. For the first time in the firm's history, the presidency was a position of influence and power. Heyst, long accustomed to being Albert Kurtz's right-hand man, quietly began to exercise the latent power of his position as president. Despite his age (56 in 1949, when he became president), he was a man of consistently good health and indefatigable energy. A thumbnail sketch in the company newspaper's thirty-fifth anniversary issue ran under the tag line, "Always on the Job," and Heyst's actions bore this out. In recent years he had frequently skipped vacations in order to remain on the job; his demonstrated competence led a number of people (in almost every department of the home office) to depend on him. Paul Kurtz and Brierley resented this "grab." Several times they hinted openly that the company ought to be run in a manner essentially similar to that of the "old regime." It was also suggested that, because Paul Kurtz and Brierley had previously occupied positions of prominence equal to that of Heyst, the actual management of the company should proceed only on *joint* decisions made by the three men. At first, Heyst appeared to remain neutral to Kurtz and Brierley's pressure, but soon he found that they were opposing him on a number of matters.

Finally, early in 1952 Heyst was forced to capitulate. The three men convened in the home office conference room and jointly agreed to run the company as a triumvirate—though each, in name at least, would keep his same position. This idea worked smoothly for a brief time only; Heyst, Paul Kurtz, and Brierley, while openly agreeing that they must work together to keep the company going forward, were able to agree on little. Each time the three met, they would emerge from the office split, two against one, on the issue at hand; the men themselves were frustrated, though not angry. They talked among each other about "communication . . . cooperation" and the like but were unable to come together. When they consulted the Board of Directors, little aid was forthcoming; the standard reply was, "You people do what you want to do. We'll agree."

This impasse continued until mid-1953 when a joint meeting of the Board of Directors and top-line executives hatched the idea of a "Development and Planning Committee." Shortly after Albert Kurtz's death, many of the older executives and board members had recognized the need to allow a greater say to some of the younger men in the company. When Heyst, Paul Kurtz, and Brierley repeatedly failed to reach agreement, it was decided to create a 14-man advisory group of younger executives, which would participate in many of the higher decisions of the company. The group was officially formed in November 1953. The chairman was James Brierley, Executive Vice President. The 14 members were all middle-management men, generally at the assistant vice president level, and their ages ranged from 29 to 44. On paper the committee seemed unwieldy, but in fact its formation led directly to the two major policy shifts that have been responsible for the recent rise in the Best Company rating. When this committee meets and decides on an issue, the company's "big three" are generally willing to accept their recommendations. In fact, they each seem relieved not to be carrying such a heavy decision-making burden. This was true of the decision to cut back writings, the committee's first recommendation, and also true of the numerous small steps in the diversification policy.

Although it appears on paper that Heyst and his top-line executives are making the major company decisions, the real impetus actually comes from this younger group. It should be added that Brierley had been quite successful as chairman of the new committee.

Two other organizational changes were effected shortly after Albert Kurtz's death. It was decided to create the position of general counsel and also the position of vice president and actuary. The general counsel position was filled by Charles Marlow, who initially came in contact with the Kurtz Company as a legal consultant in 1954. Heyst and Paul Kurtz were highly impressed with his work and hired him away from the law firm. In actuality, Marlow works as a special assistant to Heyst, and though the latter has done little to prepare a successor for his position, many of the employees feel that Marlow is "the hope of the company." He is not an official member of the Development and Planning Committee but has been sitting in regularly on their sessions.

The company also promoted Conrad Koren from the position of actuarial manager to vice president and actuary. Koren, for the most part, has merely taken up slack in a position that should have been created at least a decade ago. He stays mostly to his own business and participates in top-line management decisions only when called on to do so. His fellow workers often refer to him as a "mathematical genius," and in addition he has done much to automate his department.

Future Plans.   In talking with executives, both top-level and younger, it appeared that the company was somewhat at cross purposes on its future plans. This has been somewhat complicated by Paul Kurtz's announced sale of the family's majority stock holding. The cutback policy has not yet run its course, and it will—according to Heyst—require several more years of status quo operations before the ratio of writings to surplus is solid. After this position is achieved, the company has two paths to follow:

1. A plan that requires the company to stand essentially pat. With a reasonably solid position in the three states where it operates, the Kurtz Company can start from there to improve its earnings without much expansion. The diversification into other lines could be continued with the total amount of writings kept relatively constant. The underlying mode of thought here is to keep the business small and to handle a considerable quantity of specialized policies that the larger companies will not write because such policies lack a broad market. The diversification would continue with this line of thought in mind. The exponents of this plan, as might be expected, are the older members of the corporation. Heyst, Paul Kurtz, and Brierley have been able to agree on this and have pigeon-holed several Development and Planning Committee recommendations entailing outright expansion.
2. After a two-year allowance time, during which the preceding policy would remain in effect, the company would push for expansion. This would come through the diversification plan, with each new line comprising an increase in overall writings for the company. For the most part, this plan called for diversification of a sort that will enable a greater number of "package plans" to be sold. So far as the automobile line goes, it is agreed that the area is just about saturated, though the company is, at present, developing a sales campaign that will cover younger auto owners for an extended period of time on a prorated premium basis.

The Development and Planning Committee has recommended several specific areas for expansion, especially in the corporate surety and fidelity lines. Several fidelity requests in the past year, including several from new, expanding electronics firms, have been turned down—to the chagrin of the committee. There has also been some work done, in one state legislature, to try to alter the Workman's Compensation Law.

To date, the expansion has mostly been sketched on paper and discussed in meetings. Some of the younger men interviewed complained that the Kurtz Company was "not moving ahead as fast as it might."

THE KURTZ COMPANY IN 1961: MANAGEMENT STRUCTURE
AND ORGANIZATION

The clearest way to see the current state of the Kurtz Company's management is to break it into levels.

Board of Directors. With the topline executives, the Board of Directors appears to be the fundamental weak point in the company. At present it is, for the most part, a "yes-man" body; its average age is 66, and there have been no new appointees since 1949. A partial breakdown follows:

1. *Chairman:* Solomon Rout, retired legislator, age 87. Though sound mentally Rout has had poor health for the last 14 years. Occasionally this prevents him from attending meetings. He tends to view the company from the "old regime" perspective, and since Albert Kurtz's death in
   • 1949 he has been very silent.
2. *Members*
   (a) *Berthold Kurtz,* retired farmer and younger brother of Albert Kurtz, age 77. He takes much the same view of proceedings as Rout, though he attends the meetings quite regularly.
   (b) *Orville West,* attorney, West, West, and Huneke, age 61. West "thinks young," but his practice prevents him from giving too much time to board duties.
   (c) *Thomas Stearns,* Thomas Stearns & Son Insurance Agency, age 58. Stearns is a long-time Kurtz agent and has been consistently loyal to the company. He is probably the driving force on the board and devotes a considerable amount of his time to his duties on it.
   (d) *Axel Heyst,* president, age 68.
   (e) *Mark Leggatt,* treasurer, age 64.
   (f) *Paul Kurtz,* secretary, age 63. Bad health.
   (g) *James Brierley,* executive vice president, age 63.
   (h) *Charles Gould,* vice president, age 61.

From the foregoing, it is not difficult to pinpoint the weaknesses of the board. Not infrequently, the Heyst-Paul Kurtz-Brierley impasse dominates the meetings. Other board members are generally disinterested, with the exception of Stearns. He, however, has not been able to impart a great deal of drive and accord to the other members.

Top-Level Executives. The current Kurtz Company organizational chart is shown in Fig. 7–8. The two vacant positions have been open since Albert Kurtz's death, and it is not likely that they will be filled immediately. Paul Kurtz has continued, in a diminishing manner, to handle the underwriting work. The agency vice president is a position created by Albert Kurtz in 1947 and filled then by Robert Baines. When Baines retired in 1951, the position was left vacant pending the company reorganization. Now, Roger Wheeler, assistant agency vice president, reports to Brierley; Wheeler has seemed sufficient to the task, and his relations with Brierley have been good, so no new appointment has been made.

To summarize, the Heyst-Paul Kurtz-Brierley triumvirate runs the com-

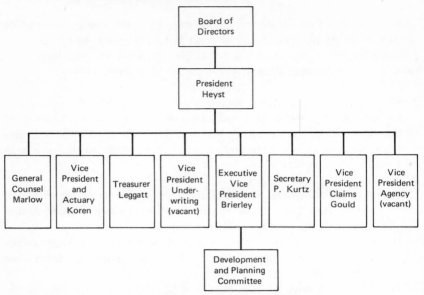

FIGURE 7–8   Kurtz Company Organization—1961

pany, primarily via the recommendations of the Development and Planning Committee. Marlow has been developing steadily as an insurance man and in recent years has been Heyst's right-hand man in many situations. Leggatt, Gould, and Koren stick mainly to their own areas; the former two often act in terms of the "old regime" and have seemed reluctant to adjust to the current organization. They are seldom consulted on major issues.

The relation between the "big three" continues to be a problem. Heyst, although he has capitulated to the three-man rule, has not forgotten that he is president and neither have the other two. Paul Kurtz occasionally feels as though he was "dumped" in the change and that he should have become president. Brierley is effective, but pressure from his wife sometimes causes him to desire more power than he has.

Development and Planning Committee.   This group, as previously described, was formed after the Heyst-Paul Kurtz-Brierley situation had become a company problem. For the younger executives of the Kurtz Company it has meant the chance to have an influence on top-level decisions. During its eight years of existence, the committee has provided a means for the development of a number of ambitious junior executives, and it is this group that presently comprises the essential strength of the Kurtz Company.

In interviews, several of them described their position as one of waiting—waiting for the "old guard" to relinquish its grip on the company. With them out of the way, those interviewed felt that the company could undergo a considerable expansion and make a success of it. Two members of the committee talked as if they had the company's management personnel changes mapped out for the next decade, but aside from these flashes of self-interest, the group seems genuinely and maturely concerned about the firm's future. In committee meetings, the members appeared to work effectively and without much of the ineffectual hassling that sometimes occurs when a young, energetic group gets together.

The members of the Development and Planning Committee, when questioned about the merger, were of varied attitudes. Many felt that such an event would give the company (and them) a chance to "go big." Others voiced distrust over the idea, apparently fearing that they might be gobbled up in the merger and that their previous position with Kurtz would mean little after the merger. As a whole, however, the reaction was favorable; the group would probably work well within the framework of the Atlas Company.

Total Employees, Agents, and Brokers. The Kurtz Company presently has a total of 350 employees. Two hundred of these work in and out of the home office, and there are another 50 working in a regional office. The remaining 100 are scattered in smaller service offices throughout several regions. Selling is done through independent agents and brokers, and generally the company is regarded as having a better than average agency plant. Twenty-nine large agents and brokers are responsible for 74 per cent of the company's total writings.

CASE DISCUSSION QUESTIONS

The Atlas Insurance Company Case

The price of the Kurtz Company's majority stock is well within the capabilities of the Atlas Company. Thus the financial aspect of the purchase would not be a major problem. The problems to be resolved are

1. Should the Atlas Company decide to merge with the Kurtz Company?

2. If the merger occurs, how should the merged company be organized, what problems should be faced, and what plans should be made?

3. What general context problem would indicate a training need?

4. What specific programs could you see if you merge? If you do not?

8 Task Analysis— Finding the Training Objective

A problem is an unwanted effect, something to be corrected or removed.
— KEPNER AND TREGOE

BECAUSE training in the systems approach means moving toward an objective from some previous position, this can be called *training by objectives*. It also means that training achieves objectives or should attempt to do so. This is a kind of discipline that liberates training from the many kinds of activities that it could become bogged down in, and makes it purposeful, meaningful, economic, and possible to evaluate. Conventions of trainers often ask the question "How can you evaluate training?"

The answer we propose here is that you cannot evaluate training at all if you wait until after the training is completed and then try to apply some kind of measurement. You must inevitably find yourself inventing the yardstick after you have decided to measure under such a system. The only possible way to evaluate training is to construct a yardstick before you enter the process of training and conduct the training. One of the most convenient yardsticks, and perhaps economically the best one, is to define a behavioral objective you intend to achieve through training, and when the training is complete, check to see if you have reached it.

Simon has made an immense contribution to the science of decision making and problem solving in his small book *The New Science of*

Management Decisions published in 1960.[1] A computer man, Simon worked many years attempting to simulate on the computer the thought processes of the human mind. As a result of this research he has proposed a definition of a problem that is systematic. It suggests that a problem is a *deviation from some standard.* This implies that there are two dimensions to a problem, the present level and the desired level (or standard). If you do not know where you are, then you cannot know what your problem is or even if you have one. If you know where you are and like it there, you do not have a problem. If you know where you are and wish you were elsewhere (at another objective), then you have the distance to travel to get there, which comprises the problem. It is easy to see why this would fit a computer analyst's mode of thought. In making management decisions the computer is essentially a user of *comparison.* There is no need, however, for you to be a computer, because the computer is merely simulating what you do when you think clearly.[2]

In an earlier book, I spelled out some further extensions of that definition, proposing that a "problem is a deviation from a standard, important enough to be solved, and to which somebody will be committed to a solution."

Simon's definition of a problem, many suggest, is too limiting. The problem that is merely a variance from a standard leaves much undone in terms of achieving new goals. Management expert Joseph Juran has proposed that "breakthrough" to newer and higher levels of excellence, therefore thought beyond the realm of the possible, is a more germane concern. Peter Drucker adds that managers should be more concerned with exploiting opportunities than merely solving problems. The distinction can be useful at the same time it exploits the systematic and logical methods of systems analysis proposed by Simon. This is done by dividing problems as objectives for training purposes into two major categories.

1. Objectives that restore the status quo. These are problems that are caused by some change that has produced a deviation from a norm, important enough for somebody to think the variance is important enough to close up. Somebody then is made responsible for closing the gap.
2. Innovative or breakthrough objectives that move the present level to new levels of excellence. The use of objectives is similar to plain

[1] Herbert A. Simon, *The New Science of Management Decision* (New York: Harper & Row, 1960).
[2] G. S. Odiorne, *Management Decisions by Objectives* (Englewood Cliffs, N.J.: Prentice-Hall, 1969).

problem solving: define the present level and then choose a new desired level. This new sought-after level of behavior becomes the training objective.

If the difference between the two kinds of objectives seems subtle, their differences in results are gross. The training program that merely restores the status quo never improves things; it merely prevents them from getting worse. Innovative and breakthrough objectives make quantum leaps in performance even though the present level is considered satisfactory.

If this kind of specific definition of a problem seems to be a trifle esoteric, we should hasten to note that actually it is a great time-saver in the end. All too often the average person, asked to define a problem, will respond by stating its cause, rather than specifying the problem exactly.

"What is your training problem?" "Motivation of workers."

"What problem does that cause?" "Our people don't come in on Monday."

Thus at the first question he indicates that the problem as he originally stated it is not the problem but the cause of the problem, which is apparently absenteeism. What the exact level of Monday absenteeism may be and what a desirable or objective level might be are not stated. These would be required before an effective statement of the training objective could be made. It would also be needed if the effect of training were to be evaluated later.

Specific definition of a behavior change objective requires that present level and desired levels be defined. In training, the difference between the two comprises the objective of training, sometimes called the training need.

Task analysis means defining present and desired behavior of a specific population of trainees; in other words, it means a very detailed and specific spelling out in behavioral terms of the present behavior and the desired behavior. Let us use the example of a trainer who wants to do a task analysis on a proposed course that will improve the delegation skills of some middle managers.

A Model for Task Analysis—Using a Systems Approach

1. *Name the behavior change area.* To increase managerial delegation to subordinates.

2. *Nature and size of the group to be trained:*
   (a) Nature and size of the group: about 30 middle managers ranging in age from 30 to 35, most having college degrees, usually
   in engineering, chemistry, or business administration, often accounting or finance.
   (b) Prior training or coaching: little if any, except for some possible
   outside reading. Several have taken management courses in colleges, but this has been at least seven years ago. Few, if any,
   have been coached by their superiors.
   (c) Situational facts: strongly technical business, frequent changes
   because of product short run and technical obsolescence of
   product. Must work frequently with nontechnical personnel
   such as pipe-fitters, millwrights, and the like.
3. *Present level or condition:*
   (a) Supervisors are often seen (ratio delay shows 50 per cent
   frequency of occurrence) doing work themselves while their
   subordinates are standing by, or doing other work.
   (b) Few, if any, coaching and instructing actions by the supervisors
   are observed. Subordinates never seem to be instructed in procedures that are repetitive, and that supervisors perform for
   them.
   (c) Supervisors often omit reports and other administrative requirements of their job. Fifty per cent of supervisory reports are late.
   Supervisors report themselves too busy to prepare reports and
   do them at home or on Saturday.
4. *Desired condition:*
   (a) Supervisors would be observed in less than 10 per cent of
   observations doing work of technicians and mechanics and then
   for instruction only.
   (b) Supervisors should be seen engaged in coaching workers in procedures that are repetitive using job instruction training (JIT)
   technique for teaching. At other times should be supervising
   and directing, not doing.
   (c) All supervisory reports would be prepared on the operating day
   scheduled and only emergency reports at home.
5. *What would be the favorable end operational results if the training
   were successful?* Productivity would increase and down time between
   production runs would be reduced 50 per cent. Turnover among
   skilled people would be reduced 20 per cent. Amount of actual work
   done by technicians would increase, freeing supervisory time by 50
   per cent. All supervisory reports would be in on the day prescribed,
   making administrative decisions and upward reporting more timely
   by 20 per cent.

6. *What indicators could you use to determine changes from present level to desired level?*

   (a) Do ratio delay studies of activities of supervisors and note the percentage of time they are engaged in the technical work part of job descriptions of lower ranking persons.

   (b) Do ratio delay study of supervisor (same study) and note percentage of time being spent in teaching, coaching, or JIT.

   (c) Count frequency of late reports from supervisors as per cent of total report due by day.

   (d) Count frequency of delays in outgoing higher-level reports and show percentage delayed because of late supervisory reports.

Presuming that you had previously analyzed the situation behaviorally to determine that the cause of the behavior you are studying was not in the situation itself nor simply a matter of enforcement but had concluded that they did not *know how,* or cannot do it, your task analysis prepares the stage for breaking the training down into steps with criteria of achievement for each. As noted in Chapter 7, this appears to be a training objective because it involves the behavior of people (the supervisors) that is caused by lack of knowledge, insufficient skills, wrong knowledge, or insufficient information.

In a more narrative style this would read somewhat as follows:

Most of our supervisors were hired from college with emphasis on technical education for plant supervision and accounting or finance for the office and administrative tasks. After a tour of duty in technical engineering or staff accounting work, they are promoted to supervisory positions. In the past we have done little to prepare them for the change in duties from technical expert to supervisor of others. Their experience, thus, has been rewarding when they excelled at technical matters, and this has often been the reason for their promotion—technical excellence. It is not surprising that they continue to pursue the very thing that led to their immediate success, promotion into management.

We find, however, that they cling to technical work rather than teaching technical work to others and to doing the supervisory planning and administrative work that is necessary in their departments; this leads to two ill effects. The first is that they usurp all the technical work in the departments while the aides and assistants stand around watching. This has caused some technicians and mechanics, who feel that they are not being well employed, to quit. The second effect is that the necessary work of reporting and doing similar managerial tasks are being left undone.

Not an uncommon story. What is the value of the task analysis, what are the key ingredients, and how is this task analysis used?

1. It described in specific, quantitative terms, in places where that is possible, what the present behavior consists of (see Part III).
2. It described the desired behavior in terms of quantitative differences, and the quantification of the behavior change problems comes out smilar to the following:
   (a) A reduction of 40 per cent observed instances of supervisors working.
   (b) More observable instances of coaching and training going on. This rate of observations would be a declining curve, because the early evidence of coaching would allow tapering off and permitting the subordinates to be working independently after they had been trained. This could be described as a learning curve rate of observation.

Figure 8–1 illustrates how progress might be noted in the reduction of supervisory work observation. (Ratio delay is a sampling of random observations of specific behaviors observed, made over a several-day period by an observer who notes his observations and records them according to category of activity being engaged in by supervisor under observation.)

This decline in supervisory work should be related to an increase in the amount of time or number of observations, using the same ratio delay study, which indicates that the supervisors are engaged in coaching and training subordinates in how to perform tasks. Figure 8–2 indicates the changed behavior that could be observed with respect

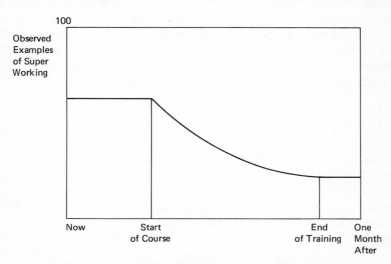

FIGURE 8–1   Curve of Observations of Supervisory Behavior Change

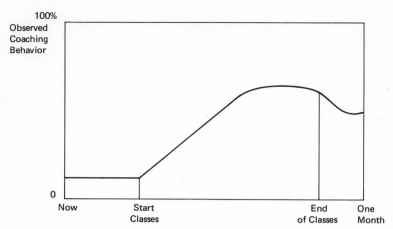

FIGURE 8–2   Curve of Observations of Supervisory Coaching Behavior

to coaching behavior. In this case the coaching behavior that is to be sought is the well-known method of job instruction training.

The two curves represent learning curves for the outcome of the proposed training. The practical hard-working trainer might protest: "You mean I have to do ratio delay studies on every course I run to be able to prove that my training is economic?" Clearly not.

The first time a course is conducted, such studies can define behavior change sought (the training objective) and establish a positive means of evaluation of effect. After that, given a similar population and objective you can simply rerun the course, confident that it has worked in the past. One task analysis can serve for hundreds of students if you have defined the training objective adequately, evaluated it after the first session, and demonstrated that you have found an effective means to reach the training objective through your training action.

ARRANGING THE ENVIRONMENT

After such a general task analysis is done, a review of the general behavioral change pattern sought should be measured against the environment to be sure that it can be supported back on the job. A review of the task analysis to this point could be reviewed with the plant manager to determine whether or not he and the production manager and superintendents will permit or endorse the behavior change specified if it appears after the completion of the course. Suppose, for example, the following were some of the responses you received after presenting these two behavior change curves to the top management.

1. Plant Manager: That's fine in theory, but we are making food and drug products of great purity, and I don't intend at any time that mechanics and technicians should be doing work on machines and processes which I could have done by a graduate chemist or scientist doing the job right without any errors.

   If such is the response, cancel the course and see if some other arrangement can be made for getting the reports and administrative work done.

2. Plant Manager: That's a fine idea, and I sure hope it works, because we are not getting maximum use out of our technical supervision. We are paying them to be managers, but they keep doing work at lower levels. We should also try to beef up the knowledge of the technicians to make them more technically competent too.

   If such is the response, you may proceed with the course and furthermore have a suggested training need for classroom training of technicians in chemistry and pharmacology. This should not be done until a task analysis has been done for this need also to determine whether it really exists.

3. Plant Manager: That's such a fine idea that I want to have a first run through the course myself. Then when the guys take the course I will start checking on them. When they are through with the JIT I will supervise them in such a way that if they should slip back into doing and not teaching I will correct them to be sure we don't let the curve slope off too badly. I think we should all take the course one week ahead of them, lesson by lesson, then watch their behavior when they come back from each class and if they aren't doing things right do some coaching of the supervisors to be sure they apply what they learn from the first crack.

   If you get this endorsing support, press ahead with a more detailed step-by-step breakdown of the course; present it first to the top-management group and then to the supervisors.

4. Union President: That's all very fine, but if you guys are going to ask for technicians and mechanics to be doing a higher classification of work, then they should be paid more for the higher skill and experience level required. The company isn't going to get any free rides off our back.

If this comes to your attention, talk immediately to the labor relations manager, the wage and salary administrator, and perhaps the plant manager regarding a decision over how such a grievance might be handled if it arose.

The point of these four kinds of response might well be a determinant of whether or not training should be offered, whether it should be offered in the form proposed at first, whether it should be reworked, or whether it should be canceled and some other arrangement in the system be considered.

BREAKING THE TRAINING TASK DOWN INTO TEACHABLE ELEMENTS.

The genius of a systematic approach to training is that you have a beginning, which is where you start; a middle, through which you proceed; and an end, toward which you move. You might construct some major stages of the task of teaching along these lines. Breaking the training task down into steps consists of defining each major teachable punctuation point in the progress from present condition of behavior to the desired condition and defining indicators of successful achievement. A step is any movement that makes an appreciable movement from the present to the desired. A key point is an vital point that could make or break subsequent behavior and is an issue of highlight and special reinforcement in the task.

For example, a step-by-step task breakdown for the preceding task analysis might look something as follows:

Step 1. Accommodate the Learner to the Learning. Spell out the objective of the training to the learner. Stress the feature of the training and the benefits to him, his opportunities for growth, the importance of delegation to his demonstrated managerial capacity, and the importance of demonstrating administrative skills if he is to make progress and grow as a manager.

Simply launching to lessons and stages without this accommodation may require redoing. Give the student time to get used to the idea of training, much as the behavioral scientists permit a mouse or primate a chance to get acclimated to an experimental cage or box before starting conditioning.

Behavioral Criteria Objective of Step 1. If this step is well done you should see the following behavior change:

1. The class members will come back for the following session and all of the succeeding sessions. (If not well done, they might not come back or might find other more pressing duties.)

2. They will, in some cases, discuss the course verbally in the class, citing objections or difficulties that they foresee, and will also discuss it with their boss on the job. The boss, having been through the course first, will reinforce this aspect of the course.
3. They will verbally add features and benefits that they see to themselves from successfully completing the course.
4. They will refrain from complaints about the necessity of the course, and enter into all its exercises and requirements affirmatively.

At this stage the devotee of what we have identified as soft criteria in learning will ask: "But aren't you really saying that they will be motivated to learn?" Perhaps so, if you want to discuss it in that language, but why bother? If they behave in the four specific ways listed as spelled out in the behavioral criteria and are not motivated, would not that be better than having them motivated and not behaving that way? The point is that if they behave so that you could generalize their internal state as being "motivated" such a generalization really does not make much difference. It is the behavior and its consequences you focus on. If you focus your attentions on generalizations, you may find you miss the criteria. As noted in Chapter 4, it is the behavior we are after, not explanations of it.

Step 2. Conduct Skills Development Instruction in Job Instruction Training. Job Instruction Training is a specific course of instruction that has two major divisions and five major steps for teaching the worker a specific task or set of tasks on a job. As a result of this part of the course, the supervisor should be able to perform the following things on his job:

1. He should demonstrate that he knows how to prepare a training time table for the task to be taught, showing how much skill is to be taught in what time. This should be done using an actual job or task from the plant.
2. He should prepare at least one and probably more job breakdowns, listing important steps and key points.
3. He should have prepared materials, tools, and supplies to teach a job.
4. He should have the work place arranged just as the worker will be expected to maintain it.
5. He should demonstrate skill at preparing the learner to learn. He should put him at ease, find out what he already knows about it, state things that should raise his interest in learning the task, and place him in the correct position.
6. He should demonstrate ability to present the task by showing and telling patiently one step at a time. He should always stress key

points during presentation and have him repeat it back. He should avoid teaching more than the man can learn at one time.

7. He should demonstrate that he can conduct a performance try-out of the trainee, having the learner do the job, correcting his errors, praising his successes, and having the learner tell him what he is doing. He should show that he can answer ordinary questions by the learner during the performance try-out. He should demonstrate that he continues teaching until he knows that the student can perform the task.

8. He should demonstrate how to taper off, by putting the man on his own, checking frequently, telling the learner where to go for help, and tapering off with extra coaching.

It is important that the desired job behavior be simulated in all important respects in the training session. The task analysis is a detailed statement of the problem, broken down into major behavioral stages as it is proposed the trainee behave on the job.

Step 3. Reinforcement by Superior on the Job. An important part of the task analysis is to establish means by which the endorsing kinds of supportive behavior by superiors of the trainees actually occur. In the first class, which is for the higher-level managers, reports weekly on what actual on-the-job reinforcement of the delegation and job training program was inspected and reinforced by the higher-level people in the previous week should be called for.

Step 4. Specification of the Completion of Administrative Duties. As the JIT portion of the program is completed, provision should be made for the presentation of the reporting and other administrative duties that will supplant the working activities of the supervisor, which have now presumably been supplanted by having trained subordinates do the work previously done by the supervisors. As a result of this, the supervisor should be able to produce the following:

1. A schedule of the desired reports, with samples of well-done reports.
2. Statements of results expected, or activities to be performed in the administrative category, approved by his immediate superior.
3. Statements by the higher-management group indicating that the achievement of specific administrative programs, schedules, timetables, and objectives have been complied with as shown by higher-management inspection and checking.

The task analysis, then, has two major ingredients:

1. Use the six steps of the task analysis model for the whole definition of training objective, including a statement of the conditions that would exist if the training were to change behavior.
2. It breaks the learning task down into manageable, teachable steps, with criteria for successful completion defined for each of the steps.

THE JUGGERNAUT JENNY CASE

Jeanette "Jenny" Compson is one of the true fixtures in the home office of the Amherst Insurance Company. A cousin to old President Long who died in 1947, she came with the company in 1928 as a secretary. She later took time off for more specialized training, and Long also had several of his associates spend some time working with her. Since 1939 she has run the Accident and Health Division's Special Risks Section, tending such matters as automobile insurance for taxi companies and various policies that come to Amherst via the assigned risk pool.

Jenny has done and does her job with a fearful, sometimes frantic, amount of energy. Some of the people in the office call her "Juggernaut Jenny," a name that she knows and is openly proud of. She is also very efficient, and the Special Risks Section has proceeded without the slightest bump or ruffle for a number of years. The office staff seldom bothers Jenny, it being generally thought a wise thing just to leave her to herself. She occasionally goes and clucks with some of the girls but usually stays to herself and her special risks. Jenny is an old maid and has sometimes been known to preach "Marriage is tommyrot"; she lives alone with a housekeeper in an old colonial home on the west side of town.

In early 1955, as part of an overall company expansion, Jenny's responsibility was enlarged and she was given an assistant. Some of the office staff feared that things would go completely askew—that Jenny and Midge Bickel, her assistant, would hassle day in and day out and would allow the Special Risks Section to go to pieces. Nothing of this sort happened, however; after a brief period of adjustment the personalities dovetailed and work went ahead as smoothly as ever and on a larger scale.

This continued until August 1955 when Midge took her customary two-week vacation. An interim assistant was assigned to the section, and for two weeks everything went wrong or did not get done at all. Jenny twice cussed out Pete Drake, the assistant secretary of personnel; once she walked out of the office in a huff at 1:30 and stayed away for a day. When she came back, everyone held their breath and said nothing. Midge returned the next week, and several days later tranquility and order were restored.

This pattern of events repeated itself again in 1956 and 1957, despite the fact that different assistants were given Jenny each time, by her choice. Each time this disrupted the office, and in 1957 an error on a Checker Cab policy adjustment cost the company several thousand dollars.

This mistake and the pending departure of Midge, who was seven months pregnant, brought a stern directive to Drake from the agency vice president. The latter did not like to deal in such "mundane" affairs, but recent events had brought the Jenny situation uncomfortably to his attention. Drake was merely told to "do something."

After discussing the problem with several of his colleagues, Drake decided the best thing to do was to move the Special Risks Section into another department. There the increased work would be sensibly distributed, and Jenny could still handle certain areas by herself. Drake called her to his office and had a warm chat with her about the situation. She liked the idea of the move and felt that it was particularly good in that it lifted some of the burden from her. Intermittent bursitis has bothered Jenny in recent years, and she does admit she's "getting along."

The switch was effected smoothly, with the Special Risks Section moving in with the Service Department. Jenny worked well there for several weeks, but then grew progressively irascible. It appeared that she made a special point of not getting along with certain people in the department. With others, she was quite affable. The effect on the morale of the department as a whole was increasingly noticeable as Jenny's attitude worsened. When she again took to walking out of the office early in the afternoon, the case came back to Drake. Now his first thought is to dismiss her, but he realizes that her tenure and connections are too great for that.

CASE DISCUSSION QUESTIONS

The Juggernaut Jenny Case

1. Was Drake's first step a wise one?

2. What should he do now? Why?

9 The Goals-Oriented Lesson Plan

There are two powerful instincts which exist in all human beings, and which can be
used in teaching. These are *gregariousness*
and the *love of play*.
——Gilbert Highet

E VERY school teacher, army instructor, or industrial manager who must conduct training is
familiar with the customary steps in preparing
a lesson plan. You outline the entire course and then
pick each major topic that can be covered in a single
class period and prepare a lesson plan. This lesson
plan is customarily seen as an *outline* showing major topics in Roman
numerals, subtopics in Arabic numerals, sub-sub-topics by letters, and
sub-sub-sub-topics by numerals enclosed in parentheses.

Although this is perfectly sensible as a way of outlining topical coverage of the material, it does not meet all the requirements of lesson
planning to achieve behavioral objectives. The goals-oriented lesson plan
may be supplemented by an outline or even a schedule of what will be
discussed and by whom at what time, for example, "3:00–4:30 P.M.:
Making a Timetable." There is really no harm in preparing such
materials for the guidance of the class so they will know when class is
adjourned and can make their car pool, but it certainly does not meet
the behavioral requirements of effective goals-oriented lesson planning.
The steps in a goals-oriented lesson plan would include the following
major features:

1. A statement of *behavior change sought* in terms of what the student should be able to do after completing the lesson or training session.
2. A description of the *action that will take place* in successive stages during the session.
3. *Methods of feedback* and reinforcement of behavior for students when they are acting in class.
4. A summary *inventory of the training materials,* properties, or supplies needed for each stage of the lesson.
5. A *rehearsal and briefing* of all those who will be involved in the session to avoid duplication, delay, or self-canceling activity in training.

Let us look at each of these in some detail.

Prepare a Statement of Behavior Change Sought

At the beginning of the course the students or learner should be provided with a statement of what behavior change he may expect to be able to demonstrate as a result of attending the course and from attending the first session. This basic statement of course objectives should be handed out in written form. In other words, he gets the answers to a final examination before he starts the course. Presumably if you have sized up the present level of behavior, then nobody in the group should be able to pass the final examination before the course starts or he does not need the training (unless he is there for a refresher training). Such a statement might look somewhat like Fig. 9–1.

This could be continued of course, but the two objectives in Fig. 9–1

FIGURE 9–1

Course Title: Management by Objectives
Course objectives: *As a result of attending you should be able to perform the following actions:*
1. *Prepare* a statement of objectives for your job for the coming quarter in a specific form that will comprise a suitable standard for measuring your own performance during that quarter. The product? Specific sets of objectives that you have written, ready for discussion with your superior back on the job.
2. *You will have rehearsed* with another class member the discussion of these objectives with a simulated boss and be able to go back to your job and discuss your objectives with that boss. The product? Verbal skills in conducting a goal-setting dialogue with your boss, using your objectives statement produced in objective 1.

---

are illustrative of what might be included in a goals-oriented lesson plan. You will note that the behavior change statement includes some mention of the activity and always spells out the *product* of that part of the lesson. The difference between a product and a nonproduct of behavior change is important. The following are not products of a behavior change session because no criteria are stated in behavioral terms.

1. "This course will expose the student to some stimulating and mind-stirring ideas."
2. "This session is designed to begin to prepare the student for attitude changes to follow."
3. "This session will make the student feel like a true and genuine member of the management team through inspiring his loyalties and dedication."

Such statements are, of course, indisputable and can hardly be faulted on their merits, but neither can the trainer or anyone else tell whether or not anything really occurred or any behavior changed.

If there is some behavior that the learner should exhibit in the classroom, that may be stated. If that behavior or something similar to it should be exhibited back on the job, that behavioral product should also be defined. The preceding might be stated in such terms if there is a terminal or continuing behavior that it is hoped will ensue. The preceding statements might be converted into behavioral terms by something as follows:

1. "As a result of this session, the student will read Douglas Mc-Gregor's book, subscribe to a magazine on general management, and attend one or more other training sessions offered by the training department this year."
2. "As a result of attending this session, the student will engage actively in subsequent class sessions, including expression of opinion, asking questions in class, and debating with others."
3. "As a result of this session, the supervisor will explain the company position factually to workers, refute false critical statements by workers about company practices, and volunteer statements to workers favorable to the company when the occasion arises naturally."

Describe the Action to Take Place in the Session

The second step in the lesson plans of a goals nature will define the choice of mode and action that is to take place for each of the behavioral objectives. For example, in a course where the lesson's behavioral objective is to achieve the first of the behaviors described above (reading McGregor's book), the description of the action to take place could be as shown in Fig. 9–2.

FIGURE 9–2

Action: Conduct a Debate on Theory X Versus Theory Y
Without explaining the source or telling which is favored, list in two columns on the blackboard the following summary statements.

Theory X	Theory Y
1. The average person dislikes work and avoids it when he can.	1. The average person finds work as natural and pleasant as rest or play and is creative and productive naturally.
2. Thus at work he must be directed, coerced, intimidated, or controlled in order to make him do the company's work.	2. Thus at work he can be relied on for self-control when a reason for achieving is given.

Step 1. Ask the class to read each statement on the board carefully and to mark down privately which one he thinks is *truest.* Emphasize that this is a forced choice.
Step 2. Ask each person privately where he sits to write down three pieces of *evidence* that would back his position.
Step 3. Now instruct everyone to stand, and all of the X voters to move to the left side of the class and the Y voters to the right side of the class. Take a physical count of the number of X and number of Y and mark on the chart.
Step 4. Explain that if anyone changes his mind he may walk over to the other side (few will because they are publicly committed now).
Step 5. Call on the X men to explain from their notes their evidence that justified their position. After most of them have presented their evidence, call on the Y men to do the same.
Step 6. Now permit rebuttal and free debate from either side. Moderate the debate until most of the major issues have been discussed, a major case has been made for both sides, and evidence of rebuttals has been made. When the discussion seems complete (usually 30–45 minutes overall), call for a halt and open the discussion of the implication of the subject matter debated.

1. What difference does it make in supervision what you believe?
2. If most people are Y, must you still use X?
3. What kinds of policies and procedures follow from one or the other?

At the end you may summarize by holding up the book by Mc-Gregor. Point out that a detailed discussion of the X and Y respective positions is found in chapters four and five, and that if they want to read it, there are copies in the company library. Ask them to sign up for distribution of the book. Pass out the distribution slip.

The objective as stated: "As a result of this session the student will read Douglas McGregor's book."

The hope here, of course, is that he will read all of it after he gets started, and this could be stated. More self-development through reading this and other books might be expected.

Such action plans could extend to other forms of action training including cases, role play, incident process, and management games. The action technique itself is meaningless without the specific behavioral objective in mind, but combined with it it adds purpose and excitement to the learning process, in addition to being vastly more effective in output than lectures.

A separate chapter on action training methods (Chapter 13) follows in Part III, so further examples may be deferred to then. The important point is that the action follows the simulation of real-life behavior sought.

Method of Reinforcement and Feedback

The third segment of a goals-oriented lesson plan is the provision of feedback method by which the student will learn whether or not his class behavior is correct. Because behavior change is a product of the student behaving in an instructed manner and then receiving direct communication of a favorable or unfavorable nature, the method of feedback should be considered when planning the lesson. Some illustrative methods of providing such feedback are shown in Fig. 9–3. Assume that Fig. 9–3 represents a single lesson, part of a course that is designed to teach job instruction training. The session is one in which

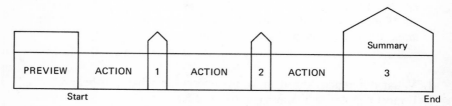

FIGURE 9–3   Model for Feedback in Training

the student is learning the second step in JIT, presentation. In previous sessions he has broken the job down into steps, has prepared the training site and the learner, and is now ready to show and tell the worker patiently one step at a time until he has learned. The instructor breaks the class up into three distinct action training phases, each broken by a feedback or critique step, and summarized by a general review and feedback of what has been learned.

1. *Action step.* Instructor teaches a specific simple task to a worker, for example, a four-step materials-handling job. He uses the correct JIT procedure in this teaching.
2. *Feedback.* He then has the student instruct him, using the same method. During the process he may use other members of the class to critique (feedback right and wrong moves as praise or criticism) his application of the technique.
3. *Action step.* The whole group is then divided into groups of three. Each person in turn goes through the JIT presentation procedure.
4. *Feedback.* At the end of each person's turn as instructor he gets comments from (a) the simulated trainee, and (b) the third party who serves as observer. The trainee thus gets four exposures to learning the procedure through action. The first is when he observes the class instructor demonstrating the procedure for the first time and again when his original demonstration learner becomes the instructor. During the three-man action practice session he functions as the learner, the instructor, and an observer. In each instance he is acting as an observer, student, or teacher.

The final feedback is a summary statement and comment by the class leader to the entire group regarding what they have learned, praise for things done right, and cautionary feedback for the most common errors observed in the session. Some of the methods that might be employed for feedback, which is an integral part of action training, might be the following:

1. When the student behaves in the appropriate manner, he is verbally rewarded by praise; and when he behaves improperly (makes a mistake), he receives negative verbal statements and perhaps has to repeat the step until it is done right. This verbal behavior could come from the instructor, or it could come from members of the group who have before them some sort of standard of behavior.
2. He could hear his own behavior fed back to him through a tape recorder, on video tape, or in an audiolingual instruction center such as a language laboratory. The language laboratory in its most com-

plete form would include a model source (the machine utters "nyet") that the student then imitates. He then gets a quick feedback that plays back the immediate sequence; the model sound followed by the student's response. He hears both sounds in short series and can compare his sound with the model. He keeps repeating the sound until the two are indistinguishable. This could also be combined with a visual display in which he must at the same time write out the word in Cyrillic script, which is then compared optically with a model form of the script.

3. Variations of this kind of learning have been applied in training operators in assembly at the Micro Switch Division of Minneapolis Honeywell. A series of 2 by 2 slides showing the exact sequence in which a task is performed, such as writing a bank of relays, is accompanied by a verbal set of instructions played on a coordinated tape over earphones. This set, a small screen projector box with coordinated instruction tape, is actually placed at the workbench and the new or untrained operator turns on the equipment and dons the earphones. A picture flashes onto the screen of the display box, which pictures the workbench and tools almost identical with the one that he is actually seated at. Three things occur:

Visual Display on Screen	Tape Instruction Over Headphones	Worker Actually Does This
1. Show operator's hand picking up soldering iron and testing temperature on solder	1. "First pick up the soldering iron as shown, and touch the tip to the end of the solder coil."	1. Picks up soldering iron and touches the tip to the end of the solder coil

Each step, key point, and instructions on what to do if a problem or special action is required are fed to the operator. He sees the ideal picture, hears it explained, and can see his own behavior duplicate it. The first time through the foreman can stand beside him and point out any errors that he makes in imitating the tape. After he has imitated the tape exactly, he tapers off his observation, permitting the operator to continue imitating the tape and following the instructions. At a point where repetition has fixed the desired behavior into a learning behavior, the operator turns off the equipment and continues to work according to the proper pattern.

4. Computer-assisted instruction programs tie the worker's response to a series of programmed comparisons within a computer, which compares the actual response with the proper response. An improper response will result in the computer stopping the sequence and turn-

ing the program back for a repetition of that teaching segment for redoing. In some instances it may route him through a branch that makes up for certain apparent shortcomings that caused the failure. For example, in a mathematics program the machine may instruct the student "Now take the square root of the resulting sum." The student responds improperly, because he does not know how to take a square root. The computer then branches him back to a remedial program that instructs him on how to take a square root. Having learned this, he now gets the question once more. This time he should be able to respond correctly, in which case he goes on to the next step or frame. If he still responds improperly, he may be re-routed through the sequence of learning square root calculations and so on until the machine is certain that he knows how.

5. In certain social skills, the group may be armed with a questionnaire or checklist that it uses in observing the behavior of the trainee as he demonstrates his skill at making a speech, leading a conference, or conducting a demonstration of some similar nature. At the end of the session each member of the class reads his findings, and the checklist sheets are collected and passed to the trainee for his further study.

Inventory the Training Materials

A fourth part of the goals-oriented lesson plan is an inventory of the materials, equipment, and supplies that will be needed for conducting the instructional session. The purpose of the inventory is simple. The training session should not be interrupted in the middle to discover that the instructor has forgotten to obtain and have at hand some important tool, aid, property, list, or piece of equipment. This list is constructed after the definition of behavior change has been made, the action plan described, and the method of feedback decided on.

This stage includes the design and construction of visual aids, which should be relevant to the training, should not be overly complex, should faithfully reproduce the job materials and supplies, and should be manageable, attractive, and necessary.

The inventory may include choice of the room and its arrangement with respect to properties, lighting, ventilation, and other details. There are two guiding rules for this room set-up:

1. Every student should be able to see and hear everything that he came to see and hear that contributes to his learning. This requires that the room and the student's work area be lighted, that the dis-

plays and aids be visible to everyone without strain, and that the acoustics be satisfactory and free of distracting noises.

2. The student should be comfortable and free of distractions that draw his attention away from the purposes for which the training is being conducted. Hard chairs, lack of ventilation, glaring lights, open windows that create an uncomfortable draft, unusual noises, lack of ashtrays, closely packed seating, no writing space, glare on the blackboard, or obstructions to vision would fall into this discomfort-causing category.

Rehearsal and Briefing

Action training is actually a form of dramatization of real life in simulated form. As a slice of life and a play in which people are being equipped to function better in the real world of business, a more effective performance will come from rehearsals. The instructor, having assembled his props, his aids, and his teaching assistants, should "walk through" the parts, try out the aids, and note any shortcoming before the session begins and his audience is on hand.

Changes in the method of presentation can still be made and any inconsistencies in the action that would cause it to fall below desired behavior change levels can be uncovered. The management of time can also be built in through realistic estimates of class time required.

The possibilities of unpredicted response to certain class behavior may be uncovered.

1. A rehearsal of a role play brought out the possibility of the group being silent and not cooperating because a higher member of management was present. After considering this possibility in rehearsal, the instructor decided to discuss it with the manager involved, explain the possibility, and suggest that he not attend during the role play session.

2. A preliminary rehearsal of using a case study tied to role brought up the question "Suppose the group hasn't done its reading prior to coming to the first session?" Because the group was to be gathered from around the country and the lesson plan had called for them to receive the first case by mail prior to arrival, with stern instructions "please read before coming," much of the first session was based on the assumption that the instructions would be followed. The very realistic question "Suppose they don't?" was asked. As a result a lengthy case was replaced with a short one-page case that served a similar instructional purpose. The shortness of the case served two purposes. It increased the likelihood that it would be read before

coming, and it opened a possibility that if it had not been read only a short time would be required to halt the class and instruct everyone to read it on the spot. It was subsequently discovered that the fears were well founded, because many had received notice that they were scheduled on short lead time, and the first session was actually interrupted while the case was read. Because the possible delay was planned and foreseen in the rehearsal and walk-through, the instructors were enabled to carry out their first session as desired. Without such a preview session, the course might have started badly, with possible harmful effects to the entire course as a result.

3. Several instructors were assigned to conduct an incident process program. By rehearsing they were able to better tie the groups together so that uniform progress by several groups could be achieved in the action phase, which might have been uneven and perhaps self-canceling if such a rehearsal had not taken place.

Summary
The goals-oriented leson plan will have several distinct differences from a lesson outline. The end product of such detailed objectives planning of each lesson is that the probability of behavior change is appreciably enhanced.

THE BOOTHBY MANUFACTURING COMPANY CASE

In the spring of 1956, the Boothby Manufacturing Company was preparing for the installation of an electronic data-processing machine. This device, the company's first computer, introduced a number of new problems in the company's operations, many of them having personnel ramifications.

The Boothby Company, one of the nation's oldest corporations, had been engaged principally in the production of basic consumer goods since the mid-1800's. Certain of its products had found industrial applications, however, so that by 1956 sales were made not only to household consumers but also to other manufacturing concerns. Throughout its long corporate history, the company had experienced depressions and booms and had continued to progress in both circumstances. Its record of dividend payments had helped win wide respect in business circles for the company's management, and its reputation for quality products had made its name well known to consumers. The company had taken numerous pioneering steps within its industry, notably leading in matters such as product packaging and display and in the "styling" of products in which fashion had previously been generally regarded as inconsequential.

Executive offices were maintained in Philadelphia for corporation officers of the purchasing department, the insurance department, the traffic department, the office of the vice president in charge of advertising, the general accounting office, and a special sales office that sold the company's products to particular industries and could also contract to purchase products outside the company for resale to those industries. The general sales office of the company, which served as headquarters for the vice president in charge of sales, was located in New York City and was complemented by nine additional sales offices throughout the United States. The general sales offices provided facilities for the product sales managers, the director of market research, the director of product research, an order-processing department, a sales accounting office, and a mill department, the last furnishing production control and liaison between sales and the production plants. Manufacturing plants, of which there were nine, were located chiefly along the East Coast. Total employment of the company numbered about 9,000, and the sales volume amounted to nearly $100 million in 1956.

Although there was no single director of personnel for the company who might serve as a coordinator of overall personnel programs,[1] the company had laid down certain personnel policies and practices to be followed throughout its organization. Generally, up-to-date personnel practices were observed, with an extensive concern for employees being evidenced, notably in the brochure distributed to new members of the Philadelphia office. In this brochure a brief history of the company and description of its principal products were followed by employment policy statements, information on insurance programs, vacations, hours of work, payroll records, company tearoom service, and similar matters. The company had a limited profit-sharing plan in operation. Other employee benefits included physical examination, financial help with certain educational courses, and a library of company books and business information.

Each of the plants had a personnel manager, reporting directly to its plant manager, whose functions dealt chiefly with matters affecting the productive work force. Labor relations were particular concerns of these men, not only in the unionized plants in the North but also in the non-unionized plants in the South. Where plants were unionized, contract negotiations were conducted by the plant manager, permanently retained (outside) legal counsel, and the personnel manager. The plant personnel managers acted fairly independently of centralized authority.

In the New York office, where 125 to 150 persons were employed, most personnel administration functions were handled by line executives. The sales department controller had responsibility for most of the clerical personnel in the New York office, including the recruiting and interviewing of such personnel. If a vacancy occurred in a merchandise department, the final hiring decision rested with the departmental supervisor. The employment of supervisory employees and salesmen was generally done by the coordinator for sales. No central source dealt with hiring other members of the supervisory force; the usual practice was for a department head to deal with such matters through inquiries in the trade, calls on executive employment agencies, and similar means. New jobs of a supervisory nature required the approval of the company president before the position could be established, and it would then become the duty of the supervisor to find the man for the position.

The Philadelphia offices similarly followed a decentralized pattern of personnel administration. A total of about 100 persons were employed in these offices, most of them performing tasks in the general accounting office.

1 During a discussion group meeting of second-level executives a suggestion was made by a plant personnel manager for yearly conferences of personnel officials. This suggestion was incorporated in the executives' report to the policy committee (president, sales vice president, advertising vice president, and the retired treasurer), but no action on it had been taken at the time of the case.

This office maintained centralized accounts receivable, accounts payable, and company-wide statistical records. No overall personnel officer, as such, was employed in the executive offices, and personnel matters for this office generally developed on the company controller, Mr. Bruce, whose department was numerically the largest. Mr. Bruce was familiar with many personnel policies and procedures, but time limitations prevented his conducting a large-scale personnel program. In his opinion, there would have been insufficient work for a full-time director of personnel, although he believed that such a position might advantageously be filled as a part-time function.

Among his personnel duties, Mr. Bruce served as a coordinator for the hiring of clerical personnel for the executive offices, departmental requests for such personnel being routed through his office. It then became his task to find and screen suitable applicants, who would be referred to their future supervisors for approval. For vacancies occurring above clerical levels, the employment process would fall to the supervisor of the proposed job, unless this vacancy occurred in Mr. Bruce's departments. In the latter case, Mr. Bruce had full responsibility.

For all company positions over a salary level of $4,000 a year, the company president maintained a personal history file. The president himself passed on the promotions and salary increases of such persons, though he generally followed the recommendations of the immediate supervisors. The president's office also kept on file the scores registered on a well-known "temperament test," which was given to all personnel and which was used as a guide in employee selection and in considering personnel for promotions. These tests were administered by the president's secretary and by the treasurer of the company, both of whom had been qualified by the designer of the test to interpret the results. In addition, the president's office approved recommendations for new supervisory positions.

In considering the purchase of a computer, Boothby first conducted a detailed feasibility study. A "Survey Committee," consisting of Mr. Bruce, the director of operations research, and a cost accountant from one of the company's plants, was established to investigate exhaustively specific operations that could be appropriately adapted to electronics processing. Systems and procedures were analyzed, and the possibilities for programming the machine were explored. In essence, the committee was to determine which machine, if any, to obtain. A comprehensive study of the electronics processing equipment field ensued. After studying machines of all manufacturers, the conclusion was reached that the company should rent, with an option to buy, a medium-size computer. Cost factors, displacement of personnel, and personnel training for the new operations were all included in the committee's considerations.

Personnel planning for the computer was considerably complicated by a location factor. The machine was actually to be installed in the New York offices of the company, but most of its work would supplant tasks being performed currently in the general accounting office in Philadelphia. Moreover, there was no real "mechanization" of office functions in the New York office, whereas the Philadelphia offices were well mechanized with adequate tabulating, keypunch, and similar equipment. It was clear that a certain measure of employee displacement would follow, to the extent that the jobs of some of the Philadelphia employees would be eliminated.

The decision to locate the computer in New York was made in compliance with the president's desire for accelerated service to the sales department, especially in the development of information not presently available. Initially, computer applications would concentrate on keeping track of orders and inventories for the sales department: what had been ordered, delivery dates, what the company needed to sell, and what it needed to manufacture.

The Survey Committee, in a final report submitted to the president and the treasurer of the company, recommended that steps be taken to reassure employees who were in danger of losing their jobs, in order to maintain employee morale. In the committee's opinion, it was desirable to say that "no employee was to lose his job" because of the advent of the computer and either to state or imply that normal turnover and attrition would take care of personnel reductions. Although the committee felt that normal turnover *would* compensate for displacements, it was thought that the company might have to request employees to transfer to other jobs. In any event, the committee believed that its recommended policy of reassuring employees could be followed easily by simply not replacing employees who left in the normal course of business.

This recommendation, however, was not followed. Top management took the position that it was unrealistic to provide employee reassurances: Jobs *were* to be eliminated and "this fact should be faced by the company."

Subsequently, the employees were told that (1) the company had ordered a computer; (2) the computer would be in New York and would perform functions currently executed in Philadelphia; (3) the company would make every effort to see that employees who were affected were offered other work within the company if suitable openings existed and, where no openings existed, efforts would be made to help the employees to locate elsewhere; and (4) the company expected no jobs to be affected during the coming 12 months, the present personnel were performing satisfactorily, and they would be needed for at least an additional 12 months' period.

This message was transmitted to the employees by means of a bulletin, in which it was stated also that the company would lease the computer, which would perform functions in the ordering, sales analysis, accounts receivable, and inventory record-keeping areas. Following distribution of this bulletin, Mr. Bruce personally talked to the employees of the two departments to be most affected, telling them substantially what was outlined in the bulletin.

This talk was given after supervisors had reported unrest and discontent concerning possible effects of the computer. It was Mr. Bruce's opinion that earlier timing of his talk would not have helped dispel such unrest and that only specific reassurances would have been of real value.

The effects of these decisions and announcements on the general accounting office were not long in appearing. Actual installation of the computer and the commencement of its operations were not scheduled until a year later; but, following the announcement of the plans, morale in the department dropped appreciably, according to Mr. Bruce. This drop in morale was evidenced by diminished work efficiency, a more careless and unconcerned attitude, and a general feeling of "I'm not going to be around here long, anyhow." There was no immediate *mass* upsurge of resignations, but the company felt reasonably sure that some employees began to look for other employment. Exit interviews were not a practice of the company, and, accordingly, it was not possible to be certain of precisely what resignations were caused by the computer. It was estimated by Mr. Bruce, however, that, over a period of about one year, some ten resignations were tendered as a result of the computer planning.

Vacancies occurring after such resignations were very difficult to fill. Applicants were reluctant to accept jobs that in all probability would not be permanent, while supervisors felt handicapped because they had less of a future to offer a new employee. Shortages of adequate personnel compounded the department's difficulties, requiring longer hours of work, overtime pay, delays in data handling, and progressively lower employee morale. Furthermore, the introduction of changes in methods and systems in order to prepare for the computer became quite difficult. The usual problems of getting clerical personnel to accept changes were complicated by lowered morale deriving from a sense of the futility of "learning a new job for only one year." This situation, Mr. Bruce believed, was one that would have to be "lived with" until the computer actually commenced operations.

The precise number of persons who would be released because of the change in operations could still not be determined. In some instances, it appeared possible that initial computer operations would reflect the desirability of returning to some manual operations. For a time, it was certain that there would be a need for parallel systems of data processing, until the new computer center was thoroughly "proved out."

In looking forward to terminations the company expected a gradual "phasing out" process to release the pressure of wholesale eliminations of jobs. (The company's termination policy, as stated in the *Employee's Handbook,* is given in Exhibit I.) It was anticipated that terminations would not be made by seniority but in inverse ratio to merit. With only one exception, no one who would be released was near retirement age, and this one exception had already exceeded the retirement age that was to become compulsory in 1960. The usual termination policy had been modified in the case of four supervisory-level employees, by reaching an agreement with them that they would receive their regular pay until they found other employment, up to a maximum of six months, in the event that their positions were eliminated.

In preparing for the computer, the Survey Committee had given consideration to the training that would be provided by equipment manufacturers to those persons selected for operators. All members of the Survey Committee had attended equipment manufacturers' schools, and it was expected that the computer manufacturer would train personnel to the company's satisfaction.

The first step in the selection of computer personnel was to find a man who would be in charge of the installation, reporting to Mr. Bruce. Recommendations for the position of supervisor were made by the Survey Committee. The final selection was made by the company president. A former plant manager, with no previous knowledge of computers, was finally selected, primarily because of his administrative ability. This man was designated the "chief of the computer center."

The second step involved the selection of programmers who would study systems and actually write the instructions for the machine. Plant managers

Exhibit I. Boothby Manufacturing Company—Statement of Termination Policy

---

Termination, Resignation, or Retirement

If, under ordinary conditions, the company finds it necessary to terminate your employment, two weeks' notice or salary will be given to regular employees with at least three months' regular full-time employment unless termination is caused by misconduct or illegal action. Severance pay in unusual circumstances is left to the discretion of management.

If, for any reason, you should resign, the company expects to receive reasonable notice.

All Philadelphia or New York office employees who retire on or after January 1, 1957, and who at the time of retirement are at least 65 years of age, will receive from Boothby one week's salary (base rate only, at the time of retirement) for each full year of service with Boothby. Years of service will be determined by Boothby. After the total of past service credit has been determined, payments to the retired employee will be made semimonthly until a total of 24 equal payments have been made. These payments will be continued even though the retired employee may have secured other employment.

You should consult with the insurance department before leaving to ensure proper handling of your Blue Cross-Blue Shield and life insurance.

---

were asked for names of personnel who might be suitable, and recommendations also were received from the Philadelphia and the New York offices. Nominees first were interviewed by Mr. Bruce and the chief of the computer center and then given a series of tests. These tests included the "temperament test," previously referred to, given by company personnel; an arithmetic test for logic and accuracy, developed by a West Coast manufacturer; and an aptitude test for electronics data-processing machine operators. This last test, prepared for a manufacturer of computers, was designed essentially to test the applicant's ability to follow instructions, to read series of numbers, and to think logically. Following the tests, the nominees were told that, if they finally were selected, they would have to move to New York at company expense and what the salary would be. This salary was considerably higher than that presently being earned, in most instances. No other promises were made, but the advantages of higher salaries and the opportunities of entering a new and interesting field were emphasized. The fact that the computer would be located in New York City had to be taken into consideration in interviewing employees.

From the overall group, nine persons were finally selected to be sent, with the chief of the computer center, to the first training course. These nine were told that four of them would ultimately be chosen, based on their performance in the training course as evaluated by the computer center chief and the teachers of the course. It was pointed out, however, that all nine were honored by being selected for the course and that by no means would the five not finally chosen be considered "black sheep." Of the four selected, two came from one of the northern manufacturing plants, one from the New York office, and one from the Philadelphia office.

Courses in the manufacturer's school included programming, theory of electronics data processing, logical operations, and "flow-charting." The courses were generally satisfactory, except in the area of flow-charting, where it was felt that a more extensive treatment would have been justified. Added training here was subsequently given by Mr. Bruce and the director of operations research, using their experience gained in this field in another manufacturer's school.

After this course was completed, the Boothby company held one-day sessions for most of top management to outline what could be expected from the computer installation. These sessions were scheduled as a part of regular quarterly meetings.

In the new installation, the computer center chief and the four programmers were to be joined by four or five keypunch operators and probably two tabulating machine operators, one of the latter a working supervisor. The keypunch and tabulating machine operators were to be new employees, as there were then no tabulating or similar machinery in the New York office.

In addition, a systems and procedures man, employed from outside the company, was temporarily assigned to the computer installation, in view of the systems problems arising there. Although competition for programmers was expected to become keen in the future, the company up to then had no problems in retaining its personnel. It was aware of the possibility that other companies might ultimately seek to draw away such trained personnel, but it expected higher salaries to help guard against this possibility.

CASE DISCUSSION QUESTIONS

The Boothby Manufacturing Company Case

1. Prepare statements of the training needs you see in the Boothby Company.
2. Prepare a goals-oriented plan for one of them.
3. Present and defend your plan.

10 Evaluation of Training Effectiveness

What if thine eyes refuse to see,
    Thine ear of Heaven's free welcome fail,
And thou a willing captive be,
    Thyself thy own dark jail?
                            —WHITTIER

BEING systematic in evaluation does not mean that you throw out old methods of testing; you merely supplement them by having a more firm set of criteria in mind. The systems approach suggests that the criteria for measuring training effectiveness is the set of objectives that you started out to achieve.

The Futility of Ordinary Testing

One of the more fruitless activities of customary classroom teaching is the folklore that somehow testing is a necessary part of the learning process. The teacher lectures to the students, assigns readings, and periodically sits the class before a blue book, away from books and notes, and tests his ability to reproduce verbally or in writing what his memory and reading skill have produced as a residue. Where the course consists of certain skills such as performing an experiment, the learner may actually perform such an experiment in the presence of the instructor. The vast majority of tests, however, are required demonstrations of verbal (oral or written) behavior, which may or may not reflect itself into some visible and productive behavior at a later time outside the classroom environment.

Although this may serve many useful purposes in the school and college, it serves far fewer useful purposes in management training. The standard variations of verbal behavior testing—essay, true-false, multiple-choice, comparison, and definition questions—when applied to a subject such as human relations, is most likely to prove anything more than the student's ability to recognize certain written symbols dealing with the language of human relations. Because human relations or other managerial training is most apt to be a complex kind of behavior, or repertory of behaviors, success on the verbal or pencil-and-paper test can hardly be described as proof of learning, as a measurement of the degree of learning.

The systems approach to evaluation of training starts with a definition of behavior change objectives sought through a conscious development effort. This definition then remains a yardstick for measurement throughout the course, and achievement against the stated goals is the measure of success. All other forms of evaluation measure the internal character of the activity itself, not the effectiveness of training.

Behavior and Its Consequences

One of the procedural hitches that can occur in evaluating the effect of a training effort is that of sorting out behavior change from the results that that behavior produced. This can be illustrated in Fig. 10–1 in which there are shown three separate ingredients of the behavior change process.

A training program (2) is conducted which is designed to change the behavior of the trainee from old behavior (1) to new behavior (3). As a result of the course or training effort, the new behavior actually

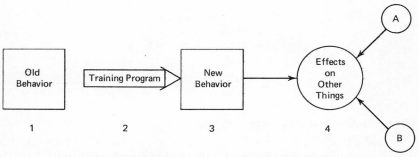

FIGURE 10–1   Ingredients in the Behavior Change Process

ensues. This new behavior affects something else in the environment (4) of the trainee when he behaves that way.

We note that it was the fourth effect that was desired before we started; that is why we organized and planned and executed the training effort. Yet a limitation on the evaluation of training effectiveness lies in the possible existence of other forces (A) and (B) that might have occurred at the same time or in concurrence with the training. Thus the effect cannot be wholly or accurately ascribed to the training unless we can be certain that no other influences were at work. For example, if we conduct a cost reduction course for foremen and costs go down, we cannot assume that it was wholly caused by the training. It might have been caused by better purchasing, longer runs in production, an easier product to make, better engineering, or a change in suppliers. Neither could we call the course in cost reduction a failure if after the course costs *rose*. They might have risen for any of the reasons cited above: other influences at work. It might also be true that costs went up but would have risen even more if the cost reduction course had not been conducted and the skill brought back to the job and applied.

From Fig. 10–1 we might reasonably conclude that the best way of evaluating training would be to confine the evaluation to items 1, 2, and 3. Evaluations of item 4 might well be done, but if the first three have been used and proved effective, then 4 must be used cautiously. Perhaps it can give insights into whether or not the course objectives were properly designed, but even here there are many limitations.

If a course defines its intentions as changing specific old behavior to specific new behavior and this change actually occurs, the training must be considered successful. The evaluation of training is limited to assessing or measuring as accurately as possible how much of the desired (objective) behavior was actually attained and applied: first, in the class, and, second, back on the job.

If training actually changed behavior in the class then it must be considered a training success from the class standpoint and instruction technique standpoint. If it fails to convert back to the job, then the analysis of system support of that behavior may be at fault and not the training, but the prior planning and task analysis are probably at fault.

Cost Effectiveness Studies of Training

Because a business or any other form of organization where money is a limiting factor places an economic dimension on training, cost effectiveness studies comprise a valuable kind of evaluation of training. Training effectiveness depends on many factors, including the morale and enthusiasm of the trainees for training, the purposes and position of the company in its industry, and the skill and ability of its employees and managers. There is, however, an economic factor that sets a limiting condition on how much training can effectively be supported. Although other factors such as learning theory must also be considered limiting factors, in this section we shall consider a systematic manner of evaluating cost effectiveness of training. This should not be considered simply cutting the costs of training; it has a rather specific meaning. Two definitions should be borne in mind when using the term *cost effectiveness:*

1. *Cost* is the dollar outlay, both direct and indirect, of planning, executing, and evaluating the training and of the consequences of that training in affecting other costs when the trainee uses it back on the job.
2. *Effectiveness* is a shorthand word for the contribution to objectives of a specific effort.

The reason cost effectiveness studies of training have been so sparse in the past is that trainers seldom calculate the actual costs of training and, further, do not define objectives and therefore cannot weigh achievement against such objectives. With both necessary ingredients missing, the only kind of evaluation possible is to obtain opinions of students with respect to their attitudes, opinions, and perception of the training process itself or to obtain opinions of others about it. These methods, with their great limitations, will be discussed later.

The problem of training could theoretically be handled as a large economic problem. The firm or organization has certain resources that it can dispose of or allocate among alternative uses. These resources (or inputs) are sometimes classified as labor, materials and supplies, and capital. These resources could be used to hire salesmen to enlarge the market, or poured into scientific research to obtain monopolies and cost reduction in process or product, or into advertising to capture a larger share of the market. They could also be spent in varying amounts for training employees with a goal of changing their behavior. In effect, the cost of training could well be expressed in terms of the other things that could be produced if that behavior had not been bought at a cost.

Two weeks of sensitivity training for 50 people could have
 Bought full scholarships for 25 Negro students at Tuskegee . . .
 Or paid for six new salesmen for a year . . .

Or paid the rent for five sales offices for a year . . .
Or paid for a new numerically controlled machine tool.

The choice among these alternatives, of course, could be screened on the basis of a number of criteria. Because they all are approximately the same cost (use up the same amount of resources), some other criterion is required to screen them. This criterion, it is proposed here, should be *contribution to objectives*.

Thus, in the preceding examples, if the objective of the firm was to maximize immediate profit during the forthcoming accounting period, one choice might be made. If it were to enhance the long-run profitability of the company, it might be another. If it were to make an immediate and long-run contribution to the social climate in which it must function, it might be still another choice.

The sequence in which these two steps define the objectives and list options is important. The statement of objectives should be clarified before the optional means of solution are fixed. Otherwise the objectives will be invented to fit the choice of method.

Cost effectiveness studies, it should be noted, do not start with the totaling of dollar costs. That is merely one of the criteria. The starting point for a cost effectiveness study is a clear definition of objectives.

Let us use a simple example to illustrate why this is true.

THE CASE OF THE SPOILED WORK

In an assembly department the rate of rejects on assembled components has risen sharply. It is discovered that most of the rejects can be traced back to two subcomponents, which are manufactured in two different departments. An investigation reveals that in the first case the cause can be traced to materials supplied by a new vendor. In the second case it can be traced to a work group of women of whom more than two thirds are newly hired. The work they perform is precise and involves working in small areas with great accuracy. The records show that all the ladies involved passed the personnel department screening for dexterity, vision, and coordination. All were trained in assembly and soldering. The supervisor of the assembly department is in a huff. He suggests "Run them all back through the screening tests and the training again to see if they can't be straightened out. It will cost a lot less than the rejects we're getting now."

The training director becomes involved in the problem at this point.

He notes the facts and attempts to define what behavior change he would affect through the training portion of the assembly manager's suggestion. The language used by that irate fellow could be mistaken for cost effectiveness language, but if it were, it would be in error. The training director does the following:

1. He finds that the women doing the work alternate between various tasks by day. Thus it is difficult to trace bad work to any single individual or pair of them. As it now stands the work can only be traced to a group. To alleviate this condition he arranges for a simple system of inspection tags, which accompany each box of completed work. This tag shows the operator's number and the date.
2. It becomes very apparent that one lady is the cause of most of the rejects. Her work is defective far more often than any of the others. When a box with her tag is used in assembly, the reject rate goes up sharply. When several components that she worked on are used in assembly, the reject rate of assembled products is outrageously high. This is illustrated in Fig. 10–2. The five ladies in A, the subassembly department, rotate among the tasks daily, each turning out a specific subassembly according to the station they occupy. These are all placed in storage, B, from which assembly draws them for use on the lines. After the identification tags are initiated it becomes possible to identify whose handiwork was being used in assembly and whose was defective. A simple experiment followed. Production run C was made using material out of storage, all of which was produced by operator I. A second run was made using material assembled by everyone *but* I. A third run was made in which I's work was used proportionately with everyone else's work. The results in reject rate

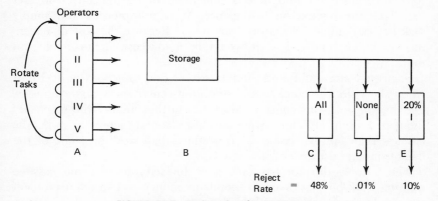

FIGURE 10–2 Design of a Plant Experiment

under each of the three test runs are as shown in the figure. The conclusion? There is something about I's work that causes defect in final assembly, no matter what subassembly or station she works on.

3. At this stage the training director performs a simple cost effectiveness study. He lists three alternatives, as in Fig. 10–3.

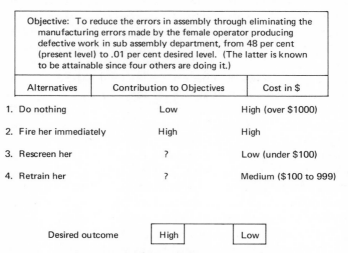

Objective: To reduce the errors in assembly through eliminating the manufacturing errors made by the female operator producing defective work in sub assembly department, from 48 per cent (present level) to .01 per cent desired level. (The latter is known to be attainable since four others are doing it.)

Alternatives	Contribution to Objectives	Cost in $
1. Do nothing	Low	High (over $1000)
2. Fire her immediately	High	High
3. Rescreen her	?	Low (under $100)
4. Retrain her	?	Medium ($100 to 999)

Desired outcome	High		Low

FIGURE 10–3   Model for a Cost-Effectiveness Study

From Fig. 10–3 it becomes apparent that the next move from a cost effectiveness viewpoint would be to run operator I through the screening examination once more. Here is why. Alternative 1, do nothing, contributes little to objectives and the cost is high for the continued rejects. Firing her would indeed contribute to the objective—in fact would be the highest on first glance. Why not proceed and simply sack her (a common managerial solution)? Because the cost of screening one more time is low, it would be a low-cost, high-possible-gain move.

She is screened and found suitable, except that somebody notices that when she visits the employment screening center she wears eyeglasses. On the job she wears contact lenses. On further inquiry the spectacles prove to be bifocal. Thus, when she wears contact lenses at work, she has less than optimal vision. This produces bad work on some of the fine operation in subassemblies.

The training director has thus done himself out of some possible training work but has saved the company money and solved a problem through his analytical methods.

The essential parts of a cost effectiveness study for training can be shown in Fig. 10–4. The first step is a definition of the objective in specific, quantifiable, measurable terms (I). The next (II) is a list of the alternative solutions that might be followed in changing the behavior or achieving the objective. The next (III) is a rating of each of the alternatives against the criteria of "contribution to objectives." Following this, each of the criterion is rated against some cost figures (IV). You might, for example, simply list the total cost of each in dollars, or you might rate them as high, medium, or low, with a definition of the ranges for each of these words.

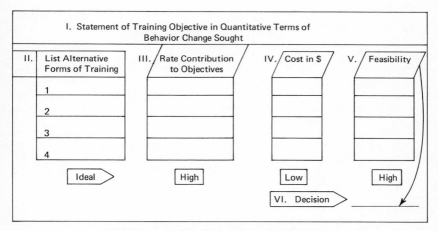

FIGURE 10–4   Decision Matrix for Training Programs

This rating according to objectives (high, medium, low) could be a source of error and merely reflect a general sensitivity to the criteria rather than rigid quantifiable analysis. Another screen for effectiveness would be that of feasibility (V), which is an estimate of whether or not that solution could be done at all. For example, it might be concluded in a government agency that cost effectiveness shows that sending people to a university program would have the greatest cost effectiveness, but the administrator knows that a ban from higher headquarters has been put on anyone leaving the office for the next three months, for some reasons known only to the top people who initiated the order. Thus the feasibility of getting the most effective solution implemented is low. The decision (VI) is that alternative that survives this screening with the closest approximation of the ideal outcome. After this is implemented, it can be evaluated against the objective (I) for conformity. If it achieves the objectives then the training was successful.

Cost effectiveness studies then comprise perhaps the best form of evaluation of training, because they force the requirements of defining present behavior, designing training to change it, and statements and examination of several alternative ways of training. These alternatives are then screened down to the one that shows the most sensitivity to criteria of contribution to objectives and cost.

Stating costs as a level of high, medium, or low could be fraught with dangers, because there has been no attempt to calculate exactly what these costs are. If there is any doubt about them, the construction of an added worksheet to estimate the various cost levels should be undertaken, especially where the sums may be significant. A sample of what might be included in such a cost estimation is shown in Fig. 10–5. The items of cost are listed down the left-hand column and the respective

Cost Comparison of Alternative Forms of Training

I	Name of Training Problem					
II	Training Objective (Behavior Change Sought)					
III	Expense	**Alternatives**				
		1	2	3	4	5
(a)	Wages of Trainees	$	$	$	$	$
	___ X ___ X ___ NO. HRS. HRLY Rate	___	___	___	___	___
(b)	Staff Time					
	___ X ___ HRS. HRLY SAL RATE	___	___	___	___	___
(c)	General Supervision					
	___ X ___ HRS. EST. RATE	___	___	___	___	___
(d)	Direct Materials					
	Books and Materials Visual Aids Announcements Travel Tel & Tel Instructors					
(e)	Other					
	Consultants	___	___	___	___	___
	___					
	TOTAL	$	$	$	$	$

FIGURE 10–5   Cost Comparison of Alternative Forms of Training

items are posted according to the various alternative approaches that might be considered.

Five major expense categories are listed:

1. The highest expense is the time of the trainees. This cost should be calculated as estimated hours in on-company-time training multiplied by the number of hours multiplied by the hourly salary or wage rate. (It may be necessary to estimate the last.)
2. Estimated staff time of planners, staff instructors, and others whose time should be figured on some kind of standard cost, such as $5.00 per hour or more, multiplied by the number of hours estimated for preparation, supervision, and evaluation.
3. General supervision is an allocated cost of general supervision of the training activity, plus any general management time that is devoted to training. This must be estimated and is a general allocation of overhead in the staff training department to each training activity based on a standard hourly charge.
4. Direct materials include books, notebooks, meals, housing, travel, telephone and telegraph, visual aids, and any other out-of-pocket chargeable costs incurred in preparing and presenting the course.
5. The final category is "Other," which would include special or unusual expenses attributable to the particular course. This would include consultants, special equipment rental such as video tape projectors, down time on a line, and the like.

Totaling these for each of the alternatives permits a more accurate figure to be used in the cost column of Fig. 10–4.

What Cost Effectiveness Does Not Mean

Many cost effectiveness studies really do not deserve the name, for they seek out mere cost figures alone without objectives being defined. Among the typical figures that are sometimes used and labeled wrongly as cost effectiveness studies are those that report the following items.

Cost per Student Trained. In this evaluation form the total cost of the course is divided by the number of students, and a per capita charge is stated. In most such statements I have seen, these costs seldom charge in true costs, including trainees' wages during the training period. Even where they do, the cost per student may not reflect true cost effectiveness because it fails to show what contribution each alternative made to the objectives. Thus a course that costs $400 per trainee could actually be of greater cost effectiveness than a $50 course that achieved only one tenth as much of the objective as the $400 course. The savings from the course is best expressed in the objective itself. Thus an objective that states that the course "will reduce the cost of credit losses from $150,000 to $85,000 by eliminating errors from 21 to 3 per cent in interpretation of credit reference services" can be useful in cost effectiveness analysis. This means that the objective should be stated in both words and numbers.

Comparison of Absolute Costs. By a simple comparison of total costs it might erroneously be decided that the one that costs the least total amount is more effective than the one that costs the most. Or, as often occurs, it may be assumed that a high-priced course will be more effective than some behavior change plan that costs little, or even nothing.

The Estimation of Potential Losses. A justification often employed is that "we can't afford not to." This may be true, but it should be pressed forward with a detailed estimate of the potential losses and a further estimate of the probability of that outcome occurring. Estimating potential losses should include a statement of the costs that would be inherent under three possibilities:

1. The costs if the worst possible outcome were to occur, multiplied by the probability of that possibility occurring. "If this course were not presented, our office might be attacked by a roving band of marauding Indians, which would cost the company the following $, and the probability of this event occurring if the $ _____ training did not take place is estimated at X:"   X _____ % Thus, the probable losses from not running are $ _____ shown as $ _____

2. Similar calculations should be performed for the   X _____ % costs of most likely outcome of the untoward event $ _____ if the course were not conducted. $ _____

3. The same estimates of costs should be made of the   X _____ % least unfavorable outcome multiplied by the proba- $ _____ bility of these results occurring.

The three figures are the expected values under each set of assumptions. Balancing risks against cost is now a matter of judgment.

How to Measure the Unmeasurable in Cost Effectiveness

It becomes apparent then that cost effectiveness studies of training require that objectives for training be set and that these objectives have the following characteristics:

1. They define the behavior change sought, stating what the present behavior is and its consequences and the desired behavior and its consequences.
2. These must be stated in mixtures of words and numbers, which calls for quantifying certain key parts of the behavioral objectives in order that they might be used later as criteria for measuring contribution of the training effort.

Yet many aspects of human behavior and its consequences do not appear readily to lend themselves to quantification. The utmost importance of quantification makes it necessary to devise measurement indicators that measure the unmeasurable. There is a descending order of reliability to measuring instruments, which goes something as follows:

1. *Hard, raw, real time data* comprise the best kind of measurement. Dollars of expense cut, pounds of tea packaged, numbers of carburetors produced, and the like are examples of such hard data. They can be readily agreed on and verified by several independent observers. Yet in the world of training it would be an error to presume that all results can be tied directly to such hard data. This does not mean, however, that measurement is impossible. Indeed in the world of the numbers we live by, most such numbers are not hard data but indices or positions on some scale designed to measure the unmeasurable.
2. *Indices and percentages* are less reliable and valid than hard data but are nonetheless more reliable than verbal forms. They comprise an extremely valuable means of noting change, including changed behavior. Batting coaches will watch the batting average of their students, their slugging average, their runs batted in percentage, and the like to evaluate the effect of their teaching. Such ratios are often said to be "hard data" by social scientists and may be relied on heavily where they have been carefully constructed in advance.
3. *Positions on a scale* comprise a third kind of measurement device that can be used in defining behavioral objectives (see Fig. 10–6). If the reader were asked at this point to rate this book on a scale that runs from 1 to 5 with 1 being low and 5 highest, the individual rating of any rater would not have any great significance in assisting

FIGURE 10–6   Scalar Measurements for Judgment Areas

the writer to determine his writing skill and the direction it seems to be going over the years. If, on the other hand, he had acquired such a rating, or were to obtain one from a large population with respect to each of his six books written to date, he might note any changes that have occurred in his writing behavior as observed by readers (for whom, presumably, books are written). The scale is meaningless unless it is used and unless it is prepared prior to the writing and decided on as a progress measurement instrument.

4. *Verbal descriptions* of conditions that presently exist and verbal description using similar words in the same way have their limitations it is true, but they also serve a valuable purpose. Not as easily agreed on as the numbers of categories 1, 2, and 3 above, they can be most useful if we attempt to use *verbs* to describe objectives before using nouns, adjectives, or adverbs. Verbs are action words, such as to check, to correct, to report, to inspect, to call, to talk, and so on. This resembles a binary system because the trainee will either be able to do something or not be able to do it, which is a choice between zero and 1. If verbs fail, use the rest of the armory of language.

5. If you cannot even define your training objective in words, do not bother doing the training at all. You will never know what happened, or indeed if anything happened, except as your impressions after the fact guide you. This is far too subject to bias and hunch to be worth very much allocation of resources.

Sampling Student Reaction

Most of the literature of evaluation of training stresses student reaction to the training experience. It generally runs along the following lines:

1. A survey of opinions at the end of the course asking student opinions of instruction, materials, arrangements, and general viewpoint. This has some value, for if students are not pleased by what occurred in the class they may not attend classes or if they do they may not pay attention to what is going on. This diminishes the likelihood of behavior change occurring. It is a measure of how well their attention was attracted by the conduct of the course.

2. Surveys of each session are a tighter version of the same method. This is often done where different "speakers" have been invited in to teach various sessions. The ratings tend to be popularity ratings of entertainment or enthusiasm inputs by the instructors rather than reflections of genuine behavior change that occurred. The instructor with energy, enthusiasm, good audience contact, and humor will

please the class members. Such qualities are *not handicaps,* but neither are they proof of good training. Many great teachers who have significantly changed the lives of students have had these qualities—and it is an asset to be sought in teaching—but the qualities are perhaps necessary rather than sufficient conditions for teaching.

3. *Third-party opinions* are another way of obtaining the same kind of information. The man's boss is asked "Have you picked any reaction from your boys to the training class?" The boss, if he has overheard anything, will report back the substance of what he has heard. Usually this is a disorganized and somewhat sporadic form of the more systematic class opinion survey. If such informants are to be used, they should be asked to cite specific examples of behavior change observed as a result of, or concurrent with, attendance at the course.

4. *It pleases the training administrator.* Far more important than it deserves is the impression that the training has on the man who planned it. If he "feels" that it went well, more trainees are apt to be subjected to this session. It may often be pleasing to the trainer simply because it meets his own needs rather than those of the groups. A sound, experienced trainer may indeed develop a "feel" for courses that work and those that do not. This feel is valuable, but it should not be relied on for total evaluation.

THE GOPHER MILLS CASE

In 1945 at the end of World War II Gopher Mills found itself entering a period of transition from war work back to civilian production. Among the many problems it faced were modernizing many of its flour, feed, and cereal plants, which required extensive capitalization, and depressed profits. Among the functions that were eliminated at that time was the training function in the large mills and divisions. The smaller ones had never had a training director but had depended on the larger units to lend them training assistance as it was needed.

By 1948 it was realized that retirement of supervisors held over during the war years had opened many new supervisory posts, and new supervisors were being added. Requests to the corporation for training were not answered, except by references to austerity and the need for economy during the period of retooling and modernization. A national downturn in flour consumption had further aggravated the problem by reducing sales volume.

By 1955 the cereal and mixed products markets had grown and it was decided by a new vice president of personnel that a training program should be initiated again after a ten-year hiatus. The new training director immediately began to survey training needs and found that during the long dry spell several key problems had grown up. The number of new supervisors was high, with over 70 per cent of the first-line managers having less than four years of experience.

In the largest division, however, he found that the general manager was resistant to any added programs, explaining that "we have made up our own program for all new supervisors which we have installed, and it is working well." It essentially provided that each manager train his own supervisors, using a manual, some training tools made locally by the sales and advertising staff, and three films written and produced by the chief engineer on a job order from the office manager of the division office. No professional training advice had been sought. The general manager added:

"I think training should be done by line managers, and this program has worked well for us. You might even find that this program would fit other divisions and we would be glad to let you use it if you give us full credit for our contribution."

The training manager returned with a copy of the manual and plan and brought it up at the next personnel staff meeting. The personnel manager refused to commit himself on either the program or the suggestion. "I would like to have a more complete evaluation of the flour division program before we decide anything."

DEPARTMENT HEAD'S GUIDE:
NEW SUPERVISOR INTRODUCTION TRAINING

PART I: INTRODUCTION

The selection and establishment of an employee as a supervisor is one of the most critical events in personnel selection. At that moment an untried person is placed in a manager's position. On his strength or weaknesses depends the success or failure, no longer of him alone, but rather of the effectiveness of a group of people and a function of the business.

A sound selection procedure will assist in choosing the person who has the greatest potential of becoming a good manager and a good leader of people. However, at this point the job is only half done. The next step is to get the new supervisor started right. Only orderly and effective training can orient him to the new situation of responsibility in the shortest possible time and give him the broader concept of the skills and techniques necessary to carry out his responsibilities.

In Part II of this guide book, there is set forth in chronological order the events that normally occur when an employee is appointed to his first supervisory position. Each of these events has a particular significance not only in determining what the most effective training should be and how it should be given but also as an influence on the quality and speed of his adjustment.

Locally developed introductory training schedules for a new supervisor may be inserted in Part III of this guide book. Such schedules will normally cover the period of one week before and one week after he takes over a supervisory job.

It is recognized, however, that today the responsibilities of supervisors and the problem of being a manager demand continuous growth and development on the part of all supervisors. New supervisors in particular should be encouraged to take advantage of evening classes or correspondence courses. Particularly appropriate are classes in conference leadership, human relations, methods, effective speaking and writing, etc. Every supervisor should be encouraged to become familiar with outstanding books and publications on subjects related to his job. A suggested reading list is included in the appendices of this guide. Every practical means available should be used to assure the continued growth and development of each new supervisor.

Training Tools Available at Each Plant and Office

1. Department head's guide (this booklet).
2. The management practices guide. This is the outline of training to be given the new man.

3. Three sound-slide films (the foundation of the training):
   A. "Off To A Flying Start" (10 minutes)
   B. "Getting It Done" (10 minutes)
   D. "The Human Factor" (10 minutes)
4. *Management Guide Book of Personnel Policies and Procedures* (all plant and office managers, department heads, and personnel managers have a copy).
5. Four pamphlets to be given to each new supervisor for his personal posession:
   (a) *How to Get Out More Work,* Elliott Service Company.
   (b) *A Short Course in Human Relations,* Dartnell Corporation.
   (c) *Basic Policies on Which Our Company Operates.* Gopher Mills.
   (d) *A summary of each of the sound-slide films.*
6. Books for each office and plant library (to be used as reference materials during the training and available to all members of management on a loan basis).
   (a) *The Foreman's Basic Reading Kit,* American Management Association.
   (b) *The Management Leader's Manual,* American Management Association.
   (c) *Do You want To Be A Foreman,* McGraw-Hill Book Company, Inc.
   (d) *Supervision In Business and Industry,* Loken and Strong.
   (e) *The Flour Business,* Gopher Mills.
   (f) A number of texts used in the management development conferences
7. Local manuals or other references (as desired).

PART II

A Management Vacancy Exists. Somehow or other a vacancy has been created in the management ranks at this particular location. How it came about is important.

1. The opening may have been created by the promotion of the previous supervisor to a position in which he directs the work of the new appointee. In this instance much of the training responsibility for getting the new person started off right should probably rest on the person who has just been promoted.
2. The opening may have been created by the transfer of the previous holder of the position. In such an instance, responsibility for training the new man will probably rest almost entirely on his department head. Some assistance should, of course, be expected from the previous supervisor, but obviously he cannot be held completely accountable for the training of the new man.
3. The opening may have resulted from either retirement or resignation. Here again some assistance from the previous supervisor can be enlisted

but the responsibility for the breaking-in training will rest entirely on the person in authority over the new supervisor.
4. The opening may have been created by death or discharge. The significance of such a situation is that it has been created suddenly and no assistance can be obtained from the former holder of the position.

No attempt is made here to elaborate on all of the possible variations in schedule, responsibility, or training methods that might be involved as a result of the various causes of the vacancy. The point is that how the vacancy came to exist is extremely important in the approach to the job of breaking in the new person and should be considered very thoroughly in planning the training in each individual case. It not only affects the determination of who shall actually do the training but in some instances may point up certain content of the training that should be emphasized. It may also indicate necessary corrective steps that must be taken in the light of recognized weaknesses in the previous supervisor.

You Have Selected Your Man. *How* you selected the new man, *where* you got him from, and particularly *what* new things you found out about him during your more critical examination of the qualifications of candidates likewise enters prominently into the picture of what the introductory training shall emphasize. It is not the purpose of this guide book, of course, to set forth any suggested standards by which candidates for a supervisory position should be selected. It is presumed that there has been a diligent effort to arrive at a yardstick of qualifications against which the prospective candidates could be measured. Certainly such qualities as apparent leadership ability, apparent capacity to grow and assume greater responsibilities, apparent breadth and depth of judgment and imagination, and his overall apparent qualifications for setting a good example have been properly taken into account. Anyway, you have chosen a man and it might be added "for better or worse." If he has had an opportunity to serve as a lead man, section leader, etc., such a background will affect the content of the training and the elements of emphasis. If, up to this time, he has never had any opportunity to experience the feeling of getting work done through others, then, of course, he will need even greater training in fundamentals. If he has had to be selected from a different area of work, then the training will have to give considerable attention to job knowledge and functional details of the area for which he is responsible. At any rate, as can readily be seen, *how you picked the man and where you got him from is an important element in developing the training.*

Now You Have To Tell Him That He Has Been Selected. Telling the new man that he has been selected is the first actual stage of getting him started. *How he is to be told* should be thought out carefully because it can have a great influence on how he starts off in his new responsibility. Generally speaking, he should be told why he was selected. His strong points, his promising qualities and characteristics, and the qualities that he has that are recognized as good supervisory qualities should be pointed out to him. In addition, his weak points should be discussed so that he can start from the very beginning to strengthen those qualities. He should be impressed with the seriousness and the importance of his first management job. This is also a good time to assure him of his job security and privileges if he accepts the new position.

Who tells him is likewise important. Certainly the man to whom he will later be responsible must have an important part in announcing the decision to give him this new assignment. In no case should such an event as this be casual or carelessly handled. It is a most important event to both the person and the company and the announcement should be given the importance it deserves.

Incidentally, the pay check adjustment should not be overlooked, and he should be told what the adjustment is to be.

In general, all of this detail should have been taken care of at least a week before he has to take over his new responsibility. This has been a particularly weak and serious item of neglect in the past. Spot checks have revealed many instances where a new supervisor was not notified until the afternoon of the day before he was to take over. When the importance of a man's first introduction to the management structure of a company like ours is considered, such lack of consideration places the appointee under an unnecessarily difficult handicap. Certainly a man should have at least one-week notice and be given some well-planned orientation instruction during that week.

Somehow or Other You Have To Tell Other People, Too. The new man is not the only one to be told about the new appointment. *Who else should be told, when they should be told,* and *how they should be told* of the new appointment can have a great influence on the way the new man gets started. Certainly the announcement should first be made to all of the rest of the local management structure. By this attention he gets his first feeling of belonging in his new status. It lets him discover with assurance that he is welcomed into the management group and that he can look for wholesome and whole-hearted cooperation and assistance.

The next group to know it should be the group that he is to supervise. Here again it should not be done brusquely or flippantly. *How the announcement is made to his group will have a great deal to do with whether he gets started off with them on the right foot.* The new man's supervisor is the one who is most responsible for establishing the new foreman or supervisor in a good employer-employee relationship from the start.

Then there is a third important person or group of persons to be considered. These are the persons who were considered but were not chosen. Particular care must be taken in announcing the decision to the people who were hoping to be chosen. No definite pattern of conduct for this situation can be given other than to emphasize that it should be planned carefully according to the personalities and circumstances that led up to the actual decision. Above all, these people should not be ignored.

Frequently, in the past, these basic considerations have been neglected or thoughtlessly handled, with the result that unnecessary problems were created.

And Now (or During the Preceding Events) You Have To Get Ready To Do Some Training. Wherever practical, the local supervisory group should formulate an introductory training schedule to be used whenever a new supervisor is appointed. But perhaps it has been a long time since a new supervisor was broken in. It is, therefore, important that the person who is to be responsible for directing the breaking-in training of the new man refresh himself on the schedule, the reference materials, and the timing to be followed in the introductory training. The general pattern calls for giving the new man part of his training during the week before he takes over and part of it during the week after he takes over. In any case, it will require some preparation to be ready to give the new man basic instruction in the fundamentals of good supervision. If he has been selected well, then, in general, he will be as good as the training he is given.

In planning the training you should think back to the time you were first appointed as a supervisor. You may have received some special training or you may have been left to find out things for yourself. At any rate, there were times during those first few days when things looked rough—times when you were not sure of what and how things should be done. Such periods as these are often referred to as "critical periods." Recent studies made by industrial management research people indicate that there are certain predictable critical periods in the early stages of every new supervisor's appointment. Obviously the most critical periods are the few days preparatory to assuming the new position and the first few days after taking over the job.

PART III

This sheet is for the department head who has just selected a new foreman or supervisor.

During the next few weeks it becomes your responsibility to get a man off to a good start in his first management assignment in Gopher Mills. Much will depend, now and in the future, on how well this early coaching and explanation of his basic managing duties is done. Here is a condensed outline for using the different aids provided to help you.

Procedure

1. *Remove this procedure sheet from this book.* This is your guide for breaking in your new man.
2. *Issue this book to your new supervisor.* Explain that during the next 30 days or so, you will see that he gets answers and explanations for every item in it and that he is to record notes for future reference as he receives his instructions.
3. *Review the procedure in the Department Head's Guide: New Supervisor Introduction Training.*
4. *Conduct showing and discussion of Film A at once.*
5. *Schedule showing of Film B one week later and Film C one week after B. Film dates:* A._____
     B._____
     C._____
6. *Begin supplying the information* called for in this book or arrange for others to supply it where necessary. (*Important:* The items do not have to be covered in the order that they appear. It is a flexible procedure.) *Try to get the book completed in approximately 30 days.*
7. *Check frequently on his progress in completing his book.* Add in any other matters of local importance that a new supervisor should know about. There are approximately 60 items in the book. This would suggest covering an average of three per day until completed.

Appointment Dates (plant superintendent, personnel manager, products control, etc.)

_____   _____
_____   _____
_____   _____
_____   _____

Date to be completed _____
Name of Foreman _____

Guide for Showing Film A

Setting: The department head, his new supervisor, and two or so other supervisors asked to sit in and assist in interpreting the film.

Subject: "Off To A Flying Start," Part I of the new supervisor induction film.

Materials Required: Sound-slide film "Off To A Flying Start"; *Management Guide Book of Personnel Policies and Procedures; Basic Policies on Which Our Company Oper-*

ates pamphlet; summary of Film A, "Off To A Flying Start."

Objectives: To establish the importance of a managerial viewpoint and the need for certain changes in mental outlook.

Introductory Remarks: Well, fellows, we're here to pass along some help to (Dave, the new supervisor) in getting started on his new job as a supervisor. All of us have been through those first days he is now experiencing and it is our aim, through a series of three conferences on effective supervision covering the importance of attitude and the need for certain changes in mental outlook, mechanics of the job, and human relations, to help to make his transition from an employee to a supervisor an easier one. To get this discussion under way, let's have a show-of the print "Off To A Flying Start," which stresses the importance of attitude and the need for certain changes in mental outlook. Immediately following, we will have a brief discussion of the key points stressed in the film. (Show film. Upon its completion, continue.)

Discussion Guide
1. Well (Dave), what impressed you most in that film?
2. (Then ask the others) What else struck you fellows as being particularly important that (Dave) should not forget?
3. The film mentioned the need for taking over the job with confidence. Would some of you fellows care to comment on the importance of this? (List on the board a few of the points brought out.)
4. Now let's look at another important point covered in the film—the new or increased responsibilities involved in the change from doing a job to seeing that a job is done. What are some of these new or increased responsibilities? (The following are some of the points that should be brought out by the group.)
   (a) Quantity and quality of production or work
   (b) Planning of work
   (c) Control of costs or expenses
   (d) Appraising work of others
   (e) Human relations and morale
   (f) Training (job instruction)
We have developed quite a list here. It might be well if (Dave) made

a note of these items before we move on to the next key point in the film.

5. One of the biggest changes in thinking that each of us went through on becoming a supervisor was the change in outlook from "my job" to "my company." In other words, we must develop the point of view of the owner or manager. Why is this important?

6. Our discussion has brought out the fact that the men's ideas of the company, management, and its policies are largely a result of their contact with their supervisor. Frankly, fellows, we have quite a responsibility in being well informed about our company and its policies. Let's take a look at the *Management Guide Book on Personnel Policies and Procedures.* Here we have a guide to assist in answering questions on policy that arise in our departments. This may be a good time to discuss some of the more common questions put to us by employees on company policy. (The discussion should emphasize further the important role the supervisor plays in explaining the company's policies to employees. Have the other supervisors present recall some typical problems or questions that they have come up against lately.)

7. Summary: Summarize again, briefly, the major changes that take place on becoming a supervisor and mention that in the next session we shall get at the mechanics of the job of supervision. (Hand out *Basic Policies on Which Our Company Operates* and the summary of Film A, "Off To A Flying Start.")

Guide for Showing Film B

Setting: Same as for Film A.

Subject: "Getting It Done," Part II of the new supervisor induction film.

Materials Required: Sound-slide film "Getting It Done"; *How To Get Out More Work* checklist; supervisor's responsibilities checklist; summary of Film B, "Getting It Done."

Objective: To establish the importance of knowing who your bosses are, what your responsibilities are, and what the extent of your authority is in each area.

Introductory Remarks: Today we are going to get at the mechanics of the job of supervision. Following the showing of "Getting It Done," we shall again have a discussion of the main points brought up in the film. (Show film.)

Discussion Guide: They certainly packed a lot of sound information into "Getting It Done" on the mechanics of the job of supervision. All of us could have saved ourselves many a headache when each of us became a supervisor if we had been well informed to start with regarding our authority and responsibilities. Let's make sure that (Dave) here gets a good start right now in how to go about getting this information. I believe the following charts may be of assistance in laying the groundwork for our discussion. (At this time draw a simple organization chart on the board to show the new supervisor his position in the line of authority and responsibility in the local organization. Follow this with a more complete chart showing him in his relationship with the other supervisors. When this has been done, continue.)

1. The film stressed the following three points as important in getting things done:

   (a) Know to whom you are responsible
   (b) Know your job and its responsibilities
   (c) Know exactly how much authority you have to carry out each of responsibilities

   To stress further the importance of these points, would some of you fellows care to relate experiences that could have been avoided when you took over as a supervisor if you had been well informed. (After a few experiences have been mentioned, continue.) Our discussion has certainly emphasized the importance of being well informed about our job. Let's make this job of getting this information as simple as possible for (Dave). It looks to me as if this supervisory responsibilities checklist in the appendix, developed out of the conference meetings that were held throughout the company, should help. Let's run over the list and discuss the best way to go about getting the information necessary to do a good job of supervision. (After discussing the list, continue.) The suggestions you fellows have made should simplify (Dave's) job. It seems to me it might be well if we all gave thought to the value of getting down into black and white our own responsibilities and authority. It certainly would give us a clearer picture of our own job.

2. One of our biggest responsibilities as a supervisor is how to get out more work. This can only be done through the proper use of men, machines, and materials. We have been furnished a rather good checklist covering these items in the booklet *How To Get Out More Work*. It would be well worth our while to run through the checklists at this time to see how we are doing and in what areas we could stand some improvement. (After running through the list, continue.) Our discussion has certainly pointed out the importance of having a checklist on the fuller use of men,

machines, and materials. It might be well if (Dave) ran over the check-list next week with his immediate supervisor to ensure he is covering all the points mentioned.

3. Summary: I believe (Dave) will agree that this session has helped him to have a clearer understanding of the mechanics of his job:

    (a) What his job is

    (b) What is expected of him

    (c) How to go about handling his responsibilities

At our next session we shall discuss the key points of "The Human Factor," Part III of the new supervisor induction film. Here (Dave) should be able to get some help on the most important phase of his job —that of handling people. Thanks, fellows. That will be all for today. (Hand out summary of Film B, "Getting It Done.")

Guide for Showing Film C

Setting: Same as for Film A.

Subject: "The Human Factor," Part III of the new supervisor induction film.

Materials Required: Sound-slide film "The Human Factor"; Books *A Short Course In Human Relations* and *The Challenge of Human Relations;* "Supervisor's Personal Evaluation Form"; JIT Outlines; summary of Film C, "The Human Factor."

Objective: To emphasize the importance of leadership and human relations.

Introductory Remarks: Well, fellows, this is our third and last film. In our first meeting we worked up the more important basic attitudes or points of view that a new supervisor needs to develop, and in the second we got at the mechanics of the job. Today, following the showing of "The Human Factor," we are going to discuss human relations, which possibly may be the most important factor of all in maintaining a smooth running department. (Show film. Upon its completion, continue.)

Discussion Guide: One of the points mentioned in the film was the need for a supervisor to gain the confidence and respect of the employees. Frankly, this cannot be done overnight, and it takes a lot of right thinking on the part of a supervisor.

1. What are some of the things that employees expect in their supervisor?

(The list developed on the board should contain among others the following.)

(a) Impartial decision

(b) Credit and praise men when due

(c) Constructive criticism when due

(d) Keep your promises

(e) Look out for the employee's interest

We have developed quite an interesting list. Would some of you fellows care to make other suggestions from your personal experience on what can be done to build good morale in a department. (After a brief discussion, continue.)

2. A second important point mentioned in "The Human Factor" was the need for knowing how to train. This certainly is an important part of the job of being a supervisor. It seems to me that this is a good time to discuss job instruction training, what it is, and how to go about using it. Would one of you fellows care to explain the background and development of job instruction training? (At this time its development and success in World War II would be covered.) We have covered the background and development of JIT. Now let's discuss its use and application. (At this time run through the sheets headed "How To Get Ready To Instruct" and "How To Instruct" in the appendices and then continue.)

3. The next point, what it takes to keep moving up the ladder, is something that holds interest for all of us. In addition *to doing a good job now,* what other factors are important in moving up the ladder? (Such things as evening school, participation in community affairs, etc., should be mentioned.) We shall wind up this session with a brief discussion of the "Supervisor's Personal Evaluation Form," to be found in the appendices. This form gives each of us the chance to rate ourselves, for our own information, in the qualities one expects in a supervisor. We all have certain shortcomings and the acknowledgment of such to ourselves is the first step in overcoming them. We shall discuss each quality first and then rate ourselves and move on to the next one. (On completing the list, continue.) I have found it quite worthwhile to check up on myself once or twice a year to see how I am doing. It is one way to ensure continued growth and development within ourselves and to improve in stature as a supervisor.

4. Summary: Well, fellows, that is it. In our three sessions we have covered quite a bit of material in the job of being a supervisor. It is quite a job and one that takes a lot of working at. However, I do feel that (Dave's) development as a supervisor has been expedited by the material we have covered. He will run into many problems during the coming weeks. Most of these he will find he can solve by thinking them through. Others he

should feel free to discuss with his immediate supervisor. In some cases he may wish to benefit by a joint opinion of a conference group. The big thing I would like to get across is that all of management is behind him in his new job as a supervisor. In closing, I want to thank you fellows for your participation in (Dave's) training. However, I do feel that we all have benefited from the discussions that have taken place on effective supervision. (Hand out *A Short Course in Human Relations; The Challenge of Human Relations;* and summary of Film C, "The Human Factor.")

APPENDIX A: SUPERVISOR'S RESPONSIBILITIES CHECKLIST

The maintenance of a checklist of our responsibilities will ensure that we have a clear understanding of our job as a supervisor. The following are some suggested items we should consider. Others may be added to ensure coverage of all phases of our work.

Responsibilities	Exactly What Are My Responsibilities in Each Case	Exactly What Is My Authority	Reports Necessary and When Due
Men			
Hiring			
Transfers			
Promotion			
Comfort			
Safety			
Labor relations			
Working conditions			
Requests and suggestions			
Materials			
Handling			
Storage			
Waste control			
Quality control			
Ordering			
Accessibility			
Machines and Equipment			
Care			
Upkeep			
Replacements			
Costs			
Accident prevention			

207

APPENDIX B: SUPERVISOR'S PERSONAL EVALUATION FORM

E — excellent
S — satisfactory
W — need to work on this

_____1. Leadership
_____2. Ability to think effectively
_____3. Desire to learn
_____4. Ability to concentrate
_____5. Sincerity
_____6. Judgment
_____7. Decisiveness or firmness
_____8. Thoroughness and perseverance
_____9. Initiative
_____10. Alertness
_____11. Accuracy
_____12. Job knowledge
_____13. Cooperation and the ability to develop it in others
_____14. Patience
_____15. Ability to inspire confidence
_____16. Ability to inspire respect
_____17. Salesmanship
_____18. Orderliness

_____19. Desire to set a good example
_____20. Fairness
_____21. Consideration of others
_____22. Good personality
_____23. Friendliness
_____24. Unselfishness
_____25. Desire and willingness to accept responsibility
_____26. Planning ability
_____27. Ability to teach
_____28. Emotional stability
_____29. Energy
_____30. Enthusiasm
_____31. Dependability
_____32. Interest in people
_____33. Self-confidence
_____34. Consistency
_____35. Loyalty to those above and below him
_____36. Foresight
_____37. Imagination

APPENDIX C: HOW TO GET READY TO INSTRUCT

1. Have a time table: How much skill you expect him to have and how soon.
2. Break down the job: List principal steps and pick out the key points.
3. Have everything ready: The right equipment, materials, and supplies.
4. Have the work place properly arranged: Just as the worker will be expected to keep it.

APPENDIX D: HOW TO INSTRUCT

Step I: *Prepare the worker*
         (a) Put him at ease.
         (b) Find out what he already knows about the job.

1 Source: Job Instruction Training, Training Within Industry, Bureau of Training, War Manpower Commission.

          (c) Get him interested in learning the job.

          (d) Place in correct position.

Step II: *Present the operation*

          (a) Tell, show, illustrate, and question carefully and patiently.

          (b) Stress key points.

          (c) Instruct clearly and completely, taking up one point at a time—but no more than he can master.

Step III: *Try out performance*

          (a) Test him by having him perform the job.

          (b) Have him tell and show you; have him explain key points.

          (c) Ask questions and correct errors.

          (d) Continue until you know he knows.

Step IV: *Follow up*

          (a) Put him on his own.

          (b) Designate to whom he goes for help.

          (c) Check frequently.

          (d) Encourage questions.

          (e) Get him to look for key points as he progresses.

          (f) Taper off extra coaching and close follow-up.

If the worker has not learned, the instructor has not taught

APPENDIX E: A LIST OF ADDITIONAL SELECTED REFERENCES FOR PERSONNEL MANAGERS AND OPERATING SUPERVISORS AND DEPARTMENT HEADS

(Normally available through city, business, or college libraries)

Broaded, Charley H., *Essentials of Management for Supervisors.* Harper & Row, New York, 1947. 239 pp. $3.00. Presents basic fundamentals of management organization and operation, including employee relations, as a basis for sound supervision.

Charm, Sumner D., *Wage Policy for Management.* Funk & Wagnalls, New York, in association with Modern Industry Magazine, 1949. 213 pp. A description of the various techniques to help solve wage determination problems both from the standpoint of how to do them and how to get them accepted.

Flesch, Rudolph, *The Art of Plain Talk.* Harper & Row, New York, 1946. $2.50. As the name implies, this is a book on plain talk. It tells you how to speak and write so that people understand what you mean.

Gardiner, Burleigh B., *Human Relations in Industry.* Irwin, Chicago, 1945. 307 pp. $4.50. An interesting analysis emphasizing the social relationships in industry.

Gardiner, Glenn, *When Foreman and Steward Bargain.* McGraw-Hill, New York, 1945. 188 pp. $2.50. A guide for foremen in developing and maintaining successful relations between foreman and union stewards.

Gomberg, William, *A Labor Union Manual on Job Evaluation.* Labor Education Division, Roosevelt College, Chicago, 1947. 80 pp. $1.00. A practical handbook for both union and management people, explaining evaluation principles, procedures, and some of the major problems that arise under the operation of evaluation plans.

Halsey, George D., *Handbook of Personnel Management*. Harper & Row, New York, 1947. 402 pp. $5.00. A guide of practical and tested methods of personnel management for not only personnel managers but also operating section, department, and plant managers.

Lawshe, C. H., Jr., *Principles of Personnel Testing*. McGraw-Hill, New York, 1948. 227 pp. $3.50. A practical treatment of the accepted procedure for selecting, validating, and using personnel tests in business and industrial situations.

Pigors, Paul, and Charles A. Meyers, *Personnel Administration*. McGraw-Hill, New York, 1947. 539 pp. $4.50. A general personnel text emphasizing the staff nature of personnel work, including many case illustrations.

Planty, E., W. McCord, and C. Efferson, *Training Employees and Managers*. Ronald, New York, 1948. $5.00. A comprehensive guide for all persons responsible for planning, administering, or conducting training—supervisors, personnel managers, and training directors.

Content of Film A, "Off To A Flying Start"

Key Points or Training Items Set Forth in the Film	Place for Instructor's Notes on Local Application (some suggestions are shown)
1. When a person is selected and appointed to his first managing job, it is an important step—important to him, to the company, and to the people he will supervise. It's a (a) New level. (b) New viewpoint. (c) Chance for new opportunities.	Localize. Point out what the local management team is accountable for and how his function fits into the pattern.
2. The days before taking over the new position, the day he takes over, and the first days following are critical times for the new supervisor.	
3. But—he can take it with confidence because (a) Of the methods used to select him. (b) Other supervisors understand and are anxious to help him get started. (c) He will be given helpful training in the techniques of being a good supervisor.	Review strong points and any weaknesses. Explain briefly.
4. From the training he should understand particularly the *changes* that confront him	

Key Points or Training Items Set Forth in the Film	Place for Instructor's Notes on Local Application (some suggestions are shown)
(a) From doing a job to seeing that a job gets done, (b) From *his* tools, *his* production, *his* safety, etc., to the production, comfort, and safety of a group of people. No longer a job he can do with his own hands, but one of helping and seeing to it that other people do their jobs well.	Review monthly payroll of his group, value of equipment under him, etc.
5. He must learn (if he does not already know) and clearly understand the mental attitude and viewpoint of a *manager*. (a) A proprietary interest (the point of view of an owner,) (b) Change from my *job* to my *company*, (c) Represent *the company to his employees—to them he now is the company*, because men's ideas about the company, the management, and its policies are largely a result of their contact with their supervisor—he is the channel through which information will flow both ways.	Local examples.
6. All this creates two big responsibilities: (a) To learn, understand, and interpret company policy in the spirit intended. (b) To make sure that his men know and understand the *why* of company policy as well as the *what*. But	Review policies he is concerned with. Issue company policies pamphlet.
7. *Policies* are not a set of rules. They are guide posts or direction signs.	Issue *Management Guide Book of Personnel Policies and Procedures* on loan for study.
8. If a supervisor disagrees with or does not understand a policy, practice,	

Key Points or Training Items Set Forth in the Film	Place for Instructor's Notes on Local Application (some suggestions are shown)

custom, or procedure, he should take it up with his superior at once.

9. To get real pleasure and satisfaction out of his new position, the new supervisor must recognize and adopt these attitudes, viewpoints, and concepts of the job of managing.

10. The next film and instructions will deal with the mechanics—the routine detail—of his new job.

Content of Film B, "Getting It Done"

Key Points or Training Items Set Forth in the Film	Place for Instructor's Notes on Local Application (some suggestions are shown)

If a new supervisor makes the mental changes suggested in the first film, is that all he has to learn?

1. No. He must find out *exactly who is his boss.*
   (a) Know the other people in management to whom he is responsible.
   (b) Know who they are and which has first call.

2. He must find out *exactly what his job is* (not the technical side—presumed to know that).
   (a) What his responsibilities and authorities are as to

   Men

Hiring	Safety
Transfers	Working conditions
Promotions	ditions
Complaints	Requests
Comfort	Suggestions
	Discipline

   Materials

Handling	Waste control
Supplies	Quality control
Storage	trol
	Ordering

How far he can go, for example. (Use form in the department head's guide and develop local responsibilities and authorities.)

Out More Work.
Issue and use as reference *How To Get*

Key Points or Training Items Set Forth in the Film	Place for Instructor's Notes on Local Application (some suggestions are shown)

Machines
Care   Costs
Upkeep   Accident pre-
Purchase   vention
Replace-   Maintenance
ment

3. Just knowing his responsibilities is not enough. The new supervisor must also know *exactly* what and *how much* **authority** he has to carry out each of the responsibilities.

         This is the most important part of the training to be given after this film.

4. He must also know what kind of *reports* he has to keep on each of the items under "responsibilities."

5. Three important jobs of a supervisor are
   (a) Organize.
   (b) Deputize.
   (c) Supervise.

6. Under "organize"
   Not much except improvement when taking over an old function,
            but
   one thing he must arrive at for sure is a *fair day's work.*

         In plants this is a leadin to instructions on performance reports.

7. Under "deputize" (or delegate)
   Tendency to keep on doing too much of what he did before—too little of his new responsibility of supervising. *Guide: Always give someone else the responsibility and authority to do something that you do not have time to do or ability to do efficiently.*

8. Under "supervise"
   This is the follow-through that ensures that the work that has been delegated to others has been done right. He should always know what progress his employees are making.

9. A good guide
   (a) *Get it done* means find out exactly who he is responsible to

Key Points or Training Items Set Forth in the Film	Place for Instructor's Notes on Local Application (some suggestions are shown)
and exactly what his responsibilities are. (b) Under *get it done right*, find out exactly *what* and *how much* authority he has under each responsibility. 10. And have some fun while getting it done.	

Content of Film C, "the Human Factor"

Key Points or Training Items Set Forth in the Film	Place for Instructor's Notes on Local Application (some suggestions are shown)
1. "The Human Factor" is most important because	
(a) A supervisor works primarily with people.	Review details of his work force.
(b) He is a success or failure based on his ability to get results through people—his ability to lead them and develop them.	Issue pamphlets *The Challenge of Human Relations* and *A Short Course In Human Relations*
2. Titles must be earned by developing the respect and confidence of the employees.	
3. Respect and confidence can be earned by (a) Not making snap decisions. (b) Not lightly reversing decisions. (c) And by items 4, 5, 6, and 7 that follow.	
4. The JIT formula is a good pattern for handling problems and making decisions. The four steps are (a) Get the facts: everything bearing on the problem. (b) Weigh the facts and decide: fit facts together and consider bearing on all involved. (c) Take action: watch timing and setting	

Key Points or Training Items Set Forth in the Film	Place for Instructor's Notes on Local Application (some suggestions are shown)
(d) Check results: did your action help production and relationships?	
5. Have a reputation for being fair and impartial. For example in (a) Assignment of special tasks. (b) Vacations. (c) Time off. (d) Allotment of overtime, etc. The supervisor must operate on the basis of *what's right*, not *who's right*.	Localize
6. Some pointers on *how to be accepted as a leader*. If you (a) Let them know how they are getting along, (b) Give praise or credit when due, (c) Keep your promises, (d) Always look out for the interests of every person in the group, then your men will look to you as their natural leader.	
7. How training fits in the requirements of good supervision (a) Few people know instinctively how to train. (b) A supervisor should learn how to do it the right way. The one best method for training another person how to do something is the standard JIT formula. The four steps are (see department head's guide for complete outline) (a) Prepare the worker to learn. (b) Present the operation. (c) Try out his performance. (d) Follow up.	Review his training responsibilities
8. When a supervisor runs into a problem not previously covered (a) Check in the policy manual. (b) Consult with his superiors. (c) Bring it up in a management conference.	
9. Managing is the orderly integration of the resources of *men, materials,*	

Key Points or Training Items Set Forth in the Film	Place for Instructor's Notes on Local Application (some suggestions are shown)
and *machines* into a profitable quality product—whether it be merchandise, a sale, or a necessary report.	
10. Every management job in the company has that same pattern. The only difference between management jobs is the size and scope—upper levels have more men, more materials, and more machines under them.	

CASE DISCUSSION QUESTIONS

The Gopher Mills Case

1. Design an evaluation study for the plan.

2. Based on the material in the manual alone, what strengths and weaknesses do you see? What other evaluative steps would be needed, if any, to determine the worth of the general manager's recommendation?

PART III ‖ **Applied Learning Theory**

Nothing is more practical than a sound theory. The atomic explosion at Hiroshima, a communication satellite, and the public opinion poll at election time are all evidence that theory is not without its consequences. In training, we rely on learning theory, and it has an impact in the kinds of training we conduct and the antecedent effects on the way people work. In this part we shall look at the major kinds of learning theory as it has developed over the years and at some of the practical effects of this learning theory in practice as we train managers, professionals, and supervisors.

11 Learning Theories— Hard and Soft Criteria

We do not, of course, know what goes on
in other people's heads.
　　　　　—James Harvey Robinson

A MANAGER of training who wants to keep
abreast of the latest development in learning theory has a difficult task. More than
the time involved, he is faced with making sense of
the divisions that exist among different kinds of
theories. The behavioral sciences are divided into
numerous camps, and the various defenders of each are not always too
helpful when it comes to advising outsiders about what the other camp
is doing at the moment. If you read the works of B. F. Skinner, for
example, he is most unlikely to have taken the time and trouble to foot-
note and thus concede the existence of alternative viewpoints such as
Likert, McGregor, Argyris, Maslow, or Herzberg. Likewise, in the works
of the last writers you would never get a glimmer of suspicion that there
are others such as Watson, Hull, Yerkes, Spence, or Pavlov who held
strongly inconsistent explanations as the causal truth about human behavior.

The question is not, of course, "Which theory is true, or even truest?"
The most important question for the man of policy and practice is
which theory will get us farthest fastest at the present stage? The two
schools of learning theory used here are this author's own classification,
suiting the purposes of this book for training managers. The classifica-
tions of learning theory into *hard criteria* and *soft criteria* will become

clear as we go along. They relate to two alternative ways of explaining behavior. The hard criteria people adhere to specific measurable stimuli and responses for the most part. The soft criteria school adheres to more internalized, subjective explanations of behavior. What difference does it make whether you think that behavior can best be explained by forces internal to the behaver or by forces external to him? It makes a difference because it will shape the pattern of the training program and training method you use. This difference can be illustrated by two examples.

The first, an example of hard criteria explanation of behavior, is shown by the unforeseen effect of the trimester plan of class scheduling at the University of Michigan on student unrest there. Several years ago that university adopted an annual calendar that provided for the starting of classes right after labor day for the fall semester. Fall classes end in December. Second semester classes end in early April. Thus, when warm weather first begins to emerge, and most student militancy and rebellion just begins to appear elsewhere such as occurred at Columbia in 1968, students at Michigan are just entering final exams. By the time the weather has really warmed up and student activity bursts forth in full bloom (the Fort Lauderdale principle of student activity as one wag has labeled it) Michigan students have graduated and gone. The result: Little student unrest appeared during the late spring in Ann Arbor. It would be attributing too much sagacity to the faculty and administration of Michigan to declare that they planned it for this effect, but the result in student behavior is the same as if they had so planned it. The system is arranged and the desired behavior follows from the system.

On the other hand it would be easy to see that internal influences inside the student could be used as persuasive evidence that soft criteria, or internally generated causes of behavior, are vital to the learning process. It illustrates what soft criteria might look like.

In a large university executive development course during the very first morning, one class member showed apparent hostility. His demeanor as he sat in the class was obviously negative. He sat turned half-around, his chin in his hand. The course director was describing what the course consisted of and what the group might expect to learn. The recalcitrant member snorted: "I didn't want to come to this course. I was ordered to come. Furthermore, you talk about all you are going to *teach* us. I'll tell you something, you can't teach me *anything*." The instructor never paused: "Of course not. But you can *learn* something, if you like."

Whether this learner learns is under his own control, not only for the reluctant student but for everyone in that group. Those who "wanted to" learn did so.

What Do We Know About Learning?

Modern psychology is much concerned with learning; some say that it comprises most of the field of modern psychology. Yet there are many theories, some of which are conflicting, about how we learn. It becomes fairly important for the training director to understand to what theory he is adhering. Although it is the learner who must learn, the trainer must manage the arrangement of the environment so that learning can take place—or even arrange it so that learning is highly likely. If he has an armory of theory he may be able to develop different learning climates to achieve different training objectives. He will know when to change. He will select a pedagogical device that fits the situation and will have more such devices at his disposal if he has mastered the major elements of learning theory.

We suggested earlier in this book that in training the learning theory is a servant of the economies of training. In turn we may propose that training *techniques* are children, legitimate or otherwise, of some theory. In this chapter we shall use seven-league boots to race across the major hard criteria kinds of learning theory. In Chapter 12 we shall look at soft criteria theories of learning.

Cognitive and Interactionist Theories of Learning

The study of learning dates from the earliest times. Primitive man, the early Romans, and the Greeks were concerned with the behavior of inanimate objects and of other people.[1] Thomas Aquinas showed concern with knowledge and its nature in 1250 A.D. John Locke's *Essay on Human Understanding* in 1690 developed a theory of the mind and how it acquired its content.

Modern learning theory begins at the turn of the twentieth century when psychology took on the manner and purposes of a science. Figure 11–1 summarizes a large number of the more prevalent learning theories in terms of a common model or set of ingredients.

It is interesting to note that not only is there some disagreement between psychologists about which theory fits into a major category, there

[1] R. Bellows, T. Q. Gilson, and G. S. Odiorne, *Executive Skills* (Englewood Cliffs, N.J.: Prentice-Hall, 1962).

1. General:	(1) What Happened Just Before	(2) State of Subject	(3) Response of Subject	(4) What Happened Just After
			(Behavior)	
2. Technical Symbols	S (Antecedent Stimuli)	O (State of Organism)	R (Response or Behavior)	S (Consequent Stimuli)
3. Communication Theorist	Input	Channel	Output	Feedback

FIGURE 11–1   Various Ways of Classifying Behavior Theorists

is even some minor quibbling about just what a theory might be. Let us use it here as being *a systematic interpretation of an area of knowledge*. In learning theory we could classify theories of learning into two major categories:

1. Connectionist theories of learning.
2. Cognitive and interactionist theory of learning.

It would be possible to subdivide these into many others, illustrated in Fig. 11–1. The first section of the figures shows the general constructions of learning theories or the elements that appear to be common to all of them.

The general construction of a learning theory as shown in line 1 in Fig. 11–1 shows that four major ingredients seem to be present in most learning theories. This can be pictured schematically as in Fig. 11–2. In the second position in the diagram (column 2 in Fig. 11–1) is man himself, or if not man some other organisms such as a pigeon, rat, primate, or other subject. He has certain basic physiological characteristics inside that impel him to make outward moves, and he also has certain acquired or secondary influences inside him called *motives*. These might also include perceptions, attitudes, values, and the like. In his existential state he is subjected to outside stimuli, shown as column 1. These stimuli bring about behavior by the organism, which is what can be

(1)	(2)	(3)	(4)
What Happened Just Before	The Organism	Behavior	What Happened Just After

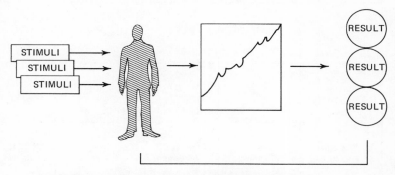

FIGURE 11–2 The Ingredients in Major Learning Theories

seen, measured, counted, recorded, or otherwise scientifically measured. Finally, in column 4 are the effects of that behavior on the organism, or its consequences to the organism. For the most part, these four ingredients comprise the arena for the differences that have been proposed for learning theories.

One of the first group of theorists are those called connectionists (see Fig. 11–3). The common ingredient among the connectionist theorists, who differ widely among themselves, is the fact that they "connect" columns 1 and 3. As Hill put it:

Connectionist interpretations of learning however much they may differ among themselves, agree in treating learning as a matter of connections between stimuli and responses.[2]

No particular definition is needed for stimulus and response beyond noting that a stimulus is any sensation. The connectionist assumes that all behavior or responses are elicited by stimuli. A response then is any item of behavior. The names shown in Fig. 11–3 are some of the more famous theorists.

IVAN P. PAVLOV (1849–1936)

Pavlov was a famous Russian physiologist whose experiments using dogs as experimental organisms discovered what has been identified as

[2] Winifred Hill, *Learning: A Survey of Psychological Interpretations* (San Francisco: Chandler, 1963), p. 28.

Name	(1)	(2)	(3)	(4)
1. Pavlov: (1849–1936)	CS (Conditioned Stimulus)	O (Organism)	CR (Conditioned Response)	US (Unconditioned Stimulus)
2. Watson (1878–1958)	CS	O	CR	US
		(Laws of Frequency and Recency)		
3. Guthrie (1886–1959)	CS	O	CR	
		(Explained by Law of Recency)		
4. Thorndike (1874-1949)	S (Stimulus)	O (Organism)	R (Response)	S (Satisfier)
		(Explained by "Law of Effect")		
5. Skinner (1904–)	S_D (Discriminative Stimulus)	O (Organism)	R (Response)	S_R (Reinforcing Stimulus)
		("Operant Conditioning")		

FIGURE 11–3   The Connectionists

the "conditioned response" theory of learning. His experiments consisted of inducing a response of salivation in dogs through ringing a bell.
Because this is not ordinary behavior for organisms, his method of
teaching this to his animal subjects is known as a conditioned response
method, or conditioning. He started with a dog that would salivate
when presented meat. By ringing a bell simultaneously as he presented
the meat and then, after some repetition, by ringing the bell without
presenting the meat, he induced salivation simply from the sound of
the bell. The salivation was conditioned.

The impact of this experiment had a widespread effect not only on
the popular mind and the glossary of everyday language but in spurring
others to conduct similar kinds of research into learning and its causes.
The bell becomes the conditioned stimulus, the dog the organism, and
the salivation the conditioned response. The details of this research are
too lengthy to go into here, except to note it as a pioneering experimental work of the connectionist school.[3]

[3] Two English translations of Pavlov's data and theory are contained in his *Conditioned Reflexes: An Investigation of the Physiological Activity of the Cerebral Cor-
tex* (London: Oxford University Press, 1927), and in his *Lectures on Conditioned
Reflexes* (New York: International Publishers, 1928).

John B. Watson (1878–1958)

One of the heirs of Pavlov was an American. He graduated from the University of Chicago in 1900 at the age of 22, his dissertation involving experimentation with rats. From the beginning of his studies he saw serious reservations to the mainstream of psychology, which up to that time had been dominated by the Germans. Their concern was with thought and feelings as it affected behavior. Watson's interest focused on what people do, and he studied them using the scientific methods used in studying the behavior of subhuman subjects. His attacks on the tendency to study consciousness, feelings, attitudes, and the like comprised a radical new movement in psychology. In 1913, then a professor at Johns Hopkins, he published his first article, in which he identified himself as a "behaviorist" and his approach to learning theory became known as behaviorism. He strongly opposed letting study of motivation and internal value systems into the field of psychology. Speech became verbal behavior. Thought became subvocalization. Love was a chemical reaction and rumblings of the smooth muscles inside the body. He denied that instincts exist except in wrongheaded theory.

All learning, he proposed, was classical conditioning; man is equipped with certain connections between stimulus and response called reflexes. We build new ones by conditioning. Complex habits are but a series of new reflexes that we acquire through conditioning. Two principles emerge as important in this learning process:

1. *Frequency.* The more frequently we have made a given response to a given stimulus, the more likely we are to make that response to that stimuli again.
2. *Recency.* A principle of learning that states that the more recently we have given a particular response for a given stimuli, the more likely we are to give it again.

Watson did not limit his theory to simple reflex action but expressed confidence that even the more complex behavior could be explained in terms of simple principles of learning. It was in this area of more complex behavior, however, that he found it necessary to fall back somewhat on heredity as a possible explanation. Emotions, such as rage, fear, and love, are patterns of movement that are accompanied by internal physiological changes. Knowledge, such as is taught in the college classroom, is merely an ability to write certain words, such as "the margin is the increment from the last added input" in a blue book, or to verbalize certain words and phrases that one could not verbalize prior to attending class. To a student who would say "I know it but can't tell you," Watson would curtly respond, "Then you don't know it."

Whatever his limitations, his contribution to learning theory was immense, for he influenced a generation of students and subsequent experimenters to reject less hard criteria and to study what man does rather than be too casual in philosophical generalizations.[4]

Edwin R. Guthrie (1886–1959)

Somewhat more of a philosopher than an experimental psychologist, but respected as both, Guthrie developed a learning theory that has often been called a stimulus-response contiguity theory. Briefly it states that a combination of stimuli that has accompanied movement will on the recurrence of the same stimuli produce the same response. Thus if you do something in a particular situation and it works, you will probably do the same thing again in the same situation.

This single theory, which looks so simple in first blush but extremely complex on closer inspection, was the major building block of Guthrie's theory of learning. He uses Watson's law of recency but not the law of frequency. This emphasis on the importance of the last response includes the problem of repetition, Guthrie stated. Learning, he says, is not a matter of the strength of the bond established between stimulus and response but a matter of eliminating the wrong conditioned response. Whereas Pavlov and Watson declared that practice and repetition is necessary, Guthrie did not—a single trial of stimulation is enough. If you want to know what an individual will learn, look at what he does. Guthrie was indifferent to motivations, attitudes, and the internal condition of the learner.

Guthrie is likewise noted for the application of his simple theoretical building block to learning situations. For example, his three methods for breaking a bad habit. The first was the *threshold method*, or presenting the stimuli so faintly that the undesirable response will not occur. He used the example of the army horse who is trained not to buck when ridden by starting with a blanket thrown over his back. When used to this, the steed is presented a light saddle. When used to this, he is mounted by a rider. By raising the threshold you will be able to ride him without bucking, whereas a saddle and rider at one fell swoop would have produced wild bucking. The second method of changing a habit is *fatigue*. Here in the presence of a bad habit the learner is presented the stimulus again and again until he gets tired of the response and just quits from weariness. His example here was a little girl who disobeyed her mother and lighted matches. Her mother forced her to

---

[4] Watson's initial article was "Psychology as the Behavioralist Views It," *Psychological Review*, 20 (1913), 158–177. A more complete exposition of his position is found in his *Behaviorism* (Chicago: Univ. Chicago Press, 1930).

light, one after another, a whole box of matches without rest. Long after she would have liked to quit, her mother forced her to continue lighting matches. The next time she had a chance to light matches, she avoided it. The third method consists of *incompatible stimuli*. A woman college student was used as an illustration by Guthrie. She found that noise distracted her from studying. By switching to a fascinating mystery novel she read steadily despite the noise level. Then, when she switched to her study text again, she found that the noise did not distract her. Habits, he suggested, are not extinguished; they are replaced by something else.[5]

Guthrie has much to offer the industrial trainer, for it suggests that learning is less a matter of inner intentions, but his law of learning sounds very practical. Put a man in a situation where he responds to the environmental cues and when he is put in that environment again he will behave that way again. This is the principle behind the flight simulator, the management game, the case study, and the role play. Read his principle again and see how it fits: "If you do something in a given situation, the next time you are in that situation you will tend to do the same thing again."

The aspect of modern simulation theory that Guthrie avoided was that of reinforcement or feedback. He simply did not deal with it. Yet simulation as a learning method owes much to Guthrie.

EDWARD L. THORNDIKE (1874–1949)

The fourth of the major connectionist theorists is Edward L. Thorndike, whose major advance over the others was the idea of reinforcement. Like philosopher Jeremy Bentham, whose "pleasure pain calculus" had been central to an economic explanation of man's behavior in the market, Thorndike adhered to the view that we do things that give us pleasure and avoid those that give us pain. His experimental subjects were cats, and his study of animal intelligence is a landmark in the literature of psychology and learning theory.

Learning, Thorndike proposed, is a stamping in of a stimulus response connection. Learning grows by repetition mainly through what he called the law of effect. Not merely exercise but a favorable stimulus that occurs at the time the response is being emitted is what produces the learning. If the response was followed by a *satisfier*, then the behavior that brought that response would occur again. If it were followed by an *annoyer*, it would not reappear. If this seems to involve Thorndike in

[5] Guthrie's major work is generally considered his *The Psychology of Learning*, Rev. Ed. (New York: Harper & Row, 1952). His theory was stated earlier in *Psychological Review*, **37** (1930), p. 216, as an article "Conditioning as a Principle of Learning."

the problems of inner states of the organism, he defines his way out of this problem. He suggests that a satisfier is to be defined as anything that follows that increases the likelihood of the behavior being repeated. An annoyer is anything that the organism is not likely to preserve. Most learning is by trial and error, in which it repeats its successes. Rewarding successful or proper responses has become an important part of the industrial training process. This is how the law of effect works in practice, wherever learning is desired. Wait until you see desired behavior; this makes the effects on the organism satisfying. Little need is seen by Thorndike for dealing with such matters as inner feeling, motivations, or attitudes of the learner. The major problem is arranging the environment so that the law of effect can be applied.[6]

B. F. Skinner (1904–   )

Perhaps the best known of the connectionist theorists of the reinforcement school is a contemporary figure, B. F. Skinner. His most notable accomplishments from the trainer's viewpoint are his development and popularization of the teaching machine and his experiments with pigeons and the dramatic shaping of the behavior of rats. He is also known as the author of a novel, *Walden Two*, in which a behavioral scientist establishes a model community based on the social application of behavioral sciences in a model utopian community. Presently at Harvard, his pupils comprise a formidable force in modern learning and teaching theory and in the application of reinforcement to such things as language laboratories, simulators, and numerous other applications.

Skinner suggests that there are two kinds of learning, distinguishable by the different kinds of behavior involved. The first of these is *respondent behavior,* such as the knee jerk reflex. Hit a person's patellar tendon with a mallet and his knee will kick upward. *Operant behavior* is that that is emitted by the organization without particular regard to any particular stimulus but that becomes reinforced by a reward. Thus if an operant (a response) occurs and then is rewarded, it will appear again. This pattern of operant learning comprises the most important part of learning for Skinner. He does not really disagree with Guthrie or Watson; he is simply interested in a different aspect of connectionism.

The reinforcers that cause operants to be learned can either be rewards (positive reinforcement) or punishment (negative reinforcers). Negative reinforcers, however, have their greatest effect when they are

---

6 Thorndike's major works consisted of his initial monograph "*Animal Intelligence,*" *Psychological Review Monograph Supplement,* 2:No. 4 (1898). His two-volume study of *Educational Psychology* was published by Teachers College, New York, Volume I, 1913, and Volume II, 1914. The latter is devoted to the psychology of learning. His text *Human Learning* was published by Century, New York, 1931.

discontinued. You teach by presenting a positive reinforcer or by removing a negative one when a particular kind of behavior (operant) is forthcoming.

One of the important aspects of learning and teaching for Skinner is the schedule of reinforcement. There are, for example, continuous reinforcements and intermittent reinforcements. These have found their application in Skinner's shaping of animal behavior through successive approximation until he has rats and pigeons performing complex behaviors not ordinarily performed by such animals. It has also produced programmed instruction, which is a method of organizing material to be taught and a method of presenting it so that learning occurs. Although others, notably Pressey, had experimented with teaching machines, it is Skinner's work that has brought it to the fore. Although it has made great strides in classroom teaching mainly through the language laboratory, industry has quickly adapted this technique of programmed texts and other programmed devices to industrial training, including some sophisticated methods of computer-assisted instruction.

One of the further features of Skinner's works is his aggressive manner of delineating his approach from the rising trend toward cognitive and interactionist kinds of theories. Such theories lean heavily on motivational, attitudinal, and perceptual causes of behavior. Skinner defiantly chose to treat the organism, even man, as an empty organism, a black box whose behavior is explained by the stimuli and the reinforcements that pressed on him. Such studies, he proposes, are not science at all, but a kind of theorizing, using constructs and abstractions as if they were real phenomena. He refuses to even consider what goes on inside the organism in conceptual terms, which he considers not essential, unmeasurable, and therefore not scientific. It comprises excess baggage in the study of behavior and merely clutters up the analysis. By his rigid insistence on hard criteria in behavioral analysis, he states the limiting condition and perhaps an extreme position in learning theory.[7]

The five theorists and theories described comprise a fair sample of the leading connectionists. Some would include Miller among them. I have chosen to include him in the next group, the cognitive and interactionist theorists.

---

[7] Skinner's initial work, written when he was an assistant professor at Minnesota, is *The Behavior of Organisms* (New York: Appleton-Century-Crofts, 1938). *The Analysis of Behavior*, written with James Holland in 1961, is prepared in programmed text form (New York: McGraw-Hill, 1961). His novel *Walden Two* (New York: Macmillan, 1948) has received more scientific literary attention.

THE CAREER STARTER CASE

Carl Austin is a young assistant comptroller with the Amherst Insurance Company, a medium-sized stock life company writing ordinary life, accident and health, and group policies. He is a Phi Beta Kappa graduate of both the University of Pennsylvania and the Harvard School of Business Administration. At the latter institution he received a special university grant for an extra year of concentration in the insurance field, doing an extensive project on hiring and training practices in the business.

It was this experience that led Austin to this present position with the Amherst Company. He spent two impressive years as an office manager in charge of personnel, expense control, and accounting in the Dallas office before coming to the home office and a position that was created especially for him by company president John Nordberg and comptroller James Mc-Coy. The reasons for this appointment are not fully clear to Austin; he knows Nordberg has recently been brought in from another firm and that the Amherst Board of Directors are concerned about their firm's lagging position in the insurance world; he also has vague knowledge of sales and economy "pushes." Not long ago McCoy charged him with a business-wide survey (for the Amherst Company's private use) of turnover among salesmen and determining factors in their being hired and fired.

During this project, which required almost seven months for completion, Austin talked with everyone from rookie salesmen to presidents of large companies. Briefly summarized, the findings of his survey are as follows:

1. 86.2 per cent of all turnover among salesmen occurs during the first two calendar years of employment.
2. In the business as a whole 77.1 per cent of the new salesmen do not "make it" permanently.
3. This is a particularly significant figure in light of the fact that it costs about $1,500 to train a new salesman.
4. Most salesmen drop for reasons that may generally be considered personal. Financial difficulties are the most frequently mentioned. Only on infrequent occasions do dismissals influence turnover.
5. The most successful company programs for diminishing this turnover rate are those that offer some kind of initial bonus for new salesmen. Three companies that have instituted such programs successfully (with percentage turnover for first two years following) are

(a) Lomax Company, 48.1 per cent.
(b) Dill Company, 52.7 per cent.
(c) Sheed Company, 54.4 per cent.
6. The Amherst Company's comparative turnover figure is 68.9 per cent.

In view of these findings, Austin, working with McCoy and the reluctant help of Russell Bascomb, vice president in charge of the actuarial and underwriting departments, devised a three-year financial inducement plan to get new salesmen on their feet. The plan, called the Career Starter Benefit Plan (CSBP), gives new salesmen gradually decreasing monthly bonuses to compensate for the lack of renewal and deferred first-year life commissions during the first 36 months of the salesman's employment. A hypothetical projection of the salesman's commission during his first three years has been mapped out.

In form this plan is similar to that of the Lomax Company in Providence, but Austin, McCoy, and Bascomb have altered it to fit the Amherst Company's own needs. Austin feels quite confident about the plan, both as a means for cutting down turnover among the new salesmen and as a money-saving policy. Over a period of time the cost of the bonuses should be far less than the repeated cost of hiring and training new salesmen.

Now Austin is preparing for a meeting with the five top company officials: President Nordberg; McCoy; Bascomb; Wesley Tuthill, who is agency vice president in charge of sales; and treasurer Robert Gray. It will be Austin's job, as the one who carried out the survey, and also the prime architect of Career Starter Benefit Plan, to present the case. He knows this will not be a simple matter, for not only will he be urging a radical departure in general company policy, he will also be facing some personal attitudes that could easily impede his plan. Austin feels sharply about "his baby"—both for itself, for his position, which is somewhat (though vaguely) dependent on it, and for the general good of the company as a whole.

Austin's knowledge of the attitudes of Nordberg, Gray, and Tuthill is mostly sketchy, consisting of bits and scraps he has picked up by intuition, in casual conversation, and through the opinions of McCoy and Bascomb. The last two are publically on record as being behind Austin on the plan, and McCoy has taken to confiding in him somewhat excessively. He knows that both are somewhat disappointed with the static position of the Amherst Company and that both have been with the company for long periods of time and have seen business going better in a more active period.

As Austin sits in his office the morning before the meeting, he mentally goes over his "battle plan" for putting across the Career Starter Benefit Plan; he breaks his problems into three areas: (1) the merits of the plan itself (no problems here, he is convinced), (2) selling a new idea (a bit of a problem), and (3) the men he must sell to (a real stickler). Under the third area he mentally jots down the following thoughts on Nordberg, Bascomb, Gray, and Tuthill. He knows he can depend on McCoy all the way.

Nordberg. He was brought in to his current position three years ago by the company's Board of Directors to help re-establish the Amherst Company's position of prominence in the insurance industry. Although he appointed Austin to his position with McCoy and suggested the survey in the first place, he has been mildly skeptical of late. Apparently he had wanted something more on the order of a full scale "crash" program, something that would bring rapid, tangible results. He has stated, somewhat hesitantly, that he feels the Career Starter Benefit Program (concerning, as it does, the development of a steadier, more loyal sales staff) is peripheral to the essential problems facing the Amherst Company. He has not, however, come out definitely against Austin.

Gray. He is the youngest of the top company executives, having been promoted to his job only a year and a half ago. It is acknowledged that he got his position because he had been a very effective pusher in his years with the company and had always produced well. Now, however, he seems to have substituted a certain amount of complacent egotism for his drive. He has been remarkably indifferent to Austin and his plan; the several times Austin has broached the subject with him, Gray has managed to shift the topic quite quickly.

Bascomb. A college graduate who has worked in the investment end of the business for many years, Bascomb is a steady, hard-working man. He started out in the middle of the depression and several times has mentioned to Austin that he "made it alone" without any bonuses. He is not sure of the advisability of such a plan now either, though he has begrudgingly admitted that "times have changed." Sometimes his counsel was quite helpful to Austin; at other times he was skeptical, and he once dismissed the Career Starter Benefit Plan as not much more than a "free gift program to lure us lackadaisical salesmen."

Tuthill. He is not a college graduate and is very much a self-made man. He came in contact with the insurance business as an agent and has assiduously worked his way up since. He came with the Amherst Company about ten years ago, from another firm, and has never felt particularly sure about his position. This is true, despite the fact that Nordberg, during his three years with Amherst, has leaned heavily on Tuthill for advice. At present he may harbor a slight suspicion that Nordberg and McCoy have sent Austin snooping into his department. He may also feel that Austin is a threat to his position, which admittedly is not producing the optimum number of sales. Tuthill has never talked to Austin much at all.

CASE DISCUSSION QUESTIONS

The Career Starter Case

1. What is the behavioral objective in this case?

2. Would training help achieve them?

3. How would you evaluate the training system as it affects

   (a) Carl Austin?

   (b) Rookie salesmen?

4. What actions would you propose? Why?

12 | Learning Theory— The Soft Criteria School

The thinker makes a great mistake when he
asks after cause and effect.
—GOETHE

Cognitive and Interactionist
Theories of Learning

AMONG scholars of learning theory the classifica-
tions of learning theory are not always
agreed on. The ideas of the connectionists
seemed to cluster them together. They connect
stimulus and response. For our purposes we shall
take the "nonconnectionists" and treat them as
another group. They are shown in Fig. 12–1, which we certainly cannot
pretend is a complete list of all such learning theorists or even the major
ones. They are perhaps representative and provide a seven-league-boots
trip through the major burroughs of learning theory of this nonconnec-
tionist school.

In lumping the two groups of cognitivists and interactionists together,
we might explain that *cognitive* explanations are concerned with cognition, which are perceptions, attitudes, or beliefs. This is, of course, the
stuff that Skinner insists either does not exist or, if it does, is sufficiently
unimportant that it can be ignored. *Interactionist* theory does not view
the person as a whole organism who is related to a whole environment.
It is concerned with the configurations or response patterns we make to
the whole experience, or response patterns to the environment.

234

	(1)	(2)	(3)	(4)
1. Miller (1909–)	Cue	Drive of Organism	Response	Reward
		Explained as "Internal Stimuli"		
2. Hull (1884–1952)	Stimulus (Independent Variables)	Drive of Organism	Response	Reward
		Explained by "Intervening Variables")		
3. Gestalt Theorists (1900–)	Perceptual Field	Tension of Observer	Reorganization of Perceptual Field	Reduced Tension Reorganized Field
4. Tolman (1886–1959)	Sign Gestalt Expectations	Organism	Response	Goal Object
		(Cognitive Map Explanations)		
5. Lewin (1890–1947)	Life Space (Vectors)	Organism Tensions (Valences)	Response (Behavior)	Goals
		E (Explain B = f(p, e)		
6. Maslow (1905–)	Cultural Situation	Organism (Needs Hierarchy)	Response (Behavior)	Needs Satisfaction

FIGURE 12–1   Cognitive and Interactionist Theories of Learning

NEAL MILLER (1909–   )

Because of Miller's work as an experimental psychologist, he might well have been included among the connectionists; some historians of psychology include him in that category, whereas others call him an interactionist. Because much of his theoretical work concerns itself with applications of his theory to personality and social and abnormal psychology, he differs sharply from Skinner. Miller is concerned with four elements of learning: drive, response, reduction in drive, and the collection of stimuli that guide the response, which he identifies as cues. These have been widely labeled and identified with Miller as drive, cue, response, and reward.

1. *Drive* is an aroused state of an organism, one that spurs or motivates the individual to act. The drive stimulus may be external, such as a strong cue, or internal, such as hunger, thirst, or emotional states

(fear, hatred, rage, and the like) that produce physiological changes in the organism.

2. *Reward* is the reduction of a drive, and this reduction in the strength of a drive is reinforced and therefore tends to produce learning. Thus whatever response or behavior tends to reduce the drive is what will be learned. In the future when that drive appears again the behavior of the individual will be similar to the response that in the past reduced the drive previously. Learning, according to Miller, is drive reduction.

3. *Cues* are stimuli that are received by the organism from outside itself. This could be any kind of external stimulus, from a boss who frowns, a rain storm, or an electric shock to disapproval of society and social approval. These are as varied and complex as life itself, because they are often multiple in nature as well as specific as a knee tap.

4. *Behavior* is the most readily agreed on ingredient in learning theory. It is activity that can be seen and measured.

Miller, in collaboration with John Dollard, theorized extensively about application of this four-part system. By explaining that group behavior of others comprises a cue to an individual when a response is called for, Miller highlighted the effects of imitation on social behavior of men. Mobs, for example, consist of people imitating each other, thus stimulating one another to gruesome deeds, which as individuals they might never have performed.[1]

Much of the material taught in early human relations courses of supervisors was drawn from the language of Miller.

CLARK L. HULL (1884–1952)

Listed as the second of the major cognitive interactionists, Hull is another theorist whose name might well be included among the connectionists. The contributions he made to learning theory are major in scope and certainly draw heavily on Watsonian traditions. Yet he moves beyond Watson and his predecessors in theory. Having been trained as an engineer, he organized his theories closer to the forms of science, using postulate and corollary along the lines of Euclidian geometry. The postulates were statements about various facets of behavior. These then were logically argued and combined into theorems, as Euclid had done. The theorems could then be compared with the various laws of learning as determined by experiments.

Whole generations of psychologists, including a few whose works drew on Hull's forms without really resembling it in rigor and logic,

---

[1] N. Miller and J. Dollard, *Social Learning and Imitation* (New Haven: Yale University Press, 1941).

were to emerge. In the latter studies of behavioral sciences of the motivational, attitudinal, and perceptual nature, the scientific language of Hull was often used to turn indications into proof and to beat opposition viewpoints over the head. Many of the studies about sensitivity training began with conclusions and worked backward using the language of science, which, as Mason Haire once put it, "it resembles not at all."

Hull's is a four-stage analysis of behavior. His goal was to develop a theory that would predict the dependent variables of behavior from the independent variables. To simplify the complexity of this task, he introduced intervening variables. Using the four stages as shown in Fig. 12–1, Hull called the independent variables such things as deprivation of food, water, sex, and the like. Other independent variables included painful stimulation, the magnitude of the reward or favorable antecedent stimuli, and the number of reinforced training trials.

Incentive motivation was an intervening variable for Hull, with the size of the reward affecting the level of performance. The larger the reward, the greater the increase in habit strength. It also affected incentive motivation. The size of the food pellet at the end of the maze increased the speed of the rat in threading through it. The worker who is paid an increasingly higher amount for added output will increase his output.

Excitatory potential, Hull proposed, was a cumulative effect of three other intervening variables. This means that there is a total tendency to make a given response to a given stimulus. In ordinary language, which Hull avoided by using formulas as a discipline, the excitatory potential consists of three other intervening variables: (1) knowing how to behave in a certain way, (2) knowing what is to be gained by doing it, and (3) wanting the thing to be gained by doing it.

Dependent variables or behavior could be measured by three major dimensions: (1) the amplitude or size of the response, (2) the speed of the response, and (3) the total number of responses that will occur after reinforcement is removed before the response fades away or is extinct. The excitatory potential increases all three.

Hull thus made an important contribution to the theory of learning of the connectionist variety, but he also alluded to matters that were more intuitive and subjective in the learner.

His constructions included numerous other concepts. His postulates and corollaries included the concept of the threshold, which is the minimum level that the excitatory potential must reach before any behavior will occur. He dealt with inhibitions to behave in a certain way in the face of identical stimuli and secondary responses. These become important in a total understanding of learning theory because they attempt to deal in a scientific way with the issues and problems that subjectivists and interactionists treat as cognitive matters.[2]

Although rigorously scientific, Hull attempted to rebut many of the popular objections to scientific causal explanations of human behavior. The view that the self, the mind, and the soul are hidden from external observations does not mean that we must rely only on intuitive methods of explaining them. Yet Hull's 133 theorems following from 17 postulates paid an unacknowledged testimony to the existence of questions of spirit, motive, attitude, and cognition. He goes well beyond Skinnerian assertions that man is an empty organism and fits the inner life into his scientific explanations of behavior. This, of course, would not satisfy those mystics and poets, or even philosophers, such as Bergson, who proposes that science moves around an object and relates it to other objects but that intuition enters into an object and grasps its absolute nature. The cognitive learning theorists went beyond Hull but were indebted to him for spelling out many of the problems to be explained.

Although the inclusion of Miller and Hull among the soft criteria school will ruffle some scholars no end, from the Skinnerian and Watsonian viewpoint, and perhaps from the more pragmatic industrial trainer's viewpoint, they are well included there. With respect to the remaining four shown in Fig. 12–1, there is little doubt that they must be considered interactionists.

Although the list is short, the inclusion of all those learning theorists and philosophers who have been concerned with the question of mental versus physical ways of behaving would be far too lengthy and not quite relevant for this book. The existentialists, for instance, drawing on Kierkegaard, contend that truth is found in subjectivity and that objectivisms of all sorts or even systems of any sort are wrong. In some ways this difference is characteristic of various cultures. The culture of the East stresses the affective immediacy of experience, whereas Western thought is concerned with conceptual understanding. The difference here could be shown thus:

Western Culture	Eastern Culture
Systematic	Subjective
Scientific	Direct
Rational	Intimate
Objective	Paradoxical
Noncontradictory	Mystical
Logical	

[2] Clark C. Hull, *Principles of Behavior* (New York: Appleton, 1943) outlines his approach. His definitive work is *A Behavior System* (New Haven: Yale University Press, 1952).

Thus a soft criteria learning theory would be concerned with feelings, attitudes, perceptions, and emotions. It might turn in training procedures for sensitivity training, to psychoanalysis, or even, in a few outlying instances, to LSD. It tries to teach by changing personality. The soft criteria trainer not only adheres to the measurement of effect through subjectivist means but often is concerned with training objectives that design change of attitudes and the achievement of empathy, awareness, and unfrozen attitudes.

The differences are not only methodological, reflecting logical conclusions about direct experience and rational understanding, but also philosophical.

Gestalt Theorists (1900–   )

The early German psychologists were mainly concerned with explaining the mind and its functions. Watson proposed one basic attack on this approach. Another was begun by a contemporary of Watson, Max Wertheimer (1880–1943). Wertheimer moved in a different theoretical direction from either Watson or the early Germans. He proposed that rather than breaking the structure of the mind down into fragments psychology should be concerned with seeing things as a meaningful whole. Wertheimer proposed that the breaking down of the mind was useless and misleading. As evidence he cited the *phi phenomenon*, as exemplified by the apparent movement of light in an electric sign. What appears to be movement is, in fact, the turning off of one light and the turning on of another next to it quickly. This apparent impression does not exist in fact but in the eye of the beholder, or more accurately in the mind of the beholder. Starting from this base, Wertheimer was concerned with perception, and the word *gestalt*, which may be roughly translated as "configuration," as it applies to dynamic wholes, was brought into the field of learning theory.

The point of the gestalt approach was that the sum of specific figures was greater than the individual parts. Three dots are nothing more than three dots. Yet in the eye of the observer they form a triangle. Two major ingredients comprise the whole. The *figure* and the *ground*, with the figure being the gestalt in any perception and the whole that stands out. The ground is the largely undifferentiated backdrop against which the figure appears. It is possible to analyze and identify the specific elements that make up the figure, but to the gestalt psychologist the important thing is the fact that we see the figure rather than the individual dots that comprise its configuration.

Wertheimer and Wolfgang Kohler (1887–   ) and Kurt Koffka (1886–1914) comprised a group that came to be known as the Berlin School, the center of gestalt theory. Their contribution to learning theory was quite unlike the Watsonians, from whom they differed sharply. The perceptions of the learner were considered more important than what he has learned in bits.

Two major building blocks of the gestalt theory of learning might be mentioned. The first of these is the idea of *insight*. The gestalt *laws of learning and forgetting* are the second. Insight is the sudden feeling that now you really understand. The sudden flash of insight when the atom was split for the first time, or the RNA molecule described by Watson and Crick, was of such an obvious and clear nature that everyone suddenly saw and knew that the solution was correct. The pointing out of a design on a wallpaper that had been there all along but unseen could be a physical example of insight.

Not only are such dramatic and complete kinds of insight important, but a series of small insights can lead to larger learning on a gradual basis. The rat in a maze learns piecemeal, but the principle is the same as when all the elements are present and seen in one flash.

Two Gestalt Laws of Learning. Two major guides to learning characterized the gestalt laws of learning. The first of these was that of *proximity*. It says essentially that things that are close together and tend to form groups will be recalled because they comprise such groupings. Sounds heard close together tend to form groups. Spacing in distance and spacing in time are more likely to produce a gestalt of a grouping, and this grouping and gestalt is the basis for learning and seeing things as a whole.

The law of *closure* states that closed areas more readily form units. When a group emerges or is perceived by the individual, he is more apt to achieve a gestalt and to learn the nature of the relationship. As long as the individual is struggling with a problem, his perception is incomplete. A reward solves the problem and brings the hitherto separate parts together into a unified gestalt. This gestalt includes the problem, the goal, and the means of achieving the goal. The emphasis, Koffka proposed, was not merely on obtaining the reward but on completing the activity and bringing the tension of not knowing to relief by closing the relations of the parts into relations with one another.

The gestalt *law of forgetting* is likewise concerned with perceptual change. The memory that existed before is changed with time into a better gestalt. Familiar, meaningful forms tend to be more easily shaped into patterns by the observer than strange or unfamiliar ones. Studies on memories of figures showed that the forgetting did not take the form of simple mistakes or loss of recall as much as a tendency for the figures to be converted into something more familiar.

As a contribution to learning theory, gestalt theory assists greatly in explaining how problems are solved in complex situations. The business manager who sees things as familiar is thrown into a state of tension or uncertainty by some new element that does not fit a familiar pattern. Until the new conceptual pattern emerges that fits a gestalten occurs, he is in such a state of tension that he must continue his search for the meaning or pattern. In such matters as analysis of markets, in problems of living generally, and in achievement of goals, gestalt theory explains his learning process.[3]

EDWARD CHACE TOLMAN (1886–1959)

Like Miller and Hull, California psychologist Edward Tolman sought to merge into a unified theory of learning the connectionists and the cognitive schools. He sought to retain the objectivity and scientific basis of behaviorism; at the same time he felt that men respond to internal beliefs and feelings and are moved externally by a desire to achieve goals that are generated internally.

Called *purposive behaviorism*, Tolman's systems rest heavily on the importance of goals. This purposive behaviorism, which he defined in his *Purposive Behavior in Animals and Men* (1932), has three main characteristics: (1) It is a form of behaviorism that is concerned with activity that can be seen or measured, not with consciousness or emotional states of the organism; (2) it is concerned, as was Watson, with the effect of external stimuli on behavior; and (3) it is concerned with how behavior changes with this contact with the external world. The major difference from Watson's view of behavior and learning is in the importance of goals in shaping the behavior of the organism. The search for a goal lends meaning and unity to behavior, permitting a wide range of different behaviors while we continue to search for a route to the goal. This would mean that to explain behavior we must know the goal toward which it is directed. The unit of behavior that Tolman studied was clustered into units that Tolman labeled *molar* behavior, or behavior arranged or studied by fairly large chunks, such as the behavior entailed in writing a book, baking a cake, or merging two railroads. The specific actions, such as Skinner is concerned with, he called *molecular* behavior. Whereas Guthrie was interested only in molecular behavior, Tolman was mainly interested in molar behavior. He showed little interest in studying how molecular behavior is strung together to form molar behavior.

[3] M. Wertheimer, *Productive Thinking* (New York: Harper & Row, 1945), gives a useful statement of the gestalt approach to general learning and thinking. Koffka's works are more technical and basic, especially his *The Growth of the Mind*, Translated by R. M. Ogden (New York: Harcourt, 1925), and his *Principles of Gestalt Psychology* (New York: Harcourt, 1935). W. Kohler's *The Mentality of Apes* is an experimental book on experiments done during World War I (New York: Harcourt, 1925).

Tolman's Cognitions. Tolman sought to deal with the intuitions and beliefs as a means of explaining molar behavior; at the same time he desired to remain scientific and a behaviorist. He employed the intervening variable as a partial explanation. This was something that existed between the stimulus and that which Tolman defined as cognitions. He noted that a cognition was not a thing—nor was it a response, as the behaviorists would propose. It was to be treated as *an abstraction created by the theorist.* A need thus becomes a cognition and exists only in the mind of the theorist, but it is treated as a reality because its effects are the same as if it were real. The relation of such cognitions to external stimuli is the assumption that they are positive creations of past stimuli and changed under the impact of external stimuli. Like Lewin, Tolman treated concepts as though they were real and objective, but he relied more strongly on the existence of external stimuli as causes and explanations of cognitions. It was the cognitions of the man that determined his goals, which in turn determined his behavior. These cognitions form into *cognitive maps,* which are intervening variables, and his sign gestalt expectation, or expectation of how the world is organized and how some things lead to others.

Tolman's Six Kinds of Learning. Tolman constructed six kinds of learning, in contrast to the single systems proposed by earlier theorists: (1) *the formulation of cathexes,* which is a tendency to seek certain goals when experiencing a certain drive. The hunger drive gives rise to a demand for food, and so on. (2) Learning through *equivalence beliefs* was a second kind of learning according to Tolman. These are forms of conditioned reinforcers in which a situation is made equal to the specific reward for punishment. The athlete who has received acclaim through his prowess will find the general situation of athletic competition, training, and team play one to which he is attracted by a cognitive map. (3) The third kind of learning is that of *field expectancies,* which are cognitions about the way the world is laid out and what leads where. Cognitive maps are made up mainly of such expectancies. When Mr. Jimmy Hoffa, president of the Teamsters union, states that "the world is a jungle," he is defining his cognitive map, his expectancies, and what tools and techniques he has learned in surviving in the world. This is the heart of Tolman's system. (4) The fourth kind of learning is that of *field cognition modes,* which are ways of learning, or special emphasis on learning some things more rapidly and easier than in other ways. The youngster who has had unfavorable experience with an early mathematics teacher finds that his tendency toward engineering curricula is affected afterward. Our language skills ended certain kinds of modes in learning. The resident of the large city ghetto has acquired a certain mode of learning that may prevent him from employability later on.

(5) The fifth kind of learning is *drive discrimination*, which is an acquired ability to discriminate between certain kinds of drives. The drive of pain may be indistinguishable from pleasure and have to be learned. The early taste of wine may seem sour and unpleasant but after may become learned as pleasant. This learning is closely related to cathexis formulation, in which needs are related to goals. (6) The sixth kind of learning is that of *motor patterns*, which is represented by riding a bicycle, playing billiards, or firing a gun. Here Tolman accords explanations to the earlier behaviorists whose studies of molecular behavior can explain the finite details of the molar behavior and stimulus-response connections.

Tolman's influence is strong on later theorists of the "behavioral science" school of management. The terms he used were adopted widely by a younger generation of survey researchers of the Lewinian school, and his concept of the cognitive map was adopted, often without his stated limitation on it, as a form of reality in which this perceptual framework was treated as though it were as real as an organ such as a kidney or liver. Much supervisory training of the 1940's and 1950's drew heavily on Tolman. His social and ethical standards also had a strong effect on subsequent generations of followers. As a Quaker he was strongly opposed to war and violence, and his stands on matters of conscience often made his leadership a moral one as well as a scientific one. On occasion it becomes difficult to distinguish between scientific research conclusions and moral philosophy of some of his disciples. Although his moral posture is laudable, it also makes it difficult to separate his followers' conclusions in moral terms from their scientific conclusions.[4]

Kurt Lewin (1890–1947)

Originally a gestalt psychologist, Lewin moved in his interests to problems of motivation, perception, and social psychology. Moving to America, he was the founder of the Research Center in Group Dynamics, which started at Iowa, then moved to Massachusetts Institute of Psychology, and ultimately moved to the University of Michigan. Lewin's studies centered on the desires and the goals themselves, as they related to personality.

The *life space* of the individual became the basic building block of the Lewinian system—the totality of facts that determine the behavior

[4] E. C. Tolman's *Purposive Behavior in Animals and Men* (New York: Appleton, 1932) is his major work. His six principles of learning are contained in an article "There Is More Than One Kind of Learning," *Psychological Review*, 56 (1949), pp. 144–155. His pacifist and moral position is outlined in his *Drives Toward War* (New York: Appleton, 1942).

of an individual at any given time. This space contains the person himself, the goals he seeks or is attracted to (valences are the strengths of the attraction), the negative goals he is trying to avoid, the barriers to getting where he wants to go, and the paths he follows in getting to the goals. The life space is not merely physical environment or even conscious perception but also his unconscious perceptions. It includes everything that affects his behavior. There are both positive and negative valences that measure the strength of the attraction and repulsion of a goal for the person. Lewin did not use geometric forms but topological forms (rubber sheet geometry), and the schema that are often used by Lewinians resemble kidney-shaped swimming pools more often than they resemble block diagrams or Euclidian forms. Such life spaces are not meant to be drawn to scale but as generalized representation, which reduces the abstract and vague to resemble the concrete and real.

Figure 12–2 shows the life space of a young man who is working in a

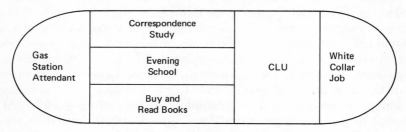

FIGURE 12–2   Life Space of an Employee

gasoline station in a topological diagram. He has a personal goal of becoming a white collar claims adjuster for an insurance company. At the left side of the diagram is the person and his present situation. He sees three other regions that are available to him. He might become a correspondence student, he might become an evening student, or he might buy and read some books and study while he is working. As a result he could then take the examination for certified life underwriter and obtain his CLU certificate, which would entitle him to employment.

There are certain barriers that seem to block the paths to achievement of his goals. Lewin used the words *vectors* and *valences* in his scheme. A vector is a force operating in a certain direction, and its valence is the strength of the attraction for the individual. Occasionally vectors will be pressing in different directions. In the case of the young man in the example in Fig. 12–2, he has a vector toward CLU, but he also has certain other vectors, such as riding cars in drag races, that take up some of the time he might use for studying. The relative valences of each goal will affect his final choice.

Although Lewin was not as important in learning theory as many of the others, he becomes very important for industrial training because of his proposed explanation of behavior and prediction of behavior itself. His work was useful in stating the result of certain kinds of learning. It also had considerable usefulness in assisting people in training to understand their total situation and to make conscious judgments about goals and plans. It was, in effect, a kind of map to self-development, which was of considerable value to many. If it was less valuable to the learning theorist in maintaining the flow of theories in the connectionist tradition, Lewin was not concerned. His purpose was to explain behavior, personality, and most especially the social relations between groups and individuals.

Behavior, Lewin proposed, was not a function of the operants, or the stimuli, or the inner condition alone. It was a function of the personality of the individual and the environmental situation within which he was functioning. $[B = f(p,e)]$ was the formula that he devised for this relationship. Tensions that are generated within the individual are partial explanations of his action, Lewin proposed. These tensions, which are similar to the drives proposed by Miller and others, may be biological, or they may be gestalt in origin, but they have the effect of requiring some behavior for relief.[5]

One of the incidental side effects of Lewin's work was the emergence of one of his experimental programs into the full-blown movement known as sensitivity training. Long interested in action training, Lewin, shortly before his death, participated in a training session to teach group members how group functions operate. Conducted in Connecticut, this experimental program in group dynamics training was expanded and moved to Bethel, Maine, under the sponsorship of the National Training Laboratories in Group Dynamics. As its purposes changed it became known as a "group development laboratory" and the group dynamics name and purpose fell away. Today sensitivity training has become a sizable enterprise with several hundreds of trainers and thousands of alumni and practitioners. The origins were in Lewin, but as is the case with many movements, its originator would hardly recognize it. Whether or not he would approve it is also speculative.

[5] K. Lewin, *Dynamic Theory of Personality*, translated by D. K. Adams and K. E. Zener (New York: McGraw-Hill, 1935) is the basic work of Lewin. *His Principles of Topological Psychology* translated by Heider and Heider (New York: McGraw-Hill, 1936) explains his application of rubber sheet geometry used in his field theory. A more recent collection of his writings is *Field Theory in Social Science* (New York: Harper Torchbooks, 1951), edited by Dorian Cartwright.

ABRAHAM MASLOW (1905-   )

Most recent past president of the American Psychological Association and a genuinely well-liked man, Abraham Maslow is the *pater familias* of the soft criteria school of trainers. His works are far less experimental than any of the psychologists outlined before, but his influence on training and the teaching practices is considerable. In the language of the learning theorist, Maslow is almost totally unconcerned with external stimuli and deeply concerned with the internal motives and personality factors that affect behavior and change it. More than any of the learning theorists (if he can be called a learning theorist), he has shown interest in personality development and the growth of the human personality. This growth, which to Maslow is the most important topic in psychology, might by some stretch of logic be called learning, or in some terms it might be called therapy. Yet Maslow appears to show little concern for such fine distinctions. He is concerned with people fulfilling their best capacities, and his interest has been in defining what that best capacity might be.

The peak experience plays an important part in Maslow's scheme of things. This is a kind of experience that produces a euphoric condition in its possessor, one in which he realizes the very best of his capacity and expresses his inner self fully. It is not ordinary triumph over success, or a simple elation over victory, or an ordinary neural pleasure. It comes from an accumulation of experiences in which the individual has grown through various stages of need fulfillment.

Needs of the human are an important building block of the Maslovian system. These needs tend to rise in a hierarchy. They are fourfold in order of significance. The lowest order of needs are those of *physical* needs such as hunger and sex. When these physical needs are fulfilled, then *ego needs* will emerge and become predominant. When these ego needs are essentially fulfilled, then *social needs*, which were present but less pressing, become highest in the needs hierarchy. Finally, when all these needs are met, there remains the highest need level for humans, that of *self-actualization*. It is in the last need fulfillment level that the peak experience becomes possible.

Maslow arranges these needs in a hierarchy, stating that the satisfaction or fulfillment of a lower-level need does not mean that the human organism comes to rest but that he merely moves to the next highest level of need. Physical needs, for example, if not fulfilled, pre-empt all other needs. The person who is hungry will subordinate his ego needs in order to obtain food. In our society Maslow points out that few physical needs are left unmet, which means that the higher-level needs are of highest importance. Given this situation, which is cultural in origin, the requirement for managing people, and the chief requirement for training managers, is to shift the emphasis away from physical needs (which Maslow often calls security needs) to the less tangible but more important needs. Thus the supervisor who would make people productive and creative will learn how these needs are arranged and will behave in such a way that the needs of workers are met. The worker in turn will be attracted to work that meets his particular need of the moment. Because industry and government have arranged to satisfy many of the lower-level needs, the dominant requirement for managing workers and professionals is the need fulfillment for self-actualization.

It would be possible to fit Maslow's concepts into the framework of other learning theorists without straining too much. It is clear that his concern with the mechanics of what Tolman called molecular behavior is small. He is concerned with the drives Hull spelled out, without the rigorous formulation that Hull used. As a theorist Maslow's contribution has yet to be assessed. His clear writing style and his willingness to use the language of the layman make him difficult to evaluate in the mainstream of learning theory. Yet there is much of the cognitive school in his work. His hierarchy of needs has little to offer in connectionist terms for explaining how learning occurs. It comes close to being an explanation of how reinforcement works and could readily be related to earlier theory. Yet the Skinnerians and behaviorists would react vigorously against what appears to be Maslow's vague and overly generalized interpretations of human behavior.[6]

If motivation is a proposed explanation of behavior as it can be observed, Maslow's greatest contribution has been a classification system of the proposed explanations of behavior.

There are numerous other soft criteria learning theorists who would be worthy of mention. Herzberg, using the method of interview and questionnaire, obtained a considerable number of responses from individuals in industry and administration by asking them to describe their most satisfactory and their least satisfactory moments. His sought-after response has some resemblance to obtaining introspective reports on peak experiences as Maslow describes them. These Herzberg then classifies into a needs hierarchy. Some experiences have a positive affect of motivating individuals; that is, they were reinforced or rewarded and are attracted by such experiences. Other experiences are unfavorable and have a negative reinforcement value to the individual. Most of the

---

[6] A. H. Maslow's *Motivation and Personality* (New York) outlines his hierarchy. His *Euphyscian Management*, a collection of fascinating articles on the application of his theory to modern management training, includes his discussion of sensitivity training and other key issues.

motivators are of a self-actualizing and self-expression nature and were found in the job itself, as when the person attempted to express his abilities and success attended his efforts. Goal achievement seems to be an important motivator for both Maslow and Herzberg. Other kinds of experience are important only in their absence in Herzberg's work. Certain kinds of experience or reinforcers have no positive effect but in their absence become "demotivators." For the employer of workers who provides these needs, such as fair pay and fringe benefits, there are no positive motivations, but their absence could be harmful to the relationship of the worker to the work and the manager. Herzberg refers to these demotivators as "hygeine" influences, in that they do not make the individual psychologically healthy but do prevent illnesses.

The major importance of the Maslow and Herzberg theories is in the possibilities they hold for individual learning in man-to-man teaching and learning situations.

This in itself is an important distinction. Whereas Miller, Skinner, Tolman, and others were often oriented toward the teaching of students in classrooms, many of the later theorists were oriented toward the work situation. Maslow is clearly convinced of the importance of work in the scheme of things, and practically all of Herzberg's studies occurred in a work environment, especially the work of managers and professionals, such as nurses, accountants, engineers, and supervisors in this country and abroad.

It is increasingly apparent that learning managerial skills and many of the advance professional skills occurs in a one-to-one teaching relationship. Job learning occurs by working for a person who is combining supervision with teaching. Thus the arrangement of policy that permits a certain style of supervisory behavior and of personal coaching behavior of superiors of subordinates calls for development of learning theory that were not required in classroom instruction in the secondary or college classroom.

Yet the limitation on this Maslow-Herzberg approach lies in its general nature. Rooted in intuition, or in generalizations from questionnaires and interviews of large groups, it often produces generalizations to which numerous exceptions can quickly be found. Perhaps the basic problem concerns this relationship between explanatory and applied science, the descriptive and the policy sciences. The generalization of the soft criteria learning theorists often deals with empty classes rather than real individuals. No matter how much theoretical knowledge we develop, we still have the problems of knowing how and where to apply this knowledge to concrete situations and of discerning and explaining differences in the situations. This *manager* behaves in *this* way in *this* situation. The changing of this behavior is the specific requirement of the trainer, and allowing this proper behavior to come about is a policy question to which his skills must be applied.

There is no doubt that basic theoretical research in learning may help us to a degree in this problem. Unique syndromes or complexes of causes repeat themselves, and we can call on tested and regular theoretical prescriptions to apply voluntarily the first time. But every syndrome and complex is unique to a certain extent, and there will always be a few dramatic exceptions. We cannot generalize about learning theory when we are dealing with a specific manager for General Motors, or Honeywell, or Aetna Life. This calls for skill and perception and above all a hard criteria in the form of training objectives in economic terms to judge which learning theory should be adopted at what time for what situation. This is the application of activity sometimes identified as an "art." The success or failure of applied art is impossible without some statement of objective prepared in advance. It is like the two ladies peering at an ultramodern painting and one asking "How can he tell whether he is getting better?" This becomes a major question for trainers when artistry and judgment are involved.

The choice of training mode and the judgment of effect cannot be readily resolved by resorting to theory alone. It requires specific goals, and learning theory is the servant of economic goals for the firm.

THE CO-WORKER COUNCIL CASE

President Smedley of the T Line Litho Company was having some trouble with his ulcer, and that usually meant trouble for some other people as well. The issue of a representation election for a union of his employees had raised its head again in the rumor mill. For several years now there had been some various alarms and passes at his employees, and in one instance the state labor relations board had held an election, under state laws, to determine whether or not the company should be required to bargain collectively with their employees over wages, hours, and conditions of work.

At the time of that first election the president had moved in very strongly and had swung a wide swath through the shop, firing people who had been active, threatening others, and promising benefits to others. This had meant that the company had won the election, but it also resulted in an unfair labor practice charge being sustained against the company. Meanwhile, during the charges and hearings the officers had gotten Mr. Smedley away from the plant on an around the world tour, had raised salaries, and had corrected some inequities that had existed for a long time. Thus, when the union won a decree from the labor board for another election, the company, using these measures plus strictly legal powers of free speech, had persuaded the employees that they should vote "no union" and had won.

Because it would be about a year before the union would have another chance, the management group decided to establish better communications with employees and thus avert a union drive before it really got rolling. One of the key attempts at this was the creation of a "co-worker council." This had been established with representatives from each department, chosen by the employees in that department, on a rotating basis. As the production manager, who was the first chairman, put it: "One of the problems around here has been too little upward communication; it's all been downward. We need to do more listening and do something about what we hear."

In its early days the council met almost weekly. Usually the agenda broke down into two parts: old business and new business. A secretary was appointed and the minutes were reproduced and made available to every employee. Some hot issues were discussed, and some changes made. Later the employees asked that the meetings be spread out to once every two weeks, because they were getting thin in matters to discuss and were turning into bull sessions. They finally settled at once a month, with additional meetings when needed.

Mr. Smedley scoffed at the whole idea when he came back. He did not veto it, however. At the time this case began he had all but ignored it. When the latest rumor of a union election came to him, however, he called a management meeting.

"Boys," said Mr. Smedley, "I heard those tramping rascals from the unions are nipping at our heels again. I want you to know that we won't take this cancerous disease laying down, and I'm prepared to fight it out with them when they appear."

"Mr. Smedley," said the production manager, "we haven't heard anything about any union drives around here."

"Perhaps you haven't heard anything, but I tell you there is all kinds of hanky panky going on right under your noses."

"Mr. Smedley, we have good contact with our people. The people are pretty happy. In fact I met a man from another litho firm the other day and he said that his union business agent was in his office not long ago and commented on how the union didn't really think they would bother with *us* this year. In fact the manager from this other firm says that the union considers it a waste of time to try to organize us at all."

"A damn trick," barked Smedley. "These union people try to plant rumors like that to soften up your sense of vigilance, make you relax your vigil, and lower the barriers of your defenses. Good thing I'm here to see through their nefarious scheme."

"Mr. Smedley," the controller said, "I'm not expert in these things, but I've had a chance to be chairman of the co-worker council and I don't think the people feel anything but high regard for us."

"Oh, you mean that gab-fest you fellows have with the help?"

"The council is a good device. I think the minutes show the candid discussion we have and that they are effective. Don't you agree?"

"I've gone along with your councils because I want to humor you people. I don't read the minutes though. Waste of time. Good thing I don't, too. Keeps me alert to any fifth columns of union organizers getting in."

The discussion continued in this vein with the managers trying to soften up the old gentleman and he scoffing at the council. Finally he agreed, however, to study some minutes and give an assessment of the council. For the next several days he went through the past minutes carefully. Finally he selected the minutes from four months and put them in his briefcase.

Down at the club he met Sam Reese, a management consultant in whom he placed great confidence: "Sam, I've got a problem for you. My managers tell me that this worker's council is a bulwark against unions and has a lot of other advantages besides. I haven't kept up with them, but I've read the minutes of all their meetings and I'm puzzled. I've selected the minutes from four months and brought them along for you. Would you read them carefully and give me your views of the advantages and disadvantages of this council?"

MINUTES OF CO-WORKER COUNCIL MEETING HELD
TUESDAY, AUGUST 1, 1961

Attended by: All departmental representatives; Ed Jones for management. Bette Davis was introduced as the new representative for Accounting.

OLD BUSINESS

Company Picnic. A comment was made that door prizes were not given out this year. It was explained that this is not an established practice. Each year the general chairman, the recreation committee chairman, and the committee discuss the subject. After discussion this year, the group decided that because we try to make our picnic a day for all employees' children, the money should be spent on prizes for the children's games and bingo.

Big League Ball Game. Ed Jones stated that arrangements for attending the ball game on Friday, August 18, have been made. Tickets were purchased through the Athletic Distributing Company. The cost per person will be $4.15, including cost for an extra ticket purchased for the bus driver as a courtesy. Ed will try to arrange for the bus to load in our parking lot, and the exact time will be announced later.

Parking Lot. Representatives of three departments reported that after discussion in their meetings the parking lot was considered adequate and we are lucky to have it.

NEW BUSINESS

Department Meetings. The matter of low morale and poor attitude toward Co-worker Council Meetings was brought up. It was reported that certain subjects or situations are brought up so often that employees lose interest in the meetings. Ed stated that he felt an overall evaluation would bring out many good things that have been accomplished by the council. In the discussion that followed, it was pointed out that the purpose of the meetings is to give all employees an opportunity to bring up, through their department representative, any subject or situation of interest to everyone. Ed then suggested that this be discussed in department meetings and that representatives report at the next council meeting on how often employees feel meetings should be held and on possible ideas for discussion at future meetings. For instance, profit sharing, waste, rework cost, safety, plant changes, and production information could be discussed.

The discussion brought out that all maintenance problems should be reported immediately to the department supervisor. In cases involving safety hazards particularly, if the problem is not satisfactorily taken care of, it can then be channeled through the council representative to bring up in the next council meeting. All production supervisors have attended a series of movies on safety, emphasizing the need for immediate action to correct hazards.

In answer to a question brought up, Ed stated that supervisors are encouraged to attend their department's meetings. These are meetings in which everyone is free to bring up problems and questions for discussion. The supervisor's presence often eliminates a minor problem being brought to the council because it can be answered by the supervisor.

Security. General disregard for security rules on restricted production areas was reported, and it was pointed out that all employees should again be reminded to strictly avoid an area that is roped off and restricted to everyone except the employee working on the job.

Reporting to Switchboard. It was reported that many people leave the building without notifying the switchboard operator, resulting in confusion about their calls. Ed stated that anyone receiving many calls should always inform the operator when leaving the building, and notify her when he returns.

The next council meeting will be held on Tuesday, August 22, at 9:30 A.M.

MINUTES OF CO-WORKERS COUNCIL MEETING HELD TUESDAY, SEPTEMBER 19, 1961

Attended by: All departmental representatives; Ed Jones for management. Ernie Hemingway was introduced as the new representative for the Bindery-Folder Departments, and Doris Day as new representative for Estimating, Planning and Purchasing.

OLD BUSINESS

Council and Department Meetings. Ed Jones asked whether department meetings resulted in new suggestions on the use of the council meetings. The response indicated considerable interest in rework, terminology of instructions, and inspection points. Ed explained that the terminology project will be a long-range one requiring work over a considerable period of time. Inspection points and inspection, he said, are being given a great deal of thought now, and there will probably be some changes made in the near future.

Rework. In the discussion of rework, Ed stated that supervisors had endeavored to point out to their departments how rework happens, thus helping employees correct errors before expensive rework is necessary. This has not been particularly effective in lowering our rework costs, and some errors continue to happen over and over again. Ed brought to the meeting a step-by-step summary of what happened on the book *Problems in Forestry*. The brief summary is given here:

1. The book was originally printed in 1960 for the two authors.
2. P. A. Greene Company subsequently took over publication from the two authors and ordered a reprint with corrections this year.
3. P. A. Greene Company submitted copy for a new copyright page carrying a 1961 copyright by them and a 1960 copyright by the authors.
4. All proof of the copyright page was sent to the authors and approved by them.
5. Late in the production process, P. A. Greene Company asked to see proof of the copyright page. Books were printed so check copy was sent.
6. It was discovered in the interim that T Line had failed to apply for copyright for the authors in 1960, and so copy in the printed text was incorrect.
7. P. A. Greene Company asked us to set up a new copyright page at their expense, and print whatever pages were necessary to correct.
8. We printed a 32-pager and failed to throw the old 32 away, and this was used when completing books instead of the new sections. The job was partially in shipping when the error happened to be noticed by a salesman.
9. P. A. Greene Company allowed us to tip in one sheet instead of reprinting and binding the whole order.

Ed stated that it took 50 hours of handwork in the bindery to tip in the correct title page, at least $347.00 cost. The total order was for 2,500 copies, but 700 had been sewed and not covered when the error was discovered. The sewing was removed, and these copies resewn with the new section in at a cost of at least $50. He further stated that it was a lucky break for us that the customer accepted a tip-in, for the Greene company would have been entirely within their rights in demanding the whole book be reprinted and bound. It was a first order from the Greene Company. "We hope it isn't the last," Ed said.

Ed went on to say that another error that will cause rework has just been discovered: a newsletter, carrying a title page for the "Hydraulic Division" rather than the "Highway Division." Part of the pamphlets were stuffed in mailing envelopes when the error was discovered. It will mean the job will have to be completely rerun, beginning with Composition Department work in correcting the title page. It will require advising the customer what happened, sending the mailings out without it, and mailing this one newsletter later on in separate envelopes with new labels.

Ed summarized these explanations with the following statement: "All of this calls our attention to the need for improving awareness on everyone's part to be more careful. Although we may need to inspect more than we do, and we're working on that subject, these are individual responsibilities in our kind of business, and we have to rely on the ability of each person to do the job right the first time. This is something that takes the effort of everybody in the building."

The two sample books, showing the incorrect book and the book with the correct tipped-in title page, will be available at the reception desk for use in department meetings.

This led to suggestions from council members about listing the costs of rework by departments, etc., but Joe explained that a true picture of rework charged to individual departments is not readily available. Discussion also brought out that figures do not really present the rework problem in a way that can lead to lowering the amount of rework, whereas examples show all employees what is occurring and gives each person a chance to sharpen up on his job to help prevent like errors in the future.

Plant Changes. Ed stated that Bill Faulkner had just completed an article for the September issue of the *House Organ* explaining the work he is doing on the new sales program. Instead of bringing Bill to this meeting to talk about it, Joe asked that if the article does not seem clear enough, or there are questions about it, they should be brought up at the next meeting.

Christmas Cards. Ed stated that instruction cards are in process for the Christmas cards and that the schedule has been established as follows:

1. Prescreen material will be due on October 16.
2. Material will be shot and handed back from the Camera Department by November 6.
3. Completed card copy should be turned in by November 17.
4. Cards will be printed and delivered to employees during the week of December 4.

No decision has been made on color of ink, but black was suggested, as it seems to be the best color and is always in stock.

Christmas Party and Banquet. It was suggested that the Town House is now building a banquet room on the second floor to hold 500 people, but it is not known whether it will be completed by December. Ed pointed out that the increase in number of employees is making it very difficult to obtain a place to handle the number of people attending. For instance, last December there were 185 employees on the payroll. Today we have 195. We were crowded last year, he continued, and chances are we will start building up the season before the banquet just as we did last year. Last year there were 34 employees who did not attend, meaning 151 attended, plus their guests, for a total of 292 reservations. He explained he had checked with other companies in the area larger than we are and found they just don't have this kind of gathering. Their activities are confined to a children's party, giving a turkey to each employee, etc. Ed said he didn't want to discontinue the banquet-dance because it does give employees a chance to get together socially and is more than just a place to get the check. No suggestions for a substitute were made, and so far the reservation is being left as is.

Phone Calls. The question was asked: Is it necessary for sales people to take incoming business calls in the lunch room; can't they take such calls at their desks? A short discussion followed, but no definite answer could be given.

First-Aid Room. The question was raised about changing the doors to the women's rest-room to enable anyone to enter the first aid or quiet room. The doors will not be changed. However, it was suggested that a folding cot be left in the men's rest-room for their use in emergencies. Ed stated a cot, which can also double as a stretcher if required, will be purchased and kept there.

NEW BUSINESS

World Series Scores. The question, "Can the World Series scores be given over the PA system?" was asked. No answer was given.

Extra Chairs for Meetings. It was suggested that about a half-dozen folding chairs be kept in the reception room closet for use in meetings when needed.

Departmental Meetings. The discussion on chairs led to Ed's statement that departmental meetings following council meetings should be held in the lunch room except a meeting scheduled at 12:00 noon. This could be held in the conference room because it is unlikely a customer would be in at that time. Conference rooms should be available for customer use just as much as possible.

Locking Lockers. In response to the question, "Why do we have to keep our lockers locked?" Ed replied, "There are two reasons: (1) Safety—if not locked, the doors don't stay shut and represent a safety hazard as someone could bump his head or perhaps sustain serious injury from it; and (2) it will prevent the continuing reports, about which we can do little, of things missing from lockers." It was stated that no reason for the request was given in the notice and was asked that all future signs or notices posted be signed so it is known by whose authority the notice is posted.

Temperatures in Plant. When a complaint was made on temperatures, Ed stated again we are in the in-between season, a difficult one to maintain satisfactory temperatures because first you heat and then quickly have to cool instead. This will even out properly when heat is necessary at all times and no cooling is required.

Language. The matter of undesirable language being used when visitors are in the plant was brought up. Profanity (or cursing) can be particularly distasteful to some of our visitors, if not all of them, because for the most part our visitors have received above-average educational opportunities and can express themselves eloquently without the use of profanity. In addition, it gives not only adults, but also children, a rather poor impression of us. We should be able to conduct our daily business without cursing and, in turn, show our customers and visitors that we are worthy of their respect in all ways.

The next council meeting will be held on Tuesday, October 17, at 10:00 A.M.

MINUTES OF CO-WORKERS COUNCIL MEETING HELD TUESDAY, OCTOBER 17, 1961

Attended by: Department representatives plus Ed Jones. Stella Dallas was introduced as a substitute for Alice Faye of the Composition Department.

OLD BUSINESS

Rework. A discussion was held on the effectiveness of the example of rework that Ed presented at the last meeting. Discussion included suggestions that a graph be put in the lunch room showing the amount of rework in each department each month, perhaps less emphasis on production and more emphasis on efficiency, that supervisors present examples of rework that concern only their own department at department meetings, and more checking on books because there is so much opportunity for error on them and rerunning seems high on them. Ed explained a graph is questionable for two reasons: (1) Dollar value of rework is not an accurate yardstick by which to measure a certain department's responsibility, and (2) it would be difficult to keep this on an impersonal basis, which is what we must do if our efforts are to be effective. He also explained that we sell jobs on the basis of so much production time, and standards are undergoing constant scrutiny to make them more accurate. Management is giving check points considerable thought right now, on books as well as other jobs, and it is expected that some changes will occur to make checking more effective in eliminating rework.

The Sales Department asked if they were to continue to watch for examples of rework, and Ed stated that sales correspondents should send him a note regarding any job they feel is a good example. These can be reviewed and the most representative examples used in council meetings.

It was decided that examples are the best way to show everyone what happened, and Ed will bring examples of rework to the meeting from time to time for discussion and review. Ed also emphasized that although rework is a management program, management is unable to solve it alone and we need more people thinking about it and giving suggestions on ways to overcome excessive rework.

First Aid. "Who pays for the ambulance when it is called?" was asked. Ed stated that in the past the person for whom it was called paid the charge, and after discussion it was concluded that this policy would continue because the individual would have to pay if the call was necessary from his home, downtown, here, or anywhere.

Christmas Party and Banquet. It was asked whether the possibility of holding this at an inn or the Armory had been checked. Ed replied that these had not been checked because it was decided it would be held at the same place again, as the reservation made early this year is still good.

NEW BUSINESS

Open House. The question was brought up as to whether any thought has been given to another open house, either for families only, the general public, or both. Ed stated that at one time we had discussed an open house for families only, but at that time interest was not great enough to warrant holding one. After discussion it was decided that representatives would ask the members of their departments whether they would be interested in a formal open house to be held on a Tuesday or Wednesday evening for families and friends only, and to report to Personnel on Monday, October 23.

Ex-Employees Entering Dock Door. It was called to the attention of the council that an ex-employee had entered the plant by ringing the bell at the dock door. As he had been an employee, the person answering permitted him to enter, only to learn later that he was no longer an employee. A suggested solution was that anyone who wishes to enter at the dock door be questioned before he is allowed to enter. Any employee should have his own key and enter at the employees' entrance, and anyone else should have specific business in the plant before being allowed to enter.

Entrance Blocked Open. It was reported the employees' entrance door was found blocked open twice recently. Each time the block was kicked out and the door closed. For security reasons, any employee finding this entrance blocked open should do the same thing.

First-Aid Kit Supplies. It was reported that many times the first-aid stations are out of certain supplies. Ed stated that he would check the stations and discuss with the dispatchers the possible cause of the situation.

United Fund Drive. The method of handling the present United Fund Drive was questioned and discussed.

New Tile in Ladies' Room. A complaint was registered on the broken tile in the ladies' room. Maintenance will be requested to check it to see whether anything can be done.

The next council meeting will be held Tuesday, November 21, at 10:00 A.M.

MINUTES OF CO-WORKERS COUNCIL MEETING HELD
TUESDAY, NOVEMBER 21, 1961

Attended by: Departmental representatives plus Ed Jones for management. Ed Jones introduced the following representatives: Carl Gray substituting for Lloyd Ball, Shipping; Liz Bruno, new representative for Camera, and Mabel Long, new representative for Layout.

OLD BUSINESS

New Tile in Women's Rest-Room. Management reported that John Black was getting in touch with the contractor to determine what could be done to resurface the rest room. He will check again with John when he comes back from vacation.

First Aid. Management reported that there is now a stretcher in the men's room, available for use in case it is needed.

Open House. Representatives reported considerable interest in an open house for employees' families and friends only. There was a thorough discussion of it, and the following decisions were made. The open house will be held on Sunday, January 21, from 2 to 4 P.M. One machine in each department should be running, i.e., one press, one folder, etc. If more than one is running, it would be difficult to talk above it to explain the operation. Visitors will be conducted through the plant by tour guides, and arrangements will be made to have someone in each department to give a short talk to each group on the operations and the machines, etc. This will not be open to the general public and will not be publicly advertised. It is not absolutely necessary for an employee to accompany family or friends through the plant, but representatives of the council are to report to Ed Jones the approximate number of people department employees anticipate will attend in order that plans may be made for serving refreshments in the lunch room at the conclusion of the tours.

Rework. The question was asked whether there were any examples of rework to be presented at the meeting. Ed replied he had no good examples for this meeting.

Christmas Banquet. Ed reported that plans are in progress for the banquet.

Entrance Open. Although the suggestion was made that a notice be posted by the employees' entrance door as a reminder to all employees that it should be closed and locked at all times, discussion brought out that it is only blocked open by painters, service men, etc., who do it to keep it open while bringing in equipment. Joe Smith explained that this will happen at times and that there's little that can be done to eliminate it, but all employees should continue to be alert to see that the door is closed at all other times.

New Business

Personal Calls.   It was suggested that a pay telephone be installed in the lunch room to be used for personal calls only. In the discussion that followed, Ed Jones explained that he did not favor a pay phone, and the group discussion also indicated that this would be ineffective in controlling personal calls. This discussion included discussion of how to handle personal long-distance calls, and the conclusion reached was that these should continue to be charged to the employees' home phone number. This can easily be done. If it is not possible to do this because of no home phone number, each employee is to notify the switchboard operator that he is making a call to such and such a place on that date. This will greatly facilitate checking the phone bill each month. Checking this bill is very difficult and time-consuming, and if a personal long-distance call is necessary at night when the operator is not here, a note should be left at her desk giving the name of the calling party, place called, date, and time of call.

Calls During Coffee Breaks.   The request was made that the operator not page employees on coffee breaks for interplant calls. After discussion, it was agreed that the operator should not carry the entire burden for stopping the calls, and that a schedule of coffee breaks should be included in a revised interplant telephone directory. It was suggested this information could be included on the side of the directory where listings are by department, immediately opposite the department name. Lunch hours also vary, and these should be included. Sales Department people have already been canvassed and the operator advised as to whether they wish to be paged for customer calls during coffee breaks and lunch hours.

Profit on Ship Flat Jobs.   The question was raised as to whether we make as much profit on a ship flat job as those we handle through completion of binding operations. Ed explained that we prefer working the whole job, but that some customers, especially New York publishers, do request that we ship flat on some things. These usually go to a New York bindery where only part of the printing is bound, and the New York bindery stores the balance of the printing flat until a later date. Storage of flat sheets would present a real problem to us. He also explained that it is jobs like this, and jobs for some customers with negatives furnished, that make it difficult to keep the work load equal in all departments. On occasion it just isn't possible to control the work load because of these, although we try to be careful and through the possible controls maintain a reasonably even work load in all departments. Ed further explained that the only way in which the ship flat jobs or negatives furnished jobs affect profits is that because we do not do some operations no profit is realized on those operations. If we did the work, our profits would be increased somewhat, of course.

Schedule of Council Meetings.   Discussion brought out that the present schedule of one meeting per month, the third Tuesday of each month, is fine except that special meetings should be called whenever the need arises between regularly scheduled meetings. One situation given as an example was regarding plans for the Christmas party and obtaining volunteers for committees. It was pointed out that some department representatives had difficulty letting everyone know that volunteers were needed because they had to contact them personally and did not have time to do it. It was felt a special meeting would have resulted in discussion, and the minutes would have carried this message to everyone so all employees would be given a chance to serve on a committee, if they wanted to. The present schedule of council meetings, with special meetings called when required, will be continued.

The next council meeting will be held on Tuesday, December 19, at 10:00 A.M.

CASE DISCUSSION QUESTIONS

The Co-worker Council Case

1. You have been asked by Sam Reese, your boss, to prepare a recommendation to Mr. Smedley. What do you think the report should say?

2. What are the objectives of the company? Smedley? The management groups? The workers?

3. How could all of them be achieved?

13 Action Training Techniques

All the world's a stage
—SHAKESPEARE

DURING the twenty-odd years since the end of World War II, the race has been on to discover new and novel techniques of teaching managers and employees. Conference and discussion methods were probably the first breakthrough from straight lectures—or even worse, papers read by executives. The trend was undoubtedly needed and may well have prevented training from being inundated under a great wave of boredom. Whatever else might be said about special methods of presentation that are akin to the theater, unless the class is willing to stay through the whole session and pay reasonable attention to the proceedings in the room, the chances of effecting any behavior change are diminished.

Despite the ever-present possibility that training can become a form of managerial entertainment on the company premises, there are volumes to be spoken in favor of such devices for presenting instruction as role play, management games, incident processes, and the like. The major virtue can be summarized in the common element that runs through all of them. The unifying thread in all of them is that they require some simulated behavior on the part of the trainee and that they afford him some feedback on the effects of that behavior from both the trainer and his peers.

In this chapter we shall move from the behavioral objectives uncovered in the task analysis and scrutinize the optional kinds of training that might affect job behavior through a planned effort.

What Is Action Training?

To make action training effective there are certain essential ingredients in the training session itself. This may be in a class, or it might just as well be in a coaching session between a single trainer and single trainee. The key ingredients are the following:

1. The desired terminal behavior of the trainee has been specifically defined.
2. His present level of behavior and performance are specified.
3. Through task analysis the specific behavior changes needed have been clearly defined.
4. During the training session he engages in some *action* such as talking, writing, walking, conferring, and the like.
5. The action that he engages in *simulates* the behavior sought back on the job.
6. The course of change in behavior is comprised of some orderly progression of small steps.
7. At each stage of training he obtains feedback that makes it known to him whether his action is successful or unsuccessful.
8. The learning is under the control of the instructor.
9. A summary evaluation, measuring actual outcome with stated objectives, is possible.

The forms that action training take include most of the major innovations in training such as role play, certain uses of case studies, management games, incident process, in-basket, as well as practice sessions and workshops. The range of these applications is wide and grows steadily.

If you understand the basics of action training, development of new forms to fit the training need is easily done.

The essentials of action training are illustrated in Fig. 13–1 and show the time stages and the important ingredients of the flow in which the training is presented to the trainee. This is not necessarily the way in which the trainer plans his action training, however. The first step is identifying the terminal behavior sought, although it appears as the final outcome on the action training diagram in Fig. 13–1.

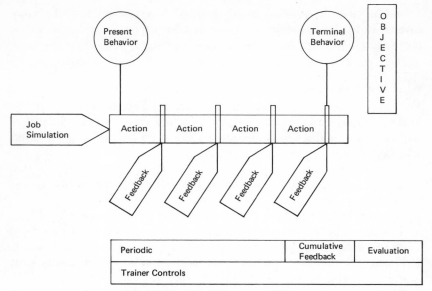

FIGURE 13-1 Model for Action Training

The Forms of Action Training

The specific forms of action training break down into different kinds of simulation. The common element is that all of them simulate the situation in which the trainee must operate in the real world and require him to behave in a way that he might behave back in that environment if he were to apply the new behavioral skills desired.

Simulation does not necessarily mean faithful, complete, and accurate reproduction of all details of the job. Completeness of simulation could be achieved only by taking the man right back to the department, the people, the machines, the problems, and the pressures of the real job. Adding to details does not necessarily add to the certainty of behavior change. Plausible resemblance in important details is more desirable than exhaustive attention to little detailed touches. The overdoing of reality usually leads only to "cuteness" in the exercises.

These things become clearer as we look at some examples that illustrate the alternative methods of action training that are often used. These methods, all simulation of life, include:

1. Role playing.
2. Case studies (with variation).
3. Management games.
4. Demonstrations.

Sticking with these four main families of action training methods permits us to use variations of them in profusion and to master a few key tools rather than becoming overinvolved in making choices among too many specific techniques. Let us study each in some detail in this chapter and in Chapters 14–16.

Role Playing in Action Training

Perhaps the form of action training that offers the quickest and surest achievement of behavior change is that of role play. Shakespeare said "All the world's a stage" and people respond quickly to the theme that they are acting out roles in this world and on their jobs. Permitting them to play a role in a relatively safe environment, the training session permits the person to receive feedback during his action and immediately afterward. It can be controlled by the director or trainer, and research evidence by Norman R. F. Maier has shown that behavior change does occur through the use of this method. What are the most useful variations of this method?

TESTING AN ACTION SOLUTION

The easiest form of role play to introduce and direct is that which grows out of a discussion of a problem or case that has been presented to the group. In all forms of role playing, somebody—either the instructor or the group—presents some situation or problem to the group and asks that people think about solutions and choose one.

Let us assume that the purpose of the session is to obtain uniform and more widespread use of a company disciplinary procedure. The procedure is a four-step procedure that moves progressively through warning, reprimand, temporary layoff, and finally discharge. The list of punishable offenses has been distributed to the class for reading and might also have been discussed, described, and explained by the instructor. He now presents the group of trainees with a situation:

You are a supervisor in a production department. You have just walked into the department and have observed an old experienced worker operating a grinder without goggles. A large sign, "Don't Grind Without Goggles," is directly in front of the machine where the man cannot miss it. What do you do?

The group then offers individual suggestions:

1. "Warn him."
2. "Fire him."
3. "Is he a union member?"

At this stage we have the stage set for some action. As a starter you might pick one man whose suggestion seems to be closest to the kind of behavior the course proposes should be taken at this point. You turn to him and ask "How might you go about warning the man? What would you actually say to him? How would you say it? Are there any limitations on your techniques? What general guidelines would you give a supervisor as he was about to engage in such a discussion with this worker?"

As the man responds, he mentally runs through some of the possible actions that he might take in this circumstance. He is then probably "warmed up" to enter role playing.

Here the director (instructor) may request him to show the group what he means. "Let's see how that would really look. C'mon up here and we'll try that out in a demonstration." At this stage he takes the emphasis and attention from the role player and turns the attention of the group back to itself.

"Now all of you people take a minute and list some of the specific steps you think Harry should take in handling this step-one case of discipline." The group works on this list and the instructor sets up a prop, perhaps using a sign prepared in advance that gives the safety instructions. He places the simulated supervisor at one side and invites another member of the group to stand by the grinder and grind without goggles.

Inviting the group's attention to the scene, the director now starts the action with some kind of introductory remark.

Okay folks, we have Bill the worker grinding away without goggles. Harry, the supervisor, is just about to walk into the department, and we'll see what happens. Ready Harry? OK. walk in.

An emphatic word or two at the end of the warm-up and instruction triggers the action and lets the role players know that they are on their own. This action prompt could be a verbal nudge to do the first thing that would get the role play under way. For a man entering his boss's office it might be a question pattern as follows:

(To the boss): "Mr. Smith, are you ready to see Jim now?"
(To Jim): "Jim, are you ready to go into the boss's office?"
"Okay Jim, Mr. Smith can see you now."

The director then fades away into the wings (one side of the room), observes, quiets the group through waving his hand to quiet them or stopping nervous wisecracks, and concentrates pointedly on watching the action. The group will very quickly do likewise. In the event of a first-time role play it might be advisable to suggest that the group remain absolutely quiet and observe during the action.

Role-Play Observer's Worksheet

Stages of Discipline	*Kind of Action Called for*
1. Warning	Get the man's attention.
	Have him stop the wrong behavior.
	Ask him why he is violating rules.
	Explain the reason for the rules.
	Instruct him in the proper way.
	State the warning and tell of subsequent steps.
	Break off the discussion.

FIGURE 13–2

As is outlined in Fig. 13–2, the trainer-director cannot use this kind of role play effectively without some kind of plan of the behavior changes desired. He might even have reproduced these guides and passed them out to the group to use as a checklist as they observe the action between the supervisor and the offending employee. At the point at which the action seems to have reached a logical conclusion, for example, the supervisor has broken contact or the discussion has deteriorated in a hassle and no further progress seems likely, the director moves back in from the wings and cuts the action. Keeping the players in their front positions he then turns to the group: "Let's cut it right here folks and discuss this action."

He might then ask the players how they would evaluate the effectiveness of the actions taken. Would the supervisor do it differently if he could do it all over from the start? Ask the worker how he feels about the way he was treated. Was the management of the situation fair? Has he learned anything? Does he have anything on his mind that he would like to have said but was unable to during the disciplinary interview?

Turning to the group, the director then asks their evaluation and comments on the supervisor's actions in the skit. Were there any essential things omitted? Were there some opportunities for extra benefits that he might have obtained? Were there any things he did that he should have avoided? During the discussion the players resume their seats in the group in order to avoid putting them on the pan too conspicuously. A summary of the action and the discussion can then follow, but it should be brief and cover only major essentials. When the players have been seated and the discussion completed, some directors have found it a good practice in encouraging future participation to enter a caveat for the players. "Of course these fellows were just role playing and perhaps we should given them some applause for their acting."

Let us recap this illustrative session. There are some terms we used that indicate the make-up for such practice sessions:

Director. The trainer becomes a director of a play.
Role. A part played by a member of the group.
Scene. Physical settings, signs, properties, environment.
Situation. The case, the problem, or the facts presented by the director.
Observers. The members of the group become observers and later feedback their observations. The feedback may be the use of a prepared guide, or it may be drawn directly from the experience and opinions of the group.

The time for conducting the preceding session will be about 30 minutes from warm-up to end of evaluation. In more complicated kinds of teaching it may run longer, but usually short specific steps are more effective.

At this point the instructor might move to the next stage of discipline, discuss the differences between the warning and the reprimand, and repeat the process. At each stage he should be constantly keeping his objective in mind and doing an assessment of the effective behavior change that he sees being demonstrated and discussed.

When problems occur, the director may take appropriate action to get the session back on the learning track. When one of the players misplays his role badly or fails to play it at all, he may let it run until such time as this is obvious and then cut and ask the group their opinion of how realistically the roles were played.

If an occasional clown engages in an elephantine burlesque, the instructor may ask the group to comment on reality or may simply tell the man "quit clowning" or "don't play to the audience and observers, play to the boss." The tendency to play to the observers can be curbed if the observers are briefed in advance not to talk or engage in banter with the players. It can also be avoided by not choosing known clowns to play a role in an early session.

This is but one example of role play, and it happens to fit the training objective. Other forms may be used.

OBJECTIVE DETERMINES TECHNIQUE

The choice of role-playing technique is not a function of what the director feels would be most entertaining but the behavior change he seeks to bring about. The preceding simple example is easy to use, and for a starter the use of an easy to apply method is sensible. After the group has become accustomed to role playing and has seen its values, more complex forms can be used.

Table I shows some of the common forms of individual, dual, and group situations in which role playing might be used. The definitions and parts played by all remain the same: the director, the protagonist, the scene, and the like.

Table I. Some Examples of Behavior Changes Sought and the Variations of Role Play Possible to Affect Them

Behavior Sought	
How to lead problem-solving conferences	Use a small group of members and assign roles to each that describe their position to themselves. Have one man be the leader and conduct the conference. Arm the observers with criteria sheets to note actual and ideal behavior.
How to get competing groups to cooperate	Prepare role sheets for several people, with built-in differences in interests. Present a specific problem and have the boss lead a conference aimed at resolving it. Use the group as observers.
	Assign dual roles to every member of the group. Divide the room into two halves, with one half holding one role assignment and the other half assuming the other role. Let them speak as they see a point to be made.
Interviewing skills	Work out your definitions of what effective interviewing behavior consists of for various situations. Present the situation and have two people enact the respective roles. Use the group as observers.
Persuading others	Give one participant a position in which he is to persuade others, assign roles to the group to be persuaded, and brief the observers.

ROLE REVERSAL

Occasionally during role play an individual takes a strong position on an issue and gets very emotional in his expressions. This may produce a counterreaction on the part of his antagonist. When this has occurred and is at a rather heated stage, the director may *cut*, and after a few words of transition may ask the participants to switch roles. The boss moves physically around the desk and takes the seat and the role of the subordinate. The subordinate moves behind the desk and assumes the boss's role. As a warm-up the director might then prime each participant: "Now you are the boss. Remember, you have just charged into him pretty hard and you know he's pretty mad. Think of what you are going to say next." Do the same for the reversed subordinate. Then start the action again. The effect of this reversal is often enlightening to the participants. As one described it: "When I moved around the desk and took the subordinate's part and got going with his viewpoint I could actually *feel* physically the difference in role positions." In any event, his verbal behavior is now governed by an ability to verbalize both sides of the disputes and a tempering of behavior that is all one-sided.

VICARIOUS EXPERIENCE

The director may be able to give the role-players simulations of experiences that the group would never have had the opportunity to experience without great risks of failure in real life. This is used with children who are about to enter the hospital. The father becomes the anesthetist, the mother the nurse, and the physical setting one that roughly resembles a hospital room. By role-playing the environment and happenings of a hospital, the fear of the unknown can be removed. A trip on an airplane can have its unknown aspects removed by having mother become the stewardess, father the pilot, and brother another passenger. Ticket arrangements, baggage checking, luncheon serving, seat belt fastening, and other unexperienced events can be simulated and become familiar.

This has numerous values in shaping behavior. Executives who will be visiting college campuses for recruiting students may find it invaluable to run through a couple of interviews with some recent graduates on the payroll, under the scrutiny of the group and the director and with the feedback of the students themselves. This can save costly and embarrassing errors on campus.

Role-playing collective-bargaining sessions with simulated union officers, played by persons who actually know the personalities and language of the union can accelerate the learning rate of persons about to join the bargaining team. It can also aid the experienced bargainers to foresee some of the kinds of obstacles they might run into in this year's bargaining session.

Teaching sales techniques to new employees or upgrading the repertory of sales techniques of experienced sales personnel can be done very effectively with vicarious experience that duplicates the real world and that has a pattern of behavior in mind that is preferred.

In practice, the use of role playing has suffered in the hands of trainers who have fallen into one of the following traps in the use of this method:

1. They have been hesitant to try it at all for fear of failure, and when they did, it reflected their hesitancy and was shallow, trivial, or meaningless. Be bold in directing it.
2. They did not have a specific definition of behaviors to be taught. As one training staffer confided to me, "I like role playing; you don't need to work up lesson plans and outlines." The result was an entertainment session without accomplishment of any planned behavior change.
3. The hard lesson here is that if you want to teach decision-making methods using role playing you must have a pattern of decision making in mind to teach. If you want to teach participative management methods, you must have an idea of what a supervisor *does* when he is managing participatively. If you cannot discern what that behavior looks like, you may end up in the next major pitfall in role playing.
4. Role playing as a means of selling a general proposition more often than not will merely confuse people. It is true that in amending or adding to behavioral skills you will often change attitudes, but the reverse is less likely. You probably will have little effect on behavior if you attempt to change a general attitude through role playing.

ADVANCED AND SPECIAL KINDS OF ROLE PLAY

As a working kind of training instrument the role play of the structured and planned types for individuals and groups that we have described will cover a majority of behavior change situations. Others that are available in various forms include the following.

Doubling. In this the role playing begins as described for two individuals, but by prior instruction an empty chair is left behind each of the protagonists. The observers are instructed that "any time you see one of the individuals taking a position that you feel doesn't represent a normal or completely authentic stance, you may become his alter ego, sort of an inner man or conscience, and join him. At this point you speak asides which reflect what he might really be thinking. This can be illustrated, as in Fig. 13–3.

What the protagonists say:	"Naturally I want to be fair to you."	"Yes sir, and I know you will."
The double's sotto voce:	"I'd like to break your stupid neck."	"In a pig's neck he wants to be fair."

FIGURE 13–3   Typical Verbal Expression by Role-Players Using Doubling Technique

After an experienced group gets warmed up to this technique they may triple and quadruple in a heated debate akin to the group role play. Behavior changes sought in this method include such skills as persistence in interviewing and counseling to be certain that verbal responses reflect the actual thinking of others. It serves to obtain complete information, or to uncover authentic responses to inquiries, and obtain authentic statements from persons.

Mirroring. Another variation of role playing that can be used is to arrange four persons to play two roles. The selection of protagonists or players calls for two persons for each role. Their instructions might be something like the following. Jim Johnson has been passed over for promotion and resents it deeply. He has more seniority and feels that he was better qualified than George Jones, who got the job. The boss, however, made the decision based on the fact that, of the two, George seemed to have more potential. He goes to evening school and studies data processing. Jim goes bowling and enjoys himself. Over time George will probably prove best even though they both do a good job now.

Some sample dialogue might go as follows:

Boss: Come in, Jim. You wanted to see me.
JIM: Yes sir, if you have a few minutes.
Boss: Certainly. What can I do for you?
JIM'S MIRROR: What he means is how can I do it to you!
JIM: Sir, I'd like to talk to you about my future here.
BOSS' MIRROR: What he means is he wants to squawk about getting passed over.
Boss: I'm happy to talk to you about that, Jim. Do you have anything specific you'd like to talk about?

JIM'S MIRROR: What he means is that he knows darn well that I'm sore about being gypped out of that new job.

JIM: Yessir. I was wondering why I wasn't considered for the new position that went to George.

Reading this carefully can give you the flavor of the dialogue. The boss hears two things in response to his question. He hears the formal surface response that the man makes, and he also hears the mental interpretation (or hears mirrored), his words reflected back to him from a mirror. The mirror may be clear and in agreement with the surface words, or it may distort and elongate or shorten the message the way a mirror in a fun house does. Both of these are a form of verbal behavior, one oral and the other silent but both expressible in words. In ordinary conversation only one of these verbalizations is available to the other party.

Through practice in role playing it may be possible to have both mirror and surface words coincide. The question that the trainer attempts to answer for the trainees in behavioral terms is the following:

What is needed in my verbal behavior to elicit verbal behavior, from both the other person and his mirror, that is reasonably consistent and acceptable to both of us?

VITAL IMPORTANCE OF FEEDBACK

At the end of the session where mirroring, doubling, or another variation of role playing is used, it is important that feedback relevant to the objectives be presented to the players and the observers. The observers are armed with observation guides, perhaps in outline form, or they ask questions of the director.

Without feedback, role playing becomes amusement. It is at the feedback and only there that the learning and behavior change will be effected. All else is designed to lead to this teaching point.

THE TRADE-OFF CASE

When Cosmic Container built their new plant it was greeted with enthusiasm by most employees. The old plant, built in 1898, had been crowded, dirty, and poorly laid out. One exception to the enthusiasm was Henry. Henry operated a great machine on the west side of the new building. In the afternoon the sun poured through the glass wall, and the temperature rose to about 100°. Despite complaints and requests for a shade, the boss stated, "Can't do it Henry. If we get one for your window, we'll have to get them for everyone. It would be costly and would make our new building look odd." Shortly after that the machine broke down for a week. Henry told his boss, "I knew that was going to happen. It's been acting funny." The boss was furious. "Why didn't you tell somebody?" he shouted. "Well, chief, I told 'em about the shades and they didn't do anything. I figured they wouldn't do anything about the machine either."

1. If you were boss, what would you do?

2. What would you avoid? Why?

THE NAMES AND NUMBERS CASE

Louis has been timekeeper for many years and was a veritable fountainhead of information about employees and their job, pay, seniority, and similar matters. There was one requirement, however: to get information you had to give the employee's number. "I can't go by name alone," Lou explained. "You may ask me about Jim Smith, and I give you an answer but about the wrong Jim Smith. If you give me a number I can't be wrong." One day Earl Alfred, foreman, wanted to check an hourly rate on an employee named Gregorian Kanagiopopolous. "What's his number?" replied Lou. "How the hell would I know? How many guys could there be with that name?" Louis shrugged, "No number, no info."

1. What is the problem here?

2. You are the boss. What should you do?

THE TOM AND THE PRESIDENT CASE

Tom Plank was a junior staff member at the Tri City Employees Council. He was a bachelor and very popular. The single girls in the office were all very attentive to him but he never showed any special attention to any or asked for dates. One day a new girl was hired and Tom was immediately interested and without any particular fanfare was soon taking her on dates. As far as they knew nobody had seen them, although they made no effort to conceal their dates. One day Tom's boss resigned and Tom was called into the president's office. "Tom," he said, "we're promoting you to office manager. This is a big step but I'm sure you can handle it. Oh yes, by the way, most of the girls in the office will now be under your supervision. As a friendly suggestion you'll probably find fewer complications if you make it a personal policy never to date any of the girls who work for you."

1. What should Tom say?

2. What should he do?

3. Are there any courses of action he should avoid?

THE LOVE THOSE WORKERS CASE

Adolf was noted as an autocratic and dictatorial manager. His foundries were run by tight engineering and tight discipline, from top to bottom. One day Adolf attended a conference and was exposed to some thought provoking ideas on management styles. In a discussion with one of the speakers, a professor, he showed interest and called for further information. The two made a date and Adolf invited the professor out to his plant. Over the next year the two conferred often. Adolf began to change his pattern of relating to subordinates. He asked their views on methods and listened better. He became more tolerant of error. Many of his managers were puzzled, a few were suspicious, and many were made tense and anxious by his new behavior. This anxiety increased when Adolf started urging them to be more participative with the workers. "That professor is going to screw this place up for sure," one of the old-line foremen predicted at the lunch table.

1. What is the major problem here?

2. What should Adolf do?

3. What advice could the professor give Adolf?

THE NEW SECRETARY CASE

Jack Jones was president of the Elm City Chamber of Commerce. A noted conservative, he was shocked one day when the executive secretary reported that he had hired a new secretary. "She's educated, skilled, personable, attractive—and a Negro." Jack, a local merchant who held the elected office of president but did not work full time in chamber management, was furious. "You'll have to fire her. You've made a policy decision without checking with the board and could offend half our members. Rig some charges and unload her fast." Jack was taken aback by the furious reaction. "You'll recall that I'm empowered to staff the office," the executive secretary said, flushing in chagrin. "You idiot," Jack responded, "that doesn't mean you can drive away members. I say fire her now before the news get out."

1. What are some alternatives for the executive secretary?

2. Which one should he choose? Why?

THE CHEATING BARTENDER CASE

An exclusive club had several slot machines in its bar, which were very profitable to the club. In fact, they almost balanced the budget. They were illegal, but the district attorney, who was a member, carefully avoided entering the bar where they were located and studiously arranged never to see them. "If they were invited to my attention, then I would be obliged to confiscate them." One day it was learned that a bartender had been systematically stealing petty cash from the bar receipts. Called before the board, he readily admitted it. "Remember this, if you push me I'll squeal about your slot machines and you'll lose plenty. I don't steal nearly as much as you'd lose by having your machines confiscated. Push me and I'll complain."

1. What are some alternatives for the committee?

2. Which one is best? Why?

THE DIFFERENT KIND OF GIRL CASE

In an eastern trucking firm (unionized) the warehouse manager was faced with expansion. His work force of three middle-aged ladies was overworked. He interviewed several and chose a competent, nice-appearing girl of good skills. All went well for awhile. One day the original three ladies came into his office with a request: "We don't think young Miss Smith should be retained. She is no lady." "Why, what has happened?" asked the manager. "She is running around with a married man, a truck driver. We don't like those kinds of women. Also she talks about it openly." The manager promised to investigate and called the young lady in. She admitted the relationship candidly. "My work has been satisfactory, hasn't it?" The manager agreed that it had indeed. "Then what I do on my personal time is really my private concern!"

1. Would you fire the young lady?

2. What would you do about the truck driver?

3. What are the options facing you? Which one would be best?

CASE DISCUSSION QUESTIONS
Seven Cases

1. Working in small groups, take a separate case from among the seven presented.

2. Answer the questions in the form of action, using an action training method such as role play, game, etc.

3. Critique for the other groups' presentations.

14 The Case Study and Its Variations

The rate of progress is such that an individual human being of ordinary length of life will be called upon to face novel situations which find no parallel in his past.
—A. N. WHITEHEAD

MANY of the training objectives of the management trainer that are sought by the role-play method can also be achieved by the case study and its variations. The emphasis in the case study is on presentation of facts or narrative summaries of situations that have actually occurred in business, government, or institutions. The situation is presented without interpretation, usually from the viewpoint of one observer, and may include statements by principal figures, organization charts, financial statements, copies or abstracts of reports, or simply verbal description of the situation in as many particulars as the case writer chooses to include.

Uses of Case Studies

Used extensively in university schools of business, the case method is used in a range of ways—incorporated with lectures, used to teach decision making and problem solving, in small group discussion prior to class reporting, and through the flow of feedback in case-reporting classes.

INCORPORATED WITH LECTURES

Some instructors require that a case be read in order that his lectures have as a base point certain real-life experiences or situations that flesh out the theories he presents to his class. In the instance of undergraduates, or graduate students without business experience, this contact with real-world problems by the vicarious route of the case study lends an air of plausibility and clinical reality to what might otherwise be a purely theoretical lecture, with perhaps instruction of examples and facts as part of the lecture. In such applications it is the instructor who does the interpretation. The student treats the case in the same way he would any other reading assignment. He may be asked to remember certain salient facts and report on them in class.

He may be asked to interpret the readings in the text in terms of some part of the case. "Mr. Jones, how would the application of Professor Likert's linking pin theory be applied to the style of management used by Bob Knowlton in managing the photon correlator research group." Obviously if this fellow has not read his chapter in Likert and the Bob Knowlton case, he is in the soup and gets a low grade on his recitation.

The end effect here is that the student memorizes the case, which gives him some memories of business situations, which fills a gap in his background in lieu of real-life experience. Presumably when he has read enough cases and memorized their details, he has built up the equivalent of a long business career in a variety of industries, firms, and times.

For totally inexperienced youngsters there may be some merits in this, although there is always the danger that they may interpret the practices in the case as examples of good or bad practice, and thus carry with them to their first job all the errors made in numerous companies instead of learning to make their own mistakes.

The feedback in this kind of case utilization is the final examinations, quizzes, and term papers that are part of the apparatus of academic grading plans.

TO TEACH DECISION MAKING AND PROBLEM SOLVING

The more common use of the case study in management training and in graduate schools of business is to teach the skills of decision making and problem solving in business. In early uses, especially at Harvard, the instructor did not lay out a model for decision making or problem solving for the class to follow but let the group struggle with the raw facts and figure out through painful discussion and interchange with the professor and each other the best way of coping with the case.

Presumably there is a model of decision-making behavior that the trainer wishes to see used by the members of the class, and in industrial management training the greatest likelihood of bringing out behavior change is to know what behavior change you wish to bring about. To take a typical pattern of decision-making behavior sought, the instructor might wish to have them follow a pattern as follows:

1. Master the available facts.
2. Define the objectives you would like to see achieved.
3. Specify the problem and some probable causes.
4. Lay out alternative solution courses.
5. Screen these alternatives through your criteria.
6. Select the one that seems to be most suitable in terms of the criteria that you have chosen.
7. Define some controls needed to make the action effective.
8. Where action involves interpersonal relations, role-play the action to test its effectiveness and find limiting conditions on it.

For some unaccountable reason, many users of the case method shun the definition of behavior change sought by using cases, and as a result one of the purposes of training, changing behavior, never occurs because the group is unclear on what is sought of them. Like the students in college they receive vicarious experience in many firms and situations, but they usually remember less because they customarily do not have the added incentive of a grade to force them to read the case.

The Use of Small-Group Discussion Prior to Class Reporting

The distinction between the college class and the executive development program use of cases at Harvard and elsewhere now ordinarily is found in the use of small discussion groups to preheat and intensively work over the facts of the case prior to a larger class recitation. The procedure used is to assign the case for reading, with instructions being centered around questions that would require the use of a scientific decision-making system. The groups conduct their own sessions without the direction of the instructor, using members as leaders and recorders and involving widespread participation of all the members, which is facilitated by the small size of the group.

When the entire group gathers with the instructor, each reports on its discussion or responds to questions and queries from the instructor and from the other groups. To treat this method behaviorally means that the instructor has in mind some behavior that he hopes will be forthcoming as a result of having studied and discussed the case. Let us assume that the instructor is conducting the first case session and has led the group through their first small-group discussions and is now ready to hear the results of this effort:

1. He has as his objective the achievement of behavior that he defines as "when confronted with a strange case, the first step is to obtain a complete mastery of the facts at hand and do an analysis of all of the relevant facts."
2. In his reporting session he calls for facts in the case. When hunches, opinions, problems, conclusions, or solutions are offered instead of facts, he pointedly asks, "Is that a fact?" His feedback is one of teaching discrimination between facts and other things that are non-facts. As a result of this feedback, the group is now able to make the distinction.

Fact Versus Nonfact. The group has also acquired some training that probably will result in the behavior "obtain the facts first" when dealing with cases. The hope here is that the behavior exhibited that was successful in the case studies will be carried back to the real-life job where the case-minded person will treat real-life cases in the same way he treated the vicarious ones. This teaching objective is achieved by the feedback, often of a negative or abrasive kind because the tendency of most managers is to treat cases glibly, intuitively, and unsystematically. To bring about systematic behavior you might well teach the first step in the system first. Having changed this behavior, it should appear in subsequent reporting sessions on cases, even when the training objective is somewhat more advanced: where the fact-gathering process includes such steps as working over figures for hidden conclusions that are nevertheless factual, where it requires assumptions, and where it requires putting commonly known information into use. He teaches these by the feedback process.

This means that two things are required in using the case method: (1) The instructor has an outline of the behavior changes he wishes to make, and (2) he has selected the cases because their content facilitates this kind of feedback. The cases also offer some specific possibilities, such as teaching narrower context—"Decision making in financial management"—as well as the generalized principles.

One of the more mysterious matters in the handling of case studies in management training is the inexplicable, almost mystic faith in the case itself as working a vague, intangible, beneficial effect on all those brushing its garments. As one of the purists stated it:

When you try to write out a plan or outline of what you want to teach by using cases, you destroy the pure essence of the case method itself, which is rooted in pure struggle with vague forces.

The origin of this statement is undoubtedly in its early uses at Harvard, where there was ample time to permit long stretches of frustration and "struggle" to occur before the instructor could gently steer the novice into a socratic understanding of what it was that he was supposed to learn. This, of course, does not suppose that the instructor and faculty of that institution had no ideas whatsoever about their purposes. More likely, they imposed no schoolwide pattern for decision making to be taught but left that choice to the individual instructor.

However invaluable this socratic method of defining purpose may have been for students who would work intensively at the method for two or three years continuously, it is of dubious value to the management trainer, who must make his intentions clear in the first session and go about achieving them.

The small-group discussions will inevitably become shapeless bull sessions unless they are controlled by the instructor by his directions, although not by his presence. The group is divided into small enough segments to permit free discussion and interchange, requires some practice in conference leadership by the rotation of group chairmanship, and teaches something of the group process for arriving at decisions.

THE VITAL ROLE OF FEEDBACK

The flow of the case preparation and discussion is shown in Fig. 14–1. It can be seen that the instructor has a behavior change in mind for the group that is part of a repertory of behaviors he hopes to effect in them. The case is chosen and assigned for reading by the entire group, working individuals, who subsequently meet in small groups. One of the members is a leader for that session and guides the small-group

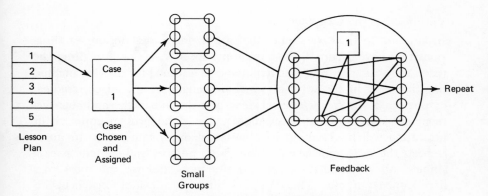

FIGURE 14–1   Flow Chart of a Case Study Session Using Study Group

discussion through its analysis and solution to the specific question assigned. The small groups then merge to form the class itself and the respective groups report their conclusions and defend them. It is at this stage that the groups obtain feedback. They get this feedback in three ways: (1) The instructor probes and questions; (2) the other groups may express doubt about, deride, or contradict the findings, conclusions, or even facts of the others; (3) the reports of other groups also

The Flow of Feedback in Case Reporting Classes

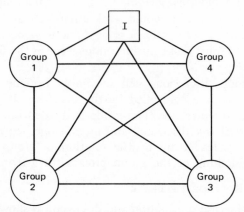

FIGURE 14–2   Flow of Feedback in Case-Reporting Classes

comprise a form of feedback, in reporting conclusions or solutions that the listening and observing groups did not find themselves. This feedback process is shown in Fig. 14–2.

Variations of the Case Method

In addition to the case studies that are narrative descriptions of situations that have occurred, there are some special ways of presenting the data in the case that meet the requirements outlined for the case method but that vary in the ways in which materials are organized, studied, or presented. These include incident process, in-baskets, and management games (or simulation exercises). The differences in approach or utilization will be discussed here, rather than its similarities. In many respects the variations have the same basic purpose and content as case studies. All are simulations of real situations and for the most part have similar purposes. The variations often permit additional behavior change objectives to be sought.

The Incident Process

Given a specific training objective, the case is presented differently by the instructor to the group. The first contact that the trainee has with the case is when the class is convened in plenary session. The instructor then opens the session by explaining the process and its purpose, which is similar to the case method. He then starts with step 1. The steps run in the following order.

Step 1. Present the Incident. The instructor reads a brief statement to the group that indicates that some critical incident has occurred. For example, he might read the following:

The quality control manager stood up and almost shouted "The hell with you and your policies. We aren't buying your shoddy quality." He stalked out of the conference room, and shortly afterward two of his associates followed.

At this stage, the instructor stops and informs the class members that he has given them all the information that he will *voluntarily* present. If they want more facts, they must ask for them by specific questions. The questions are limited to factual information. Suggested solutions, conclusions, requests for opinions, and other nonfactual data will be rejected at this stage. If the class asks questions that the instructor cannot answer, he will say, "That isn't known." If they ask questions that require extensive documentation, he may distribute supplementary exhibits, but only if the members ask for it. This exhibit material is all prepared in advance but not advertised by the instructor. Thus the first step is an exercise in asking the right question: questions that students learn to ask to elicit all the available facts that would be necessary to define the problem and solve it.

When all the available facts have been dug out by the group, or the instructor judges that the group has obtained all the information that it will probably seek (repetitious asking for the same data for example), he cuts the first step and moves to step 2, still in plenary class session.

Step 2. The class identifies "What questions must be answered here, or what problem needs solving?" The group suggests problems that need solving and questions that need answering. The instructor leads the discussion, listing the proposed problems to be solved and obtaining some kind of consensus of which ones have the highest priority. The problems may be specific and immediate such as "How to get the quality control manager cooled off" and perhaps some long-range or chronic problems that the evidence has shown to exist: "How to establish improved communication between quality and production and prevent errors from occurring." At this stage the instructor may help by defining a problem as the difference between what exists and what should be. He also leads the group into defining some objectives that would comprise solution to the problem. Having agreed on the problem to be solved, the class is now ready to proceed with step 3.

Step 3. Small-Group Problem-Solving Conferences. The group now breaks up into small groups, with a leader, a reporter, and perhaps an observer, who watches the process objectively to describe how small groups arrive at decisions. After some decisions and recommended solutions have been developed, the small groups assemble once more and the leaders or recorders report.

In some applications the small groups subsequently are asked to define the problems, breaking into small groups immediately after the fact-gathering sessions have finished.

Step 4. The small groups engage in the feedback process, defend their solutions (or problem definitions and solutions) and discuss the other groups' solutions. The observers report, their comments being designed to show how the interpersonal relations or the individual actions of group members might have affected the final solutions recommended. ("Harry conned the whole group.")

Step 5. A final best solution is sought, and a summary of the entire case is presented. ("What general conclusions could be drawn from this case?") The conclusions might be about the decision-making process itself, or they might be about a substantive area such as communications, man-boss relations, or some other management or supervisory skill.

The limitations of this method are that it requires more extensive preparation by the instructor and often the preparation of special materials. Ordinary cases can be converted into incidents in some instances. The instructor carries the burden of making step 1 work through his ability to field questions and not get cornered by his group. Commercially available materials with a complete set of instructor's guides for the incident process are available from various sources, the principal one being the Bureau of National Affairs of Washington, D.C., all written by Professor Paul Pigors, the developer of the incident process.

The In-Basket Method

Still another variation of the case method is the in-basket method of training. Also used by some firms as testing material for selection of supervisory personnel, the in-basket method is a simulation of the in-basket found on every manager's desk. The information in the case is assembled in "items" that comprise all the inputs of information. They resemble the random and unorganized memoranda, letters, brochures, and notes that might be found in the in-basket of a manager on a typical day. They are limited usually to 15 items and might include separate memoranda such as the following:

1. A letter requesting an explanation for a mistake.
2. Two phone messages, one urgent.
3. A letter from a supplier announcing a price hike.
4. A request from personnel for some personnel information on all employees.
5. A request for a donation to a local charity.
6. A confidential memorandum in an envelope marked *personal*.

The person is given a verbal statement of the situation and who he is supposed to be in the case. He might be a subordinate who has suddenly been promoted and takes over a new job. He might be a man who has come into his office and plans to work for one hour on pressing matters before taking off to an important out-of-town conference for a week. The situation is such that time pressure is important.

Each person is then assigned the task of working by himself on the simulated in-basket. Each person has the same in-basket of materials, but each works separately by himself as he might in his own office. He works over the materials, deciding what the problems are, setting priorities, and making decisions. He may defer solution, may dictate a reply, may route to others for their solution, or may make notes to himself.

Upon the termination of the one-hour work he returns to the class where the instructor conducts a discussion of how the materials were handled. There may be a discussion of how the in-basket was approached, what priorities were assigned, and how the decisions were made. Again, the instructor has a training objective in mind. For example, his first session may be designed to stress that the systematic analysis of facts is essential. If this is the case he queries the members of the class on their methods of fixing on important facts, and the group receives feedback about the propriety of its methods of handling this phase. His next session may be designed to teach problem identification. He leads the discussion through his feedback to press the group into proper systems of problem identification.

The similarities to the case method lies in the method of teaching. The differences lie in the organization of the material to simulate real-life ways of receiving information and the ways of working over the facts. Some instructors vary this method of class management by conducting study groups following the individual study of the facts. Here the small groups may seek agreement on the facts, problems, solutions, and actions taken. In those instances where action involves face to face conversations, the instructor may move into role playing. This is less suitable, however, because the in-basket method often stipulates that no contact with others is possible for the solutions.

A final variation of the case study is the management game or simulation exercise. This has several variations and will be discussed more fully in Chapter 15.

THE CARBECK DRUG COMPANY CASE

THE SITUATION

The Carbeck Drug Company is a medium-sized research and production firm located in South Orange, New Jersey. Although not large enough to compete with such firms as Upjohn, Parke-Davis, and the like, it has managed to gain a strong hold on the drug market in several specialized areas. One of these is the area of tranquilizer drugs; Carbeck's Librium has been a steady and successful seller for the past half-dozen years, though the FDA still insists that it be dispensed by prescription only.

You became president of the Carbeck Company in 1959; prior to that you headed up the company's Drug Research Division for seven years. During that period you were given two one-year leaves by the company for study in business management, marketing, and public relations. You took both these leaves at the Wharton School, where you received an M.B.A. at the end of the second year. You also have a Ph.D. in biochemistry and have done extensive research in cytology and protein chemistry.

When you assumed the presidency in 1959, one of your first moves was to persuade the board to create a new position in the company structure: Director of Personnel Relations. The title actually was somewhat ambiguous and partially a misnomer. What you wanted was a high-level position to give you a good right-hand man, more experienced than you were in various aspects of business management. Despite your work at Wharton, you felt closer to the laboratory than to the desk.

Your choice for Director of Personnel Relations was Mr. John Mecawber, an acquaintance you had made during your second year at Wharton. Mecawber was 41 years old and had worked in advertising (where he managed several national drug accounts) and later in the personnel department of the national headquarters of the Rexall Drug Company. He was a businessman, not a scientist, and that is what you wanted for this position.

Other men immediately concerned with this case are

1. *James Lydgate,* age 48, current director of the Drug Research Division, your old position. You are responsible for putting him in this position; you have no doubts about his ability as a research scientist, and his performance in an administrative position for the past three years has dispelled most of your doubts about his capacities in this area too. You have left him with much of the responsibility involved in the hiring and firing of laboratory personnel, asking him only to consult with you on

any major decision. To define Lydgate's work with respect to that of Mecawber, you have told the latter to attend primarily to personnel relations *within* the company, leaving the hiring and firing to Lydgate.

2. *Richard Kaminsky,* special assistant to the president, age 39. Kaminsky also has a Ph.D. in biochemistry, though he has spent considerably less time in the laboratory than you have. As your special assistant, you have used him primarily as a liaison with the AMA and the FDA in Washington. Thus his position is that of a scientifically informed public relations man.

THE IMMEDIATE SITUATION

In early June 1963 you took a week away from the office to attend an association conference of executives in the drug industry in Kalamazoo, Michigan, hosted by the Upjohn Company. When you returned, you found the accompanying materials in the in-basket on your desk, not including the organizational chart (Fig. 14–3). You are Ladislaw.

1. What are the major problems here?

2. What solutions do you propose? Immediate? Long run?

Item 1

Memo:
To: Will Ladislaw
From: Kaminsky

While I was in the FDA offices in Washington last week, I happened to discover that Barbour Company has just about got the go-ahead on a DNA-

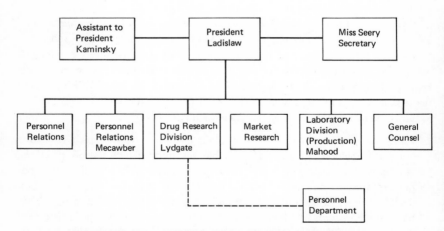

FIGURE 14–3   The Carbeck Drug Company Organizational Structure

compound tranquilizer that may well shoot the whole market. Apparently they've been working along almost the same lines as we have for the last three years, but with more success. This DNA compound was first developed in Sweden about five years ago and has been marketed there on an untested basis. Barbour, and especially a chap named Gerald Schenck, has been working on a refining and testing process for the drug in this country. Schenck is their production hope.

This may not break for awhile, but you'll probably want to act on the possibility when you get back. I'll be in on the 10th to discuss it further with you.

Item 2

Memo:
To: Will
From: Mecawber

I've just seen Kaminsky's memo to you on the Barbour-Schenck work on the DNA compound. Dammit, I should have thought of this sooner. Schenck lives down the street from us over in Ridgewood, and I happen to know that he's not too happy with his working situation at Barbour. He's talked to me a little about the DNA work he's been doing, though I don't understand him three quarters of the time. I do know that he's half on the look-out for a new position, with more freedom and less pressure.

In your absence I'm taking it on myself to talk with him. If he were to come with us over here at Carbeck, the DNA work would come with him. We might not be able to beat Barbour, but we'd get an even start!

Item 3

The Carbeck Drug Company
567 Harrelson Street
East Orange, New Jersey
June 4, 1963

Mr. Gerald Schenck
The Barbour Company
12 Princeton Street
Rahway, New Jersey
Dear Gerry:

I've tried to get you on the phone all morning. First you were busy, and then your secretary (or whoever she is) told me you'd be out until Wednesday afternoon. This will be waiting for you when you get back.

Would it be possible to have lunch with you Thursday? On me! I remember several weeks ago you told me you had half an eye out for another company and another job, and we just might have the spot for you over here.

I didn't realize how similar our DNA work was to that of Barbour's. You could give us a real lift.

Give me a ring when you get in.

Best,
John Mecawber

Item 4

June 5, 1963

Memo:
To: Will Ladislaw
From: Mecawber

Lunch with Schenck all set up. I've decided to give him the straight pitch, though, of course, no decision can be made until you return. He called this afternoon and sounded interested.

Kaminsky says that if we got Schenck we'd literally lurch ahead in the DNA work. Apparently his name is all over the FDA. He's been down there several times to discuss his DNA work with the board; they're going over his tests now.

I leave you these memos to give you a blow-by-blow account of what's going on.

Item 5

June 5, 1963

Memo:
To: Mr. Ladislaw
From: Miss Seery

Mr. Kaminsky called from Washington this afternoon. He wanted you to know that the FDA has delayed the Barbour Company on the DNA tranquilizer for at least two months. Dr. Kelly is going to Sweden to check the results over there, where some basically similar product has been on the market for several years.

It strikes me that Mr. Kaminsky and Mr. Mecawber are doing a lot of pretty hurried chasing about on this thing. What's going on anyway? Isn't our research up to par?

Item 6

June 5, 1963

Memo:
To: Will Ladislaw
From: Jim Lydgate

I've just talked with Mecawber, and he says you're planning to hire Gerald Schenck to head up a DNA section of the Lab Division. I thought Mecawber was supposed to take care of personnel *inside* the company. I've been looking around for a good DNA man myself. Mecawber won't tell me a thing. It strikes me that I'm in a much better position to judge who's to be hired in the lab. And what are we going to do about John Mahood if we hire Schenck? We can't have two men running the division. In my mind Mahood has been doing a damn good job. He just isn't getting any breaks. Our other lines will suffer if we lose him, and he insists that any new production must come under his direction.

Item 7

June 6, 1963

Memo:
To: Will Ladislaw
From: Mecawber

A good lunch with Schenck. He's definitely interested. I had to work up to it very slowly, but when I got to it, he bit like a lunker. Barbour has, apparently, been climbing all over him. Says they're making him a nervous wreck; he likes to work at a nominal, intelligent pace—none of this break-neck stuff. He insists on a free hand, however, and unless he can report directly to *you* he won't come over to talk. This leaves us a problem with Mahood.

He will call and make an appointment with you himself.

Item 8

June 7, 1963

Memo:
To: Will Ladislaw
From: Jim Lydgate

I've been thinking about this Schenck business. It strikes me as little more than out-and-out raiding. I don't think Mecawber cares a hoot about Schenck personally, and I don't think we could apply any less pressure on him than Barbour is doing. All Mecawber wants is the details of Schenck's DNA work—I don't like this. We're plunging in pretty fast on the shady side.

Item 9

June 7, 1963

Memo:
To: Mr. Ladislaw
From: Miss Seery

Mr. Schenck of the Barbour Company called this morning asking for appointment. I've put him down for 10:00 A.M., Monday. He seemed quite anxious to see you.

What's going on anyway?

Item 10

                                        The Barbour Company
                                        12 Princeton Street
                                        Rahway, New Jersey
                                        June 7, 1963

Mr. William Ladislaw
The Carbeck Drug Company
567 Harrelson Street
East Orange, New Jersey
Dear Mr. Ladislaw:

It has been brought to my attention that your company has been trying to hire away Mr. Gerald Schenck from our firm.

Knowing the particulars of Mr. Schenck's work, as well as Barbour's work on the DNA tranquilizer—plus the progress we've been making with the FDA in Washington, I am not just a little disturbed by these developments. Competition can be keen just to a point; then it becomes downright vicious. You know just what I'm talking about, so I'll not go into details.

Let me just say that we are willing to more than match any offer you make to Mr. Schenck. I should like to talk with you personally at your earliest convenience.

                                        Yours truly,
                                        Douglas N. Barbour
                                        President

DNB/aa

Item 11

Note: Clipping from *Drug Industry News and Notes*

As a result of the 1962 Thalidomide scandal, research on tranquilizer drugs has tended to move underground. There is no indication that companies are slowing up their work in this area, but—for PR purposes—they are keeping pretty quiet about it. Because of this silence, competitive tension has mounted at an increasing pace, though—as facts have born out—sometimes there was absolutely nothing for the tension to mount *about*. Rumor, allegation, and hearsay have all played their part.

CASE DISCUSSION GUIDE

The Carbeck Drug Company Case

1. Read the instructions.

2. Upon direction from the instructor, treat items 1–11 as paper received in your in basket.

3. After one hour be prepared to present your analysis and defense.

15 | Management Games

Untaught we cannot look in the right direction.

—Plato

MANAGEMENT games did not originate in business at all but in the military. The war colleges of the armed forces, flight simulators for pilot-officers and combat commanders in air combat, and field maneuvers themselves are all forms of simulation that have been used by the armed services to train realistically for the actual eventuality of war. The need for this kind of training was clear in the case of combat leadership. The number of wars to be fought is unpredictable and learning by experience could be hazardous, not only to the persons involved but to the security of the nation.

The approach taken has been to establish simulated battlefield conditions to the extent possible and then to present battlefield situations that demand a behavior that actual battle will demand. The feedback is the only aspect of the battle behavior that does not reproduce the real thing. In some models of military simulation the noise levels were equal, the physical sensations were the same—shiplike motions or gravity pull in aircraft—and the presentation of information such as enemy planes, warships, and even the odors of battle were reproduced in the model simulation. Failure to behave properly, or quickly enough, or coolly as the situation demanded produced disaster in the same fashion it would in actual combat. The only difference was that a light flashed or a referee stepped in and reported your expiration to you rather than the actual event occurring.

In simulation the only aspect of reality that is not faithfully reproduced in kind is the feedback. This is the beneficial aspect of simulation from the viewpoint of the trainee; he can learn behaviors that could hurt if not performed properly while avoiding the damaging aspects of the feedback. He does not get killed or wounded, go broke, or lose his customers, job, or employees. He merely learns that these outcomes are possible if he does not behave in the specified way in the real world.

Business Simulation

Management games were first introduced by a group of researchers at the American Management Association in 1955, inspired by the example of the Naval War College, which used computers to simulate the conditions of surface and air war at sea. Franc Ricciardi, Cliff Craft, and several others developed a game to teach decision making to managers in a simulated general management position. As a first step they selected eight key decisions that general managers must make. Prices could be raised or lowered, advertising expenditures could be raised or lowered (or kept the same), production volume could be scheduled based on estimates of future sales and present inventory levels, and so on. All these decisions worked within a competitive market. If you cut your prices and your competitors did not, you were likely to gain a share of the market. If everyone increased advertising, then nobody gained a share of the market, but if one abstained, then his share fell. This series of decisions affecting inputs were then fed by punched cards into a computer. The computer was preprogrammed to execute the variables of a model of a competitive market. Five firms, all with the same rules of play, sought to maximize profit, return on investment, share of market, net worth, and other business objectives. The influences at work in the model that guided the computer simulated those that characterize the real world of market competition. If you produced more, the costs of production per unit were lower. If you produced more than you sold, your inventories rose and the cost of maintaining inventories rose. Research and development could increase your product's attractiveness and trim the costs of manufacturing. Advertising could increase your share of the market during the period in which you spent the advertising money, but it was not cumulative. Research and development expenditure was cumulative for five years. All these conditions were explained to the contestants, who knew that they—and their competitors—were operating under similar rules.

The Five Companies

The players (trainees) in the AMA game are divided into companies of five players per firm. One of them is made general manager, and other duties may be assigned to each of the other members. One may be financial manager, another sales and marketing manager, and so on. The company has its own room where the various teams gather. They are equipped with calculators, paper, pencils, and information sheets showing the financial position of the firm and its competitors in the same market at the beginning of the game. It is assumed that all have comparable or identical products, that all are competing in the same market, and that their actions will be affected by competition.

Each company will make decisions in the required decision areas for each quarter for a ten-year simulated period. That is, the first decision will be for the first quarter of the first year. These decisions are written onto a decision sheet and turned in to the instructor. The sheets are then tab-punched on cards and fed into the computer input unit along with the decision data from the other four companies. The computer memory relates the information for that company to its past data and computes the effects of that decision against the effects of the other four companies.

It should be noted that the game using the computer deals with quantitative inputs and outputs and measures the financial and physical consequences of managerial behavior. The output that comes from the computer is returned in a few minutes and the feedback—the consequences of their decisions—is given to them almost immediately. The simulation and training effect lies in the fact that the players can discover the consequences of their decisions for a whole quarter immediately after they are made. They then turn to analyzing these results and making their decisions for the next quarter.

In company Able a dispute arose among the members about the level of advertising expense. One of the members, a college faculty member, interjected a long-standing personal bias against the expenditure of advertising. The group was uncertain, except for one experienced manager of consumer goods sales, who insisted that without advertising "we're dead." The professor was adamant and persuaded a couple of others to go along for one period with greatly reduced advertising expense and to put the same amount of money into a new plant to hire more people and make jobs. Immediately the computer came back with its result. The other four companies had raised their advertising budgets to the maximum permissible limits and the share of market held by the first company dropped drastically. As a result the added plant capacity for the company proved to be a costly burden, inventory was excessively high, and the company was required to lay off help and cut back in order to find working capital to operate. During the evaluation session inside the original firm, the professor admitted his chagrin. "I think I'll stick to teaching physics," he said.

To the extent that it teaches the key decision areas and the relationship among them, the game is a form of economic education that can provide insights and behavior that might be obtained only in the market at great cost or over a long period of time.

In another game the company that always spent the maximum for advertising and cut its prices sought to gain the maximum share of the market as a steady policy. This worked well for several quarters until it discovered that in so doing it was achieving volume at the expense of profits, and some of the firms with lower dollar volume of sales were making more money profit and adding more to their net worth. The team members summarized the experience this way: "I think our sales experience led us astray and maybe we should think more about the contribution to profit which can be made by sales than simply volume alone."

Introducing Variations

By introducing changes in the program itself during the ten-year period of play, the trainer can introduce such elements as a recession, a falling share of the market, or a leveling off. Thus the companies may be required to operate under the various business conditions that are found in the real world. They may have rising markets, stable markets, declining markets, with changes unannounced and unpredictable to the players.

In the AMA game it is also possible to purchase market research information about such competitive information as the share of market held by other firms and the like. The values of this information, which is expensive, lies in the uses that the competitive firms can make of it in shaping their own decisions. As time goes on it becomes increasingly apparent that two variables are important in the team's strategy:

1. It must have some objectives and be organized to work toward them.
2. It must do a good job of estimating what the competition has chosen as its objectives and strategies for getting to them.

Although these two hard facts are explained to the teams in advance, there appears to be a tendency to shun this advice until the market itself and the quarterly result sheets reveal the importance in practice. These lessons are better learned by the feedback from the market than they are from the lecture.

Supplementary Materials

One of the frustrations of the game is that it includes so much potential for teaching appropriate behavior but that the time pressures involved will not permit the trainer an opportunity to engage in more than the essentials. A group that was to stay together a long time and that became more sophisticated in the fundamentals would undoubtedly be able to get to some of the more advanced behaviors, such as the organizational skills required for successful operation and the skills of objectives setting.

It might also provide some excellent opportunity for feedback on the functioning of small groups, of interpersonal skills, and similar behavioral skills.

Other Games Using the Computer

Since the original game developed by the American Management Association, numerous other forms of computer-centered games have been developed for such areas as inventory control, purchasing, production, sales, and other areas.

The company that wishes to use such a game may find it possible to obtain a deck of cards containing the basic program from their computer manufacturer's service department. This deck will provide the basic pattern for the company's own computer people and avert the necessity of constructing a new program especially for the using firm. Prior to directing such a game the trainer should himself have attended a course as a participant and worked with a trainer during part of that session in order to learn the requirements for administration and conduct of the game.

In-Basket Games

Games that do not require the computer have been developed as well, some of which are possible for trainers to run by reading the materials and organizing their own groups without special consultants or advisors to conduct the exercises. In some instances companies have developed their own games using cases that have been converted into games for training purposes.

ONE-PAGE INSTRUCTION SHEETS

In Norman R. F. Maier's book is a sample of the one-page instruction sheet (akin to role playing) for each of four players called the President's Decision. Each of the role-players is passed a two-page general set of instructions that explains the organization of the company and some relevant facts about what has happened in the recent past. The firm has undergone a change of management, and the new team has attempted to build up the long-run profitability of the firm through some fairly drastic changes, including heavy expenditures. Now the president has called a meeting to discuss the future.

Role In-Basket. Each of the participants in the case receives different information. The sales manager gets instructions that would entail making certain changes to strengthen his department; the plant manager gets information that proposes expanded plant capacity; the personnel vice president has expansion plans to present; and finally the president receives instructions that place him in conflict with the others. He has received orders from the board to turn the organization into a profitable one and has one year to achieve it. The roles being set in one direction and the action designated for the president being diametrically opposed to their expectations places some demands on the president's ability to lead the group and of the group to respond to changes.

Complementary In-Baskets. The President's Decision case as a model permits the application of case methods of instruction and of role playing. The case is not presented wholly in writing but is revealed during the enactment of the roles that have been assigned to the respective players. In this sense, the case is developed out of the personal interpretations and enactments of the role-players.

The demands on the instructor here lay in the uncertainty of predicting exactly what will be contained within the case, because it will be made by the players as they interpret their roles. The patterns that will emerge in the case will tend to follow a few basic ones: The president will get tough and will try to sell the group, or he will seek their involvement and support. In such an enactment the director might have some principle or "school solution" that he has in mind as terminal behavior sought.

The dangers for training purposes in such a plan is in the assumption that a certain kind of behavior is superior to other kinds. Often the trainer starts with the assumption that participative management techniques are the only acceptable behavior and intends that his instructional design and feedback will reinforce this kind of behavior. Yet the groups placing personal interpretation on the roles may enact the parts in a way that leads the president into impossible blind alleys because he followed participative management with this particular group of players. Or another possibility is that the president might behave autocratically and succeed very well. In using complementary in-baskets the instructor might construct a diagram that lists the possible outcomes of the action training. It might look something like Table I.

Table I. Possible Outcomes of Role Playing the President's Decision Case

President Plays Role of	Possible Outcome upon His Subordinates
Dominant, autocratic	They resist him vigorously. They fight a while but then give in. They accept his direction willingly.
Democratic	They flatly refuse to go along. They go along but modify his wishes. They accept his wishes and make them work.
Laissez-faire	They flatly refuse to change. They are puzzled, angry, and resist him.

If the trainer wishes to see a certain outcome, his first step is to define what the appropriate behavior might be. For example, he might define some of the following possible definitions of behavior, but if his training situation has within it the possibility of wrong behavior, he must be prepared to apply negative feedback when that behavior appears.

Yet the use of punishing or negative feedback as a training method has many limitations and deliberately designing training that makes punishing kinds of feedback necessary is not the soundest strategy, especially with managerial trainees. This is especially true if the negative feedback or punishment comes from the trainer rather than the group.

THE APEX GAME

Perhaps the most sophisticated application of in-basket games is that of the apex-type game. Developed by Charles Kepner and Benjamin Tregoe, two psychologists with the Rand Corporation, who now operate as a private firm, the game incorporates the features of games, in-baskets, and role play.

As in the computer-based games, each team forms a simulated company. Each player is passed a general set of instructions, as well as a specific in-basket of materials relevant to his assigned position, for example, general manager, sales manager, materials control manager, and so on. Simulation is enhanced by each person working in an office with a telephone connection to the other members of his team. The director has a master listening post by means of which he can monitor the calls between the respective players.

Any manager may call any other manager, exchange information, report problems, request data, or call for a conference. Through the inputs that are contained in the items in the in-basket, certain immediate problems are introduced to the teams. The production manager learns from the sales manager of customer complaints, for example. He then talks to the materials control manager and others to try to define the problem and isolate its causes. He then may recommend solutions.

Contained within the construction of the case and diffused among the in-baskets is enough information to clearly identify the key problem and to locate the only possible logical solution to it. The group may flounder while searching for the problem, may identify and solve the wrong problem, or may identify the problem but attribute it to the wrong cause. The problem requires group action and communication to be systematically applied for the discovery of the key problem and action.

The behavior sought is a decision-making pattern that is similar to that used in other games, except that the data may resemble typical in-basket methods and cases in surface details but concealed within it may be a specific serious problem and a *single best solution*. The difference between the Kepner-Tregoe in-basket game and other cases can be shown diagrammatically, as in Fig. 15–1.

The difference lies in the way the data are converted into problem identification and solution. The Kepner-Tregoe game presents an apparent potpourri of data, spreads them among five players, and counts on the feedback sessions following the group work to make it apparent that a single best problem identification and solution exists. The consequences of failing to find the problems are received in embarrassment or chagrin at failure.

In a typical case-study approach there may not be enough information presented to have a closed loop of problem identification and ideal solution, and the group takes an apparent potpourri of data and works out plausible identifications of problems and solutions for which no positive feedback of success or failure is possible. The feedback for the conventional case for use in decision making then lies in adherence to an accepted method of attacking problems, the scientific method, for example. The Kepner-Tregoe game has been designed so that all the needed information to arrive at the optimum solution is in the hands of the players.

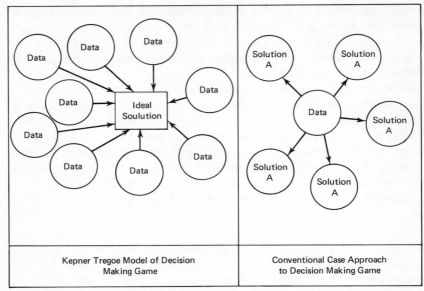

Kepner Tregoe Model of Decision
Making Game

Conventional Case Approach
to Decision Making Game

FIGURE 15–1   Kepner-Tregoe
Model of Decision-Making Game

FIGURE 15–2   Conventional
Case Approach to Decision-Making Game

The desired behavior change sought in the Kepner-Tregoe game is the application of the scientific method—especially the logical abstraction ladder—to find a concealed solution to a specific but not obvious problem. The sequence of behaviors that can lead to solution is not competitive, because all teams playing might conceivably succeed, although the complexity of the problem makes this outcome unlikely. In addition to finding the solution—the school answer—the group also will discover that following certain behaviors will enhance the likelihood of its being uncovered.

The pattern of proposed behavior is presented in Fig. 15–2; the courses are organized around the presentation of situations of the single problem type. At each stage of the course the feedback is emphatic and positive. It probably accounts for the success that the course has enjoyed in changing managerial behavior, as well as the enthusiastic response to the form of training used.

If limitations exist, it is in the preciseness of definition itself. It might create the impression that all problems lend themselves to such precision. Although this assumption has value in that it will lead to diligent search for such a single solution, it could also lead to some frustration in those problems that indeed have no such single outcome, because they were created by a dissatisfaction within some existing condition impossible to change.

Trainers who intend to use the Kepner-Tregoe game as part of their training plan should master the basic training objectives that the KT method proposes to change. There are three kinds of changed behavior that are sought in the KT exercise:

1. As a result of attending and taking part, the trainee will *analyze problems* systematically.
2. As a result of going through the exercise, he will *make decisions* systematically.
3. As a result of attending, he will *prevent potential problems* from occurring.

The trainee will be able to apply the three separate analytical procedures, one for each of the objectives of training.

Obviously a brief summary will not detail all the specific stages of each of the three separate analytical procedures. Suffice to say that they are rooted in system analysis and are action training applications that provide feedback of success and failure in applying these analytical procedures to the in-basket materials presented in the game. The text for this method is the Kepner-Tregoe book *The Rational Manager*, which every trainer should have read carefully before making a decision that this form of training will suit the training needs of his managers.

What kinds of present managerial behavior might indicate that KT training would achieve a suitable training objective? A quick generalization of the major training needs that might indicate that this program would be useful could be the following:

1. A manager who is habitually observed to make action suggestions that solve problems that do not exist or that solve the wrong problem.
2. The manager who does not specify his problem as the difference between what exists now and what should exist.
3. The manager who does not consider causes before proposing solutions.
4. The manager who does not logically eliminate irrelevant information in specifying the problem.

These are but a few examples of the kind of behavior that might be improved that KT has had a measurable effect in changing toward a more logical systematic kind of problem analysis and decision making.

It is obvious that this is not a simple kind of *act* of behavior that is being changed by training but that it is a complex kind of behavior repertory. In this sense it is practical, realistic, ambitious, and even when it misses doing all the things it tries to do it makes such substantial changes in so many behavioral areas that the entire process is usually worthwhile to the middle manager who has had no formal training in problem analysis and decision making in management.

Class Exercise on Action Training

On the following pages are five short cases. They include a variety of short incidents from managerial situations. They are intended to be used as a basis for conducting role play or simple management game sessions in training courses. Break the class up into groups of four persons per group. Each group selects a case and follows the steps outlined below:

1. Discuss the case briefly, answering the questions at the bottom of each case.
2. When some specific actions by specific characters or groups are agreed upon, the group should then write out separate role instruction sheets for each character. For example in the *case of the lengthy memo writer* the following sample role sheets might be written.

Role for Dr. Apple

You are Dr. Apple, recently made associate director of Pristine Labs. You have decided upon certain changes in personnel, hiring, supervision, cost, and so on. You wrote lengthy memos on each and sent them to all staff. To your irritation they have ignored your instructions. You consider them childish, and plan severe action if you can find the ringleader. You suspect a plot. You want backing from the Director. Fill in your own dialogue.

Role for Director

Dr. Apple who works for you was an excellent scientist but has been doing badly as an administrator. He is cold, impersonal, capricious. Morale is suffering. He has asked for an appointment to discuss a problem. Listen and ask questions before doing anything, then straighten him out. Fill in your own dialogue.

When you have completed your discussion, write out the role assignments for the major characters in your case. Each should emphasize conflicts of viewpoint, differences of understanding, and differences of perception. State each person's role as being favorable to himself and lacking in understanding of the other. After reviewing the role assignments, the entire class should gather as a group, and assign its roles to members of another study group, who will enact the roles. One member of the role-preparation group should act as director, start the action, and cut at the appropriate point. At the end of the role playing the director leads a discussion.

1. What have we learned from this case?
2. How could this situation have been averted?

Ask the players to read their roles aloud to the group as a final act. Thank the players (calling for applause from others may be appropriate). Assure everyone that the actors were merely playing assigned parts. Turn to the next group.

THE LENGTHY MEMO WRITER

Dr. Apple was made Associate Administrator of the Pristine Labs, in charge of personnel, accounting, and organization. After several months of observation, he became convinced that certain changes were needed in the way things were done. Accordingly, he drafted a series of lengthy memos on matters of personnel, hiring, supervision, cost control, and other practices. Each discussed the problems at great length and was distributed to all department heads. He waited to see if any adverse reactions followed, but not a murmur emerged. Neither did any improvement in the practices he hoped to change. "I can't understand it," he told the director. "If they disagree, why don't they reply? If they agree, why aren't they following my suggestions?"

1. What might the director say?

2. What action do you recommend? Why?

3. Prepare brief role assignments for:

   (a) Dr. Apple.

   (b) the director.

NO REPORT—NO TIME CARD

A sales office was chronically late in filing its monthly cumulative report because the boss never got the salesman's reports on time to cumulate. Each month salesmen also turned in time tickets which the boss signed so their pay checks would be drawn. These were never late. He prepared a note: "*NOTICE!* No more time tickets will be signed unless accompanied by monthly report." The problem seemed solved until a new sales manager high up heard of the practice. "You can't treat salesmen like kids. You're coercing them. This could ruin morale." The sales supervisor didn't agree. "It works," he said. "I get my reports in on time, and haven't had any complaints."

1. What policy would you advise the company to adopt?

2. What should the sales manager decide? Why?

3. Prepare roles for:

    (a) the sales supervisor.

    (b) the sales executive.

    (c) a typical salesman who doesn't mind the system.

THANKS, DAD!

Delong Smith had been chosen president of the new Plum Valley Bank from a long list of candidates. From the beginning he did extremely well. The board was delighted until one day he suggested hiring his son, Delong Jr.

"He's just graduated from Indiana Business School and would love to come into the bank" said the proud father.

"Do you think it would be best for him and for the bank?" asked one board member.

"Of course! If I didn't think so I wouldn't have suggested it!"

All of the board members felt that in a small new bank with only five officers and 20 employees the move would be inadvisable. Yet they wanted to keep Mr. Smith.

1. What alternatives can the board choose from?

2. What is your recommendation? Why?

3. Prepare roles for

    (a) Delong Smith.

    (b) his son.

    (c) an opposing board member.

PAUL THE BIGMOUTH

Twenty-three people comprised the crew on the Tiny Tots assembly line. The product was a toy for children which sold for about 23 cents to wholesalers. On a good day about 15,000 toys were finished. Because the conveyor carrying the toys from station to station was much faster, the output was under the control of the operators. Variations ran from a low of 12,000 to a record high of 20,000. In order to obtain maximum production an incentive was introduced for the whole group rather than for each individual because the problems of attributing production to a single person were too great to control. Group meetings to explain the plan were held and the initial results were excellent. Base pay was set at $2.00 per hour for 14,000 toys. On several days records were broken with 22,000 toys, and each person was paid an average of $105.00 for the week. Because of changes in another department a man named Paul was transferred to the line. He immediately began exhorting everyone to slow down. "If you don't they'll cut the rate." Despite assurances from the foreman that no such action was planned, production fell to an average of 19,000 per day and stayed there.

1. What should management do?

2. What should they avoid? Why?

3. Prepare roles for

   (a) foreman.

   (b) two neutral workers.

   (c) Paul.

THE RED CAN

A large metal working plant had many automatic machines. Output was more dependent upon the skill of mechanics and set-up men than operators. Each mechanic serviced, repaired, adjusted, and set up ten machines. There were five mechanics. Jim the foreman kept production records. One day he walked down to machine 33 which had been producing poorly and hung an empty red coffee can over the edge of the guard on the press. "I'm hanging the can on 33, it's the worst" he said jokingly. The mechanic reacted strongly. He went into the engineering office and came back with an engineer and huddled with him by the machine. Two hours later 33 was running beautifully. It wouldn't quit. The mechanic called Jim: "Come move that can somewhere else. I notice that 49 is now the lowest. Why don't you hang it on 49?"

1. Would you advise Jim to hang the can on number 49?

2. Under what conditions would it be a good idea? A bad idea?

3. Prepare roles for

    (a) Jim.

    (b) the mechanic.

16 || On-the-Job Coaching of Workers

Life, not the parson, teaches conduct.
—O. W. HOLMES, JR.

IF there is a single effect on training from taking a systems approach, it must be centered on the movement of training out of the classroom back onto the job. The important role that the boss plays in modern organizations means that his influence can be used most effectively when his main role is that of teacher of his subordinates. Faced with the steady and sometimes radical changes that occur in technology, coupled with social and environmental changes in the ways organizations run, administration is coming closer and closer to being a teaching function.

This does not mean that the typical teacher could be taken right out of the classroom and made manager of an organization. For one thing the typical classroom teacher is all too unsystematic in his management of behavior change. Often he adheres to an autocratic style of class leadership. His grading system is inextricably tied to a disciplinary code of deportment and manners, which favors the compliant and deferential student. Bad manners or poor displays of obsequiousness, and even low intelligence, are equated to lack of learning in the typical mass production education system. For this and numerous other reasons the average classroom teacher, in addition to being inexpressibly ineffective as a teacher, would make a poor manager.

Despite this condition, which describes teaching as it is rather than as it could be, the manager of the future will become more and more the effective teacher of his subordinates, and the organization of the future will assume more and more of the teaching function that is to be done.

Coaching by Objectives

By turning industry and other organizations into giant learning institutions, the importance of face to face coaching takes on added significance. For one thing, the behavior change required of individual workers and managers is such that clusters and groupings of people with identical or even similar behavior change requirements will become less significant. The assumption that five foremen, all working in the same plant for the same foreman, will have identical or common learning requirements is both unrealistic and exists only in the unrealistic assumptions of trainers who hope to cut the full range of their task down to a single session of spouting speeches at a bored group of different behavioral problems.

The increased demand for coaching on the job will remake the practice of management, as well as remaking the training of subordinates. Promotion from within as a policy will take on heightened significance if the manager at the higher level is required to assume the responsibility for training his subordinates. It means that the superior must not only know more but must be able to perform managerial tasks consciously. Three levels of managerial excellence emerge when the manager becomes primarily the teacher of his subordinates (see Fig. 16–1):

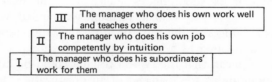

FIGURE 16–1   Levels of Managerial Excellence

1. The lowest level of excellence in management is the manager who does his subordinate's work for him as a substitute for the difficult, but more effective, method of teaching him how and leaving him alone after he has learned. This is all too frequently the level of managerial performance at the present time. Such self-downgrading of managerial work is one of the major sources of discontent among lower levels. It has been identified by a variety of names: autocratic management, centralized management, theory X management, and other similar labels.

2. The next highest level of management involves the manager who knows his proper function and does it naturally and intuitively. This level leaves something to be desired in the manager's performance, however. Because he is an excellent performer, he often limits his actions to doing his own job and relying on others to not only do their own job but to be self-taught without coaching from above.

3. The highest level of managerial excellence consists of the manager who not only does his job and does it well but who does that work consciously. Why should he do it consciously if he is doing it well already? Is there some special value in being aware of one's own behavior? Two reasons suggest that there is a reason for doing managerial work consciously. (a) The manager who manages consciously and well can amend his own behavior in segmental fashion without throwing out the good things. He can correct his own mistake by changing that part of his behavior that needs changing. (b) Even more importantly, if he is to teach others managerial and professional skills he must not only be a good performer, but he must also know what the basic elements of good performance consist of. The great football halfback may win All America awards in football by playing his position intuitively and justifiably hold onto his position on the team. If, however, he wishes to become a coach, he must learn what it is that he does when he performs at his best in order to instruct others in what they must do to reach his level of skill and excellence of performance. If feedback for right and wrong behavior is part of his function, he must not only be competent in performance but must be introspective about it before his coaching will become effective.

In fact, we find that some of the best coaches have been people whose abilities lay in their facility for seeing and recognizing the elements of excellent behavior in others, even when they did not possess all those elements themselves. The coaching function in management lies more in this skill of seeing behavioral requirements and instilling skills in others than in dazzling individual performance on a personal basis. The dazzling performer finds satisfaction in the admiration of his colleagues, but "dazzling" may or may not be a suitable means for bringing about imitative behavior. The use of imitation for learning is invaluable if it is part of a demonstration of a specific program of coaching. Often, however, it may so completely outshine subordinates that it discourages ordinary people from even trying, because it holds little hope for success. When it is used as an exclusive method of teaching it may not produce the desired behavior on the part of the learner. For one thing the learner may merely imitate some superficial aspect of the successful man's behavior, such as his idiosyncrasies, the cigars he smokes, and so on, rather than those behavioral elements that really account for his success.

Using Behavioral Technology in Coaching

Two levels of coaching can be isolated. The first is that kind of coaching in which workers are being trained to behave in specific routine fashion. The second is the managerial and professional level where the skills are symbolic, conceptual, and not routine in nature, such as might be the case where decision-making and problem-solving skills are being taught. There are some common elements to both forms of coaching. There are also some significant differences. The common elements are those that have been outlined in the systems approach. The unlike and differential elements lie in the quality of the behavior being taught.

What are the common elements in coaching for both kinds of work?

1. The behavioral objectives to be achieved at the end of the teaching process are clearly spelled out.
2. Some small local steps toward the terminal objective are defined.
3. Feedback of success or failure for each step is given the learner as he behaves in the manner desired.

What are the differences? Let us look at each of the forms of training: first teaching workers specific job skills (this chapter) and then managers conceptual skills (Chapter 17).

Teaching Job Skills to Workers

The factory or office supervisor has an important responsibility in teaching workers the routines and procedures of the tasks for which he has been hired. This breaks down into two major teaching objectives: (1) preparing the job so that it can be taught and (2) instructing workers in the proper job behavior.

PREPARING THE JOB SO THAT IT CAN BE TAUGHT

In modern factory and office occupations, the work has been rationalized in such a way that the full effectiveness of division of labor can be brought to bear on the work to be done. The detailed breaking down of the job into specific tasks usually finds that such work can be described as *cycles of behavior*. The laborer, machine operator, or the clerk will perform tasks in a fairly repetitive fashion.

1. As discussed in Chapter 9, the lesson planning for individual coaching should include a job breakdown, showing the individual steps, key points, and training timetable for each job and subordinate task to be taught. A step in a job can be considered any individual task that will help the worker make progress toward completion of the job. A *key point* is any special point of emphasis that could make or break the job. Key points are to be highlighted, emphasized, and noted specifically during the instructional process.
2. Repeating the material outlined in Chapter 9, job worker instruction calls for having all the necessary aids, working materials, tools, and arrangement in place before the instruction starts. Practice by the trainer is necessary to assure that training goes forward as planned.

STEPS IN TEACHING A SKILL

There are four essential steps in the actual teaching of any job "lesson." The instructor does not always have to do something about each of the four steps. Often the learner does it himself, but the steps are always there, and each step has its purpose.

1. *Preparation.* To get the mind of the learner focused on what he is to learn.
2. *Presentation.* To demonstrate and explain what he is to learn.
3. *Application.* To let the learner try it out and to correct his errors.
4. *Testing.* To put him "on his own" and see if he has learned it.

As the supervisor or instructor goes about breaking in new men and helping them to get started properly, he is always carrying on one or more of these four steps. The lesson may be very short—not more than two or three minutes—or it may take more time, but if it is successful, resulting in real learning, the four steps are present and accomplish their purposes in the order named. Because job instruction must be informal, it is especially easy to lose sight of the purposes of these steps, yet if any of them are neglected the worker may fail to make proper progress in learning the job. The four steps may now be explained more fully.

Step 1. Preparation. To bring a new idea or process into the mind and muscles of the learner, the instructor must capture his attention and find a way to connect the new lesson with his previous experience. The better the supervisor or instructor knows his man, the easier this step will be, for scattered through the learner's background of experience are bits of knowledge to which the new skill can be connected, with which it can be compared or contrasted, and that can be recalled to illustrate it. He understands the new by associating it with the familiar. He takes an interest in it as soon as he sees its relation to himself and to his own previous experiences. Therefore, the preparation step is nothing more than helping the learner to recall such experiences, and getting his mind focused on them, in relation to the job to be learned.

One approach is to tell him an interesting incident connected with the job. Another is to ask him questions. Better still is to begin by showing him rapidly how the job is done—not to demonstrate it in detail, but to arouse his curiosity and get him to talking or asking questions about it. Such an overall picture of the whole job helps to arouse his interest and to give him a general idea of it.

If the lesson is a simple operation that can easily be learned, this step may last only a moment or two. The harder the job and the farther it is from the learner's previous experience, the longer it will take. There is a psychological moment when this step is complete, when the learner is ready to ask, "What next?" Wherever and whenever a learner begins asking questions, trying to find out, becomes eager to know more about the job, no matter how he gets that way, step 1 is over and step 2 should begin at once.

Step 2. Presentation. Here the new operation is shown and explained. The methods and teaching devices used will depend on the job or lesson and on the learner's previous experience. Mere telling is not teaching. The skillful instructor usually demonstrates the operation slowly, step by step, especially to a beginner. After he has done so, or at intervals between parts of the demonstration, he calls attention to points about the procedure that the learner might not readily notice for himself. He cautions against common errors, using key points for emphasis. He asks questions that cause the learner to think and discover something about the job for himself. The skillful instructor uses a variety of methods to put over the lessons. The learner's previous experience is still very much in the picture, just as it was in the preparation step, for it is through his own past experience that he "gets" the new lesson.

A common mistake is to try to teach too much in one lesson. If the operation is simple, it should be presented completely. If it is complicated, it should be taught one part at a time, carrying through the teaching steps with each part. The presentation step may last only a few moments or it may require many minutes, depending on the lesson, the learner, and the number of interruptions. Its purpose, however, is always the same—to show the worker how to do something and to do it right. He probably will not be able to do it well the first time. That is the reason for the next step, application. As soon as the instructor senses that the learner understands the lesson, has caught the idea, and is ready to try to do the operation for himself, he is ready for step 3.

Step 3. Application. This is the try-out step. The principle "We learn to do by doing" is very close to the truth in learning a skill. Before he can swim, the learner must get into the water and try the strokes he had demonstrated to him lying across the piano bench. Real learning occurs when we attempt to put into use what we have been "taught." But the first attempts to "do" must be made under the watchful eye of an instructor who sees that they are correct, for without such a check on his first attempts the learner can learn to do the wrong way as readily as the right way. The employee does not stop learning as soon as the supervisor or instructor leaves him and moves on down the shop. He keeps on learning, right or wrong, as he tries to do the job he has been taught. If he does it wrong in these early attempts, he learns wrong, unless the instructor discovers his error promptly and helps him to correct it before he has formed a habit of doing it that way.

The instructor can demonstrate again if necessary by doing the operation slowly, step by step, explaining exactly what he is doing at each point. He can give the learner a chance to make repeated trials and see that he gets the correct motion pattern. He can watch him as he tries and suggest greater or less effort or changes in motions. He can see that the learner holds his tools and handles his materials correctly from the start. Just as an athletic coach teaches a correct "form," so the instructor, by demonstrating, can give the operator the correct form for a shop skill so that through practice he will acquire the "feel" of the operation as it is done in its correct or most effective manner. It is highly important also that the learner be told, as soon as he becomes curious about them, the reasons for doing the job in just this particular way. The reasons for particular quality requirements and how to recognize good and poor work should be stressed. He should see that correct form is nothing more than the kind of motions that highly skilled operators have found to be best.

Teaching thus continues in the application step. The supervisor or instructor encourages the learner to ask questions, explains further, or shows him over again the right way to do the job, but teaches no new jobs or operations. The whole purpose of the step is to make sure that the learner is able to do the job correctly without making mistakes that may become wrong habits or that may spoil materials or damage valuable machines. Step 3 is finished when it is safe for the worker to go ahead on his own.

Step 4. Testing. The real proof of good job instruction is the ability of the operator to do the job effectively without help. In step 4 he is left to himself for a longer period of time to see if he can do this. But the supervisor or instructor does not forget him. He still observes him regularly to see that he is not falling into wasteful motion habits. He checks his work. Does his product pass inspection? Is he making a reasonable growth in output? If not, some part of the instruction has failed and must be done over.

Organizing for Better Job Instruction

Although the procedures for instructing a specific worker on a specific job are sensible and reasonable, they are more complex than they might seem from this verbal picture. Certain policy-level decisions about training are required for job instruction using applied behavioral technology in improving worker effectiveness.

1. There must be a firm committment to improved worker effectiveness through training.
2. Investment in human capital must be calculated carefully to assure that training becomes a permanent method of supervision rather than a luxury or ephemeral matter used only in periods of relative prosperity.
3. The training of supervisors in training methods must be adequately prepared and executed. Merely prescribing that foremen are trainers will not complete the transition. Training as a means of supervising must be seen as more than some additional responsibility; it must be seen as a way of doing the supervisory job.
4. The supervisory functions of control and human relations, it must be noted, are best achieved through the vehicle of converting the supervisory position into a teaching one. Control comes through knowledge and imparting it. Human relations, which implies a fair and helpful face of proprietorship to the workers, comes through the same teaching relationship.
5. All this change in the supervisory position does not occur in isolation from the jobs above it in rank but begins at the top and works its way down through the ranks, with superior rank being a different kind of teaching relationship.

THE VISCOUNT STEEL COMPANY CASE

The Billet Department of the Viscount Steel Company is an intermediate preparation stage in the production of steel. Billets are received from an adjacent rolling mill. Depending on the grade of the steel and its final use (a rolling mill at the next stage shapes the billets into coils, bars, or rails), the billets undergo some combination of pickling, chipping, scarfing, or burning to length. The purpose of these preparations, other than the last, is to remove surface defects.

Scarfing, for example, is the removal of surface defects from billets by the use of a large hand torch. Billets (bars of steel having a rectangular cross section) are set down on skids in the scarfing area by a crane. A cleaner rolls out the steel into a flat position with a special wrench. He then cleans the surface. Next, an inspector marks the surface defects on the up-side of the billets with chalk. If defects have been missed, the surface is marked again and rescarfed; otherwise, the cleaner rolls the billets to the next side. This procedure is repeated until four sides are finished. A checker then marks the steel for removal.

The workers in the scarfing area are

1. One checker—acts as a group leader, being responsible for bringing the steel into the work area, keeping any necessary records, and removing the steel.
2. One crane operator.
3. Two hookers—responsible for signaling the crane operator and hooking and unhooking chains.
4. Six scarfers—two to a team.
5. Three cleaners—one assigned to each team.
6. Three inspectors—one to a team.

With the exception of the inspectors, who report to an inspector foreman, the workers mentioned receive their orders from the shift foremen. All the operations, including scarfing, require about 60 men per shift. The department usually operates 21 shifts per week. Each shift is operated by two foremen.

Mr. All, the department superintendent, assumed control three years ago. One year later the department was unable to meet production schedules and maintain previous cost levels. At this time the department was transferred into the blooming mills division (before it was a separate unit). Mr. Hat, the blooming mills superintendent, moved into Mr. All's office. From here he directed his departments and supervised Mr. All's activities. After reviewing the department's production records, Mr. Hat remarked that scarfing should be producing at least 60 tons per man per eight-hour shift. Shortly thereafter, several billet department foremen were criticized by Mr. Hat when their production had dropped below 60 tons. The 60 tons per man per eight-hour shift soon developed into an informal quota.

During a production upsurge and increasingly higher demands on the billet department, Mr. Hat transferred a young college recruit under his jurisdiction into the billet department as a subforeman. Jim White, the college graduate, was the only foreman in the department to have more than a high school education. Before Jim started working in the department, Mr. Hat expressed his philosophy of a work day to Jim: Every working man should produce at no less than his maximum effort for eight hours.

Within a few weeks Jim had familiarized himself with the department and his duties. Even during his orientation period as a foreman he was maintaining a high production record. Nonetheless, he had been put "on-the-carpet" by Mr. Hat after the latter had made a surprise visit to the production area where he found several men on Jim's shift not working at the moment. The next day Jim walked into the scarfing area around 1:30 on the 7:00 to 3.00 shift and discovered that one team of scarfers were not working. Jim went over to the scarfers.

JIM: Why aren't you working? Is there anything wrong?

SCARFER: The billets have not been inspected yet.

JIM: OK. [He went over to the inspector.] The billets are ready to be inspected. Are you going to inspect them?

INSPECTOR: My team already has their 60 tons, so why push them?

JIM: You stop work after eight hours, not when you reach 60 tons. You have high-quality steel and could easily reach 80 tons.

INSPECTOR: OK. Just don't rush. I'll get to it.

Jim went on with his tour of the other areas and returned 20 minutes later. The steel had not been inspected and the inspector was gone. A scarfer informed him that the inspector went for a drink of water. While looking for the inspector, Jim found the inspector foreman.

FOREMAN: Well, how's everything going today?

JIM: Your scarfing inspector in number 2 bay hasn't been marking his steel and my men can't work until he inspects the steel.

FOREMAN: I'll change that!

Fifteen minutes later the inspector in number 1 bay came over to Jim.

INSPECTOR: What the hell are you trying to prove? Bill (the inspector foreman) said that you told him that we have been sitting on our cans causing your men to be idle. He hinted that you are in the thick with some of the top brass and unless we shape up, you're going to make it hot for us.

JIM: Look, I told Bill that the inspector in number 2 bay was not working up to par. I said nothing about anyone else or even suggested that I was going to carry the episode further. You are not my responsibility, but when my men are waiting for an inspector, I want that situation changed immediately.

INSPECTOR: What's with you? Your men are over the quota.

JIM: You men are here to work eight hours. I don't ask you to kill yourself working, but there is no excuse for anyone standing around.

Jim ended the argument here because he had to prepare his production report for the next shift. He decided that it was too late in the shift to do anything else about the incident.

The next day Jim was in the mill to start the shift and discovered that the inspector who started the whole episode the day before was on his shift again. The other two scarfing inspectors were different and a new inspector foreman was on.

The inspector Jim had trouble with was trying to avoid Jim. As the shift started and the inspectors began their work, he called back his cleaner and told him to clean the steel again. Jim knew he was going to have trouble again with this inspector, because the inspector could control the rate of production by regulating how fast he inspected the steel. He inspected the steel over and over again, to the exact standards of the books. Not a trace of slag could be left on the billets, or he would not pass the steel. By lunch time his team's production was off one third. Jim was worried. His boss would be sure to see the drop in production if this continued and Mr. Hat did not accept excuses.

CASE DISCUSSION QUESTIONS

The Viscount Steel Company Case

1. What action by whom is called for here?

2. Prepare roles for the major action protagonists.

3. Direct another group in enacting the role play.

4. Conduct a critique and summary from the case.

17 | Managing Managers Through Coaching

There is a strong relationship between mobility and competency.

—E. E. JENNINGS

THE managing of managers differs from the managing of workers in some important ways. Among the most important of these is the characteristic make-up of the supervised. The worker has some distinctive expectations, values, and skills that the manager does not exhibit when he is the subordinate. To name a few, the worker is, for the most part, less likely to have a high level of education, such as professional or broad cultural education. His expectations will be different, having learned that work is something you do for money, which is equated to time spent on the job following prescribed practices in operating the machine or following a specified procedure. The manager, when he is being managed, has a higher level of expectation of his superior. As a manager himself he has general thoughts about the work of managing and is apt to be a more expert judge of the quality of his boss's managerial talent. He is more motivated by desire to move higher and to be willing to work for relatively long periods of time without immediate rewards in cash in the hope for promotion and recognition over his career.

The Effects of Careerism

Little has been done to uncover all the implications of managing managers as an important aspect of managing firms.

These expectations of workers and managers comprise an important social problem in the eyes of many observers. At the same time, they call for basic explanations that will help us obtain the required behavior from people in managerial positions in systematic fashion. The differences between managers and workers, as they must be considered in coaching, can be classified in three ways: holistic, functional, or by reference to goals.

HOLISTIC EXPLANATIONS

Holistic explanations treat workers as one class and the managers as another, and the differences are explainable in terms of class differences. The concepts of order-givers and order-takers, the blue bloods and the plebes, the aristocrats and the peasants, the elite and the masses, and the establishment and the mob would all be variations of the holistic theme in explaining differences. Such explanations, however useful they may be elsewhere, can only do us damage when we try to apply them to defining better ways of training and coaching managers as contrasted with coaching workers.

FUNCTIONAL EXPLANATIONS

Functional explanations of differences between workers and managers assay a kind of paternalistic explanation of differential treatment. The kind of statement that one company president made to his employees, "After all, we each have our job to do, and you should do yours and I'll do mine," emphasizing likenesses in the situation of each and thus playing down the differences as being merely that of function, would exemplify such an approach. Workers, it might be noted, perform such functions as the following: operate, manipulate, do physical work and simple mental calculations, follow procedures, and apply skills. Managers use less physical skills but apply mental and conceptual skills, such as organizing, planning, controlling, motivating, delegating, communicating, energizing, deputizing, making decisions, and solving problems. Each, you see, has some functions, and in having functions they are similar. The differences lie in the functions they perform. The functions may be divided into physical and mental as the major differences. Another way of looking at worker-manager differences functionally would be to note that workers do repetitive and recurring tasks, whereas managers do restorative and innovative tasks.

REFERENCE TO GOALS

Still a third approach to noting the differences between workers and managers would be with respect to the goals of each. Whether these goals are innate or acquired, it is proposed, they differ. Living systems, especially man, display goal-directive capacities. There is a common persistence in both worker and manager to strive for achievement of goals. Their intentions are determinations toward some specific goal, and are usually conscious in character. The goal may be reached in different ways.

In a work environment where managers and workers exist together, the explanation of goals is often subsumed under the general expectation category of *careers*. The mature worker and the mature manager may be usefully distinguished by a goal plan that is woven into a larger fabric that comprises his set of expectations, called his career.

Career expectation then comprises a useful basis for different patterns of coaching of workers and managers. For managers, careers are inextricably tied to a higher level of learning about work.

The Change from Idle Rich to Working Wealthy

In the early days of capitalism, especially in England, it was considered a prerogative of the rich, the landed aristocracy, to engage in leisure. The arts, culture, aesthetics, the classics, and pastimes such as hunting and partying were usually reserved for those who owned the land and the companies. Because they were amply financed and lived off the fruits of the labors of others without really contributing labor themselves—not even management—they could know and appreciate leisure. Well educated, that is, classically educated, cultured, and well heeled, they were able to live the good life free of the necessity of punching in at the plant, flying on the company plane, or doing other productive work. A few of the more responsible members of this set would assume commissions in the army or would enter the civil service, but for the most part this desire to pursue leisure in its purest form was their perquisite, which they held a monopoly on.

A nineteenth century Edgar Guest composed the following jingle, which reflected the locus of leisure of early capitalism.

> The golf course was near the factory and all the livelong day,
> The children at their work-place could watch the men at play.

This crisp summary of the relationship of man and boss, worker and owner, capitalist and laborer, just does not hold water any longer. Today the jingle must be revised as follows:

> The golf course is near the office and all the livelong day,
> The manager at his work-desk can watch the help at play.

Today the desirable job, the one that everyone aspires to, is the executive or managerial position, for which the 40-hour week does not apply. While labor unions strive for shorter work weeks, the manager works 55 to 65 hours per week on the average. If there was indeed a kind of guilt complex that overtook the idleness of the rich, it has been well submerged in the rise of the working wealthy, the well-paid manager who spends evenings at community activity for public relations purposes, who travels 100,000 miles a year, usually (some of it) on his own time, and whose entertainment is a tension-laden extension of his office.

Even the holders of inherited wealth hit the campaign trails of politics or accept appointed posts in government. Vigorously pressing into recreational pursuits with the zest that they manage their business, leisure has become a way of doing business or a form of temporary therapy to mend the tissues in order to return to the fray with increased drive and zeal.

The Roots of Guilt

The vague sensation that there is something indecent about doing nothing, or doing something purposeless, pervades the world in which people must "make things happen." Much of this can be traced to the early economic theories that underlie many of our beliefs today.

David Ricardo made it amply clear in his Iron Law of Wages that there was little hope for leisure being achieved under capitalism for laborers. Extra time and well-being would merely result in their reproducing offspring faster than before, thus increasing the supply of labor in a few years. This surplus would drive down the price of labor until wages fell below subsistence. At this turn of events the workers' time and physical well-being would decline and their fertility would become diminished until a labor shortage resulted. This dwindling of the labor supply would bring about a rise in wages, and the cycle of the iron law would work its natural laws once more.

Thomas Malthus, the gloomy parson, in 1798 wrote a classic essay on population that suggested that population would always press on the food supply in a way that would bar workmen from ever achieving the kind of prosperity that would permit leisure to workers. Because his wages could not buy back his own production, certain other classes would serve the useful function of consuming the gluts that must occur in the economy. This would, of course, be a leisure class. The solemn outcome then would be a world in which the hard-working poor must always labor at the brink of subsistence concurrently with a leisure class

of landed aristocracy and upper middle class who would be well educated and accordingly would be qualified for the ranks of government
official, army officer, or country gentleman.

The theoretical effects of such an expressive system were incorporated
into Marxism, and the clarion call to workers to strike off the chains of
such a system was embedded in early socialist movements. The rise of
democracy and the spread of popular suffrage led to the popular con-
viction that the competitive market system struck hardest on the bearer
of the labor power and made an attack on capitalism (and the leisure
classes it engendered) a defense of man.

Thorstein Veblen wrote at about the turn of the century that "the
leisure of the leisure class is still in great measure a predatory activity,
an active assertion of mastery." This myth of predatory unpinnings to
leisure still may be found in the statements of certain politicians and in
the cartoons that sometimes appear in labor union periodicals.

Ida Tarbell and the Muckrakers of the turn of the century could
report on the evil opulence of America's 60 families with intense moral
fervor, thereby generating long after such analysis had little pertinence
a sense of unease at being sufficiently free of the requirement for work
to permit pure leisure.

Still, as time went on it was not the equalitarian moralists who proved
to be the prophets for the latter half of the century. By the end of
World War II the gains of unions and the decline in numbers of the
unskilled workers had made leisure a privilege of the worker and longer
hours a characteristic of the technical, managerial, and professional
classes.

The Cushion for Blue Collar Workers

Joseph Schumpeter, as time has proved, was the most accurate of the
economic theorists of our system and its workings. Capitalism, Schumpeter had pointed out, provides silk stockings for the worker and not
simply for the queen. He might have added that it also provides leisure
for the worker—however reluctant he might be to accept it—rather
than the bosses.

The 1964 automobile company contracts with the United Auto Workers were strongly geared toward implementing early retirement of
workers. For those who would retire at age 60, there was offered the
prospect of 70 per cent of their normal pay up to $400 per month if
they had accrued over ten years of service. Workers with 30 years or
more of service might retire at age 55 at $200 per month. In the Kaiser
Steel Company, on the docks of the West Coast, and for firemen and
shopmen on the railroads, the specter of unemployment because of

technological employment was reduced by a guarantee of continued pay, even when the job had been eliminated, negotiated by the employers in return for the right to automate operations without restriction.

The possibility of "complete career security" became a specific bargaining demand of a million steelworkers as the new year rolled around, supplementing an already generous package that includes sabbatical leaves for workers of long service in steel mills and can companies.

Clearly the world of leisure was one that already existed on an enlarged scale for many blue collar workers and that will undoubtedly be expanded. It is not as clear that all workers who are paid for work no longer performed will accept this condition as added leisure, because many are already joining the ranks of moonlighters, persons with two jobs. Many of those freed from the economic insecurity of job loss will accept their paychecks won from prior employers and immediately attempt to find another occupation and second career as worker to enhance their incomes.

This is obviously not a simple by-product of a sense of guilt carried over from the worker's cultural heritage of needing to work. It is more likely a need for extra income to live the kind of life that he knows can be financed only by higher pay. To send his children to college, as an increasing number of working men are doing; to underwrite the costs of home ownership, which have risen rapidly; and to engage in middle-class living in the mass consumption society demand that he be interested in more pay.

The desirable life that he aspires to requires that he add a layer of new income to the amounts paid him for work he no longer must do in his original occupation. It also points up the plain fact that he would, in all likelihood, be willing to undergo the pains of professional hours and stresses in order to get the pay attached to such life if he were able to get it.

The New Careerism
Although the steelworkers' union may adopt "complete career security" as a collective bargaining objective, such a phrase is probably nothing more than a catchy phrase and a play on the complete meaning of the word *career*. Careers, in our society, have come to mean professional, technical, and managerial work more than simply a lifetime job. As professional work it usually begins with a college degree or its equivalent in practical experience and training on the job.

Studies by sociologists have shown that of 8,000 top managers in this country over three quarters of them have baccalaureate degrees and 20 per cent have graduate or professional education beyond that level.

Rising enrollments have created pressures on the colleges for admissions, and the better schools are already turning away many qualified applicants. This has raised the academic standards through selective admissions and in turn has placed more pressure on the high schools for higher levels of achievement to qualify graduates for admission.

This chain of events, careerism leading to pressures on the colleges, reflects back into the high schools until the pressure on high-schoolers today far exceeds that of the high schools of an earlier generation. Accelerated programs in mathematics and science, greater loads of homework and outside study, and the tighter planning of the student's time to fit some extracurricular activity into a jampacked educational curriculum have eliminated the careless happy days of youth that are sometimes associated with the teens.

The typical high-schooler in a modern suburban high school lives the life of an executive in many respects. His date book is sprinkled with appointments for committees, clubs, counseling sessions, organized activity, lessons, and developmental programs of all sorts that would tax many executives of past years. The simple purposeless spending of time is increasingly being reduced until high school today resembles more and more the life of the careerist as it will be lived a decade hence when he has accepted a position as a junior management trainee, rising young lawyer in a large law firm, or cadet engineer with the giant corporation.

Careerism may even extend into the grammar schools, when parents begin to sharpen the careerist tendencies of their children at an early age. A frenetic form of lilliputianism pervades many school systems in which 11-year-olds are pressed increasingly to behave like small-sized adults. Fencing lessons, tennis lessons, French lessons, and junior achievement fill the days of carefree youth; they have a blocked-out calendar of activity.

Nor do the oldsters who have arrived in careers find themselves escaping the pressures of careerism. The self-developer is the model man of the careerist movement. Self-help courses send people to adult education courses to study everything from certified-life underwriter programs to Sanskrit. "How to Improve" books comprise the staple item in the book lists of a number of large publishing houses.

Less optional than many of the self-help courses are those educational efforts that are designed to retrain obsolescent professionals. The engineer of today, for example, finds that he needs to be retrained in his profession several times before he retires. The curriculum that he studied ten years before is now over 30 per cent changed, not simply in courses, names, and numbers but in entire new concepts of science that are now taught. The 20-year veteran is more obsolete than up to date, as the changes have wiped out more than half of his undergraduate curriculum.

For the trained accountant the computer brings similar effects. In every profession new systems, new methods, and new technology unsettle established patterns of behavior. The life of the careerist is one of re-training and frantic scrambling to keep up. Younger men race past older ones, and formerly fast-rising careerists are placed on a shelf as the substance of the careerist life is changed.

The Life of the Careerist

Whatever else might be said of the careerist drive, it has wiped out leisure. A turmoil of change has left the careerist with an option of falling behind or of working long hours in his job and in keeping abreast.

Vance Packard has described the pressure-laden life of the Pyramid Climbers in executive positions. He might well have used the same title to describe the life of all pyramid climbers in the arts, the sciences, and the hard scramble to the top in any line. The concert pianist, the artist, the labor leader, and the bishop of the church achieve their rank by careerism. Five main characteristics attend on the life of the careerist:

1. He works longer and harder than people who are not careerists. Studies by the American Management Association have shown executives to work in the neighborhood of 60 hours a week. This 60 hours include time in the office, in meetings, in conferences, on planes, and in face to face contact with people. If he is allowed to fly on the private company plane he will discover that it often leaves on Sunday.
2. Careerism competes with family life. The model father must work at it, usually at times and places where he can be with his family. The careerist often finds his working time cuts into the time he might spend with the kids while they are growing up. He is heading for the coast on Sunday night when he might be assisting his son with algebra. Protracted vacations of several weeks every two years do not provide a genuine substitute. The model father must today be considered limited to those whose highest career aspiration extends up through the skilled man. Working hours of 9:00 to 5:00 permit (but certainly do not assure) normal family life. No careerist rises on such a meager work schedule.
3. It is a life of tension. Because it is constantly competitive, the tensions and anxieties of executive life are constant if not somewhat less than hectic. Maintaining outward aplomb while inwardly seething with ambition and drive is hardly conducive to serenity.
4. It is accompanied by physical abundance. The executive seldom punishes himself in terms of physical wants. He lives in the most comfortable hostels when he travels, dines at the finest restaurants,

and surrounds himself with comfortable, functional fittings, some of which are of the highest aesthetic quality.

5. It has many intangible rewards. The pressure toward the top in careerism is not impelled by tangible rewards as much as by the recognition, sense of belonging to important groups of people, feelings of adequacy, and the reinforcements of success for effort expended. The ego and social satisfactions make the efforts expended seem worthwhile. By contrast, leisure seems to be a pale competitor for the time, effort, and aspiration of the careerist.

The Significance of Careerism for Coaching

If such a lengthy discussion of careerism might seem to be a trifle overlong, there is a very sensible reason for dwelling on the subject.

The importance of careerism, mobility, and guided experience as the means of management development on the job almost eliminates conventional face to face preaching as a means of coaching.

Studies by Eugene Jennings on the career patterns of men who reach the top reveals that the mobile manager, one who remains in a position only long enough to have mastered some 80 per cent of the elements of the position before moving outward or laterally, is the fastest moving man. His competence is directly tied to his mobility, for the overall learning exposure from several positions in a firm in a ten-year period is vastly greater than sticking with one area of responsibility for the whole ten years and becoming complete master of it all.

This suggests that situational management of the careers of oneself and one's subordinates is more relevant to behavior change for managers than being exposed to homely little pep talks and platitudinous statements about "when I was in your position" and the like. This implies several things that managerial coaching is not:

1. It is not a specific set of instructions about activities or behavior of the subordinate by a superior.
2. It is not a set of tasks to be performed with demands for vaguely determined outcomes such as "hitting the ball" and the like.
3. It is not some action or policy that inhibits movement, requires sitting overly long in one position, or exhorts achievement of the virtues of patience and humility.

These three, however, are often the bulk of the activities of the superior who imagines that he is coaching his subordinates:

1. The plant manager who daily calls his staff together and pours forth his wisdom about the mistakes of the day before, with somber warning about "Let's watch that one, boys," is seriously attempting to coach but is lamentably bad in his effectiveness as a coach.
2. The sales manager who uses his sales management meetings to divulge deep insights about top-management goals and thinking in the form of ten-minute speeches to his men is often doing nothing more than using communication as a club to beat down any incipient rise of new ideas or change from his subordinates.
3. The staff manager who counterpunches with his staff, insisting that they produce new ideas, but shoots them full of holes when they appear, may be utterly sincere but is also utterly incompetent in coaching.

The effective coaching function is more apt to take the form of working on forward-looking plans and objectives for his subordinates, in a fashion that keeps them moving constantly toward new areas of experience, new demands for personal skill development, and application of ingenuity and problem solving.

Coaching Through Establishing Objectives

The positive aspect of managerial coaching is that of requiring that annual and quarterly objectives be established.

The subordinate who makes a commitment to try to produce something is practically obliged to try. Such a commitment may not always be successful; in fact it will almost always fall short in some respects. In the process of trying, however, the subordinate will learn more than under any other kind of managerial system.

In *regular responsibilities* the superior has several questions that comprise a key to enlarging his subordinate's viewpoint of the job and to shaping his behavior to attack his objectives of a recurring nature with realistic energy. Such questions as the following might be considered germane with this category of objective:

1. What is the present level of output?
2. What trend does it seem to be showing?
3. What is the minimum acceptable level?
4. What is the record high we have ever seen in this objective area?

In *problem-solving objectives* the superior spends little, if any, time with futile lectures on the theory of problem solving or job instruction on decision making. He induces these skills by asking questions and using the replies as commitments and as a basis for framing new behavior in subordinates. Such questions might include the following:

1. What is the present condition? What are the facts in the situation and how do you know them to be facts?
2. Given these conditions, what would be a satisfactory level or substitute for these conditions?
3. What time element would be realistic for arriving at these desired conditions?
4. Given this gap between present and desired, what are the causes of the problems? Has anything changed recently that could have caused the undesired condition? Is one cause more important than other causes?
5. What are some alternative solutions to the problem? Have you considered others?
6. Which one would give us the greatest contribution to objectives? Which one would be least costly? Which one is most acceptable to the people involved?
7. What is your final decision? How will you measure effect?

Such questions are designed to force the individual into a pattern of problem analysis, much the same as was used in the class session describing the use of the case method.

Innovative or improvement objectives entail a dialogue between superior and subordinate that forces the subordinate to define some improvement goals that will bring about breakthroughs to new and better levels of achievement, even though the present might seem satisfactory from a historical viewpoint. Such questions as the following could be involved in the dialogue between superior and subordinate:

1. Exactly what is the present condition? Why?
2. Is that condition the best that could be achieved?
3. What is a possible level of improvement?
4. When could it not be achieved?
5. How could it be done?
6. Who should do it?
7. Is it being done in the right place at the right time by the right person?
8. Could we combine, change sequence, simplify?

What kinds of growth potentials exist?

1. If you were to have your expense budget cut 10 per cent, what would you eliminate?
2. If you were to have 10 per cent more income to spend, where would you apply it?
3. Who else would be affected by such a change?
4. What acceptance conditions must be achieved?

From these and similar questions the superior indicates a general dissatisfaction with the status quo rather than a specific discontent over some condition gone wrong. He transmits this discontent to all his subordinates in order that they will apply their best talents to achievements of new levels of excellence. The agreements are shaped in a dialogue and firmed up in a memorandum confirming the agreements to try to innovate.

The conclusion about managerial coaching is that it differs from coaching workers in the manner of presenting objectives. The worker is presented objectives through specific telling of the job in steps. The manager learns by the questions his boss asks him.

Asking the Right Question in Coaching

The general framework of managing by objectives goes beyond the specific questions outlined, which are aimed at obtaining commitments at three levels of excellence. They are framed within a context that serves to facilitate career growth for the subordinate. The following questions about the careers of subordinate managers are asked about the subordinate by his boss.

Is He Matched to This Organization?

Some managers have too much talent for the kind of organization in which they are employed. The MIT engineer who works in a small firm may find that unless he can get to the top he will be frustrated. The young boss with a young subordinate may find that he has a superior man who will become stale because of his position in a dead-end position. On the other hand, a firm that has a high technology base may find that it cannot find a suitable position at a higher level for a man without sufficient formal education to learn new technology fast enough.

The managerial misfit should not be hired, but if already aboard should be assisted in moving out, either inside or outside the firm.

The alternative to this is to coach him to become a shelf-sitter and enjoy it.

Does He Complement or Supplement His Boss?

The broad generalist may need a detail man to handle things he cannot do well. Other managers may have so many projects they need a second hand, an alter ego to pitch in and do the same things as well as he does.

The manager who complements his boss should be asked questions that move his goals in identical direction to the superiors by doing things that the boss cannot do. The manager who supplements his boss should be pointed by questions toward activities and goals identical to those of the boss, working in harness to add to the strength of the boss.

Is He Clear on His Specific Objectives?

Does he have a clear map of his major areas of responsibility and in each area a knowledge of the outputs required? In terms of coaching managers the ascending scale of coaching must begin with regular objectives, after which problems may be identified and committed and finally commitment to innovative behavior can be discussed.

Are His Relationships Clear, and Is He Using Them Effectively?

Does he understand his relationship to his boss? Is he clear on what matters should be acted on without approval, and what should be cleared? Is he clear on how frequently he is to report results and in what form? Does he know what the exception points are in his performance that call for explanations? Is he clear on where his areas of responsibility end and those of other managers begin? Are his jurisdictional boundaries clear? Does he know where his areas of joint accountability lie, with whom, and for how much?

Are His Aspirations Matched to His Promotional Potential?

The young man with a long working life and demonstrated ability to learn may require that his aspirations be raised. The older man, or one who through past failures has caused his acceptance in the organization to be lowered permanently, may have aspirations that cannot realistically be attained. The coaching situation for each is different. The superior should temper his coaching programs accordingly. The general tendency is to coach only the highest potential and not to develop others whose ultimate level of attainment is not quite as high.

DOES HE HAVE ACCEPTANCE AND A GOOD NAME AMONG HIS COLLEAGUES?

The subordinate manager who works silently and anonymously may not be promotable until he has become more visibly identified as competent by his peers and colleagues in the organization. The coaching process entails enhancing achievement but calls for more. The good works must be made known to others before his promotability is assumed to be legitimate to the rest of the organization. Part of the coaching process may be in enhancing those skills that make his acceptance higher.

IS HE GETTING CONSTANT FEEDBACK OF HIS RESULTS?

A natural product of managing by objectives should be the ability of the man to see how well his results measure up to the objectives he agreed to produce. Coaching may be a refresher and a testing to ascertain whether or not he is reading these indicators himself and functioning under self-control during the period of operating results. This can be supplemented by summaries of these results at periodic intervals, concurrent with the establishment of new and revised goals.

Managing as a Learning Experience

The operating decisions that one manager makes with respect to the managers who work for him are coaching (behavior changing) in effect. These include such chronic areas of concern in managing managers as the following:

1. *Compensation.* Merit increases, bonuses, commissions, and other forms of compensation are designed to reward certain levels of excellence in performance and to withhold those rewards for failure to perform. The compensation system itself coaches managers. He is apt to repeat that behavior that the compensation system rewards and is apt to avoid or be indifferent to that behavior that it overlooks or fails to reward.
2. *Performance records.* Annual reports of performance, accurately reported and filed regularly, are a form of coaching, in the sense that they affect behavior. The knowledge that good work will be recorded periodically will elicit more of that kind of behavior. Blank personnel records have no behavior change effect on managers.
3. *Selection and promotion.* Where selection for important new lateral positions or promotional movements will have a profound effect on the behavior of the manager and of his peers who note the relation-

ship between performance and promotion. Where competence and results are obvious criteria for promotion or favorable assignments, more good performance will follow.

The general guide to coaching is that managers will behave in ways that produce favorable consequences in their career.

THE AMHERST INSURANCE COMPANY CASE

In the fall of 1962 Carl Austin, executive vice president of the Amherst Insurance Company, attended a seminar run by the Insurance Information Institute of America. The theme of the seminar was "improving personnel evaluation," and it was attended by a number of personnel executives from insurance firms throughout the country.

In the keynote lecture Mike Campbell, co-chairman of the institute, raised an issue that lodged itself firmly in Austin's mind: "It is a basically unsound practice for an insurance executive—or any executive, for that matter—not to let his people know how they are doing and what is expected of them." Austin was thoroughly impressed with this and reflected back to some situations that had recently occurred in his own office. He recalled that there had been several instances where promotions and raises had come up. When the decision was made to promote one man or another, someone always seemed to be ruffled. He even got wind of a complaint that "Austin promotes people by rolling dice." It occurred to him, as he thought over Campbell's lecture, that if a systematic method of appraising personnel performance —and letting the employees know how they were doing—were devised, then the office might run more smoothly. The appraising and informing could be done on an annual basis; it surely would make for less surprises and gripes when the better men got raises and/or were promoted and the less able men were left behind.

He discussed this with several other executives and they all agreed that this was a serious problem in their companies as well. At one juncture in this discussion Bert Ashley, a personnel manager from the Lomax Company in Providence, Rhode Island, reached into his briefcase and produced a form that was being used to this end in his office.

"I'm not saying you should use this in your company, and if you do you'll surely have to make some modifications. It has worked well with us, though. We are about the same size as Amherst and our problems are no doubt similar. We found that the big rub was not so much promotions as it was salary increases. We haven't grown too much lately, and since we are a stable organization we can't give everyone promotions every year. So we set up this system—as orderly and rational as we could make it—for determining who should get a raise and who should not. We decided we'd do this on the basis of actual performance—much better than random impressions, personal prejudice, favoritism and so on.

"So we set up this thing—rate the individuals from 'doubtful' to 'outstanding' on performance in each of these categories. Again, I'm not saying you should use this. It might give you a few hints on how to get rolling though."

Austin took the form and studied it carefully. The more he looked at it, the more he thought it might work at Amherst.

When he returned to the home office, he circulated the form among several of the top-level executives and directors. It was discussed at the next directors' meeting, and it took only about a half hour to agree favorably on the use of the plan. The form would be changed slightly from the Lomax pattern and sent out yearly to each employee, who would then know exactly how well he had (or had not) performed during the past year. The sample letter sent out read as follows:

Dear _____ :

Your Board of Directors is most happy to give you the raise in salary indicated below. We appreciate the fact that you, as an employee, are an important cog in the Amherst's continued success, and we hope that you will continue to make our company successful—both through your work here and your contact with the public.

Several years ago we put into effect a grading system designed to recognize more accurately those individual traits necessary and commendable in this business. Believing this method to be the most equitable one for recognizing your abilities, we listed fifteen categories covering the above-mentioned traits. We then graded each employee according to our best knowledge and belief. Besides giving us a yardstick on which to base your salary raises, this also gives us a basis for judging promotions. We also think it will give you an index on which you might improve your own work. This year we are adding an additional item—attendance in business, insurance, etc., courses—any of which will add to your usefulness at Amherst.

Our scoring system contains seven degrees ranging between doubtful and outstanding. See attached "Employee Appraisal" sheet for the results [Fig. 17–3 in this case].

Based upon an average score for all employees, your salary raise for this year is $ _____. In addition to the above points, we feel that we must recognize certain activities by employees that are especially outstanding and outside the scope of your regular jobs. If you qualify for this additional recognition, your total raise for this fiscal year is $ _____. We expect you to keep this letter confidential, since it is intended only for your own information. This same system will be used in the future.

Yours truly

YOUR BOARD OF DIRECTORS

Austin's system was circulated and each officer was asked to study the seven-degree system. The questionnaire was, by and large, well received, and the various area supervisors looked forward to the task earnestly. There was, however, a loud dissenting voice from Robert Cohn, one of the senior executives who had been with the company a number of years. He criticized the wording of the letter, saying that it had been copied almost verbatim from the Lomax Company—even to the point where the second paragraph read, "Several years ago we put into effect a grading system." This, Cohn pointed out, just was not so; Amherst was just beginning the idea. He felt that the employees would know it was "stolen" from another company, and therefore the whole thing "should be scrapped, and Amherst should make its *own* beginning with its own standards."

Austin pointed out that at this time the letter was sent out only for discussion, that the heart of the matter was the rating scale. If the supervisory staff would rate their people in the manner suggested, the wording of the letter could easily be changed before it was sent to the employees. Cohn was finicky and defensive about the whole thing in Austin's opinion and went on to ask, "One thing I'd like to know: Am I going to get one of these things?"

Austin replied, "Since the idea originates with the Board of Directors— and since I'm only here to help execute the decisions they make—yes. Every employee should get one, even the officers." On hearing this, Cohn fell silent, and there was no more discussion.

The suggested changes were made in the employee letter, and Austin prepared a four-page questionnaire form which the rating supervisors were to use in making their appraisals. Page 1 (see Fig. 17–1) was a direction sheet, page 2 (see Fig. 17–2) was the "Employee Appraisal" grading sheet, page 3 (see Fig. 17–3) took care of promotional status, and page 4 was a blank sheet for remarks. In reading over the completed forms, Austin noted that Cohn had rated his people much higher than had the other executives. After thinking this over for a couple of days, Austin dropped over to Cohn's office and mentioned this observation. "Are all these people that good?" he asked. "What about Dave Gill, for instance. Isn't he as sluggish as you can get sometimes?" Cohn asked him to shut the office door so they could discuss this privately. A heated exchange followed.

"I don't think you're in a position to judge my employees as well as I am," Cohn said. "You high-tail off to some conference and come back with a lot of hot-shot ideas about forms. Then you try to tell me I don't know my employees on the basis of a form you swiped from the Lomax Company. Don't you know this is a different office? Or do you think we're Siamese twins? OK. OK! If you want to change my employee ratings, you just go right ahead. But don't expect me to hold responsibility for this any more. I'm an insurance executive—not a head mistress in a finishing school. Don't

EXHIBIT I
PERFORMANCE APPRAISAL AND INVENTORY OF
EMPLOYEE POTENTIAL

Appraisal Date _____

Name _____   Date of Birth _____

Title _____   Date appointed _____

Department _____ District _____   Local Area _____

Date of Discussion with Employee Appraised _____

Instructions for Appraiser

The care and accuracy with which an appraisal is made will determine its value to you, to the employee, and to the company. It deserves as much care and thoughtful attention as you would wish from someone who might be appraising you.

In using this form, the following procedure is strongly recommended:

1. Record the name of the subordinate being appraised.
2. Consider the first AREA OF CONSIDERATION and make a check under the most appropriate degree.
3. Proceed in the same manner with the other areas, treating each one independently of the others.
4. Review your appraisal and make any adjustments desired.
5. Consider the overall results of your new appraisal in the light of the subordinate's performance and/or development progress since the previous appraisal. Determine his current status of promotability and check the appropriate block under PROMOTIONAL STATUS.
6. Based on this new status and considering also the information provided on the employee's department personnel record, suggest a specific COURSE OF DEVELOPMENTAL ACTION that will serve the best interest of the company and the employee for the future. Indicate your thoughts briefly, yet completely.

In preparation for the group review session and also for subsequent discussion with the individual, it would be well to have in mind particular results and specific incidents which would give support to or illustrate an expression of the individual's ability.

FIGURE 17–1   Performance Appraisal and Inventory of Employee Potential

be surprised if some of my people get sore about this—especially if the word leaks out that you are changing the rating of their immediate boss."

Austin decided to let the thing cool off for several days and see how the other department heads and officers were making the form work. Most of them appeared to have tackled the job conscientiously, doing the best they could to rate their subordinates accurately. He did discover, however, that one individual did tend to rank his people very much on the low side—that in several instances he had given some quite able people oddly low rankings. In one specific instance, young Jake Barnes, an accountant considered to be an excellent man by almost everyone in the office, had received only a "satisfactory" average from his boss. He compared this with Bill Gorton, a clerk in Cohn's department and a rather marginal employee, who had come

EXHIBIT II

EMPLOYEE APPRAISAL

Name_____ Appraisal Date_____

AREAS OF CONSIDERATION

	Doubtful		Satisfactory		Good		Outstanding

1. **Obtaining Results**
   Application of time and facilities. Amount and quality of work produced. Direction of subordinates.
   ☐ ☐ ☐ ☐ ☐ ☐ ☐

2. **Knowledge of Work**
   Knowledge of functional skills for job and company practices.
   ☐ ☐ ☐ ☐ ☐ ☐ ☐

3. **Reasoning and Judgment**
   Mental alertness. Critical observation. Logic. Soundness of decisions.
   ☐ ☐ ☐ ☐ ☐ ☐ ☐

4. **Expression**
   Ability to state point of view clearly in written and oral presentations.
   ☐ ☐ ☐ ☐ ☐ ☐ ☐

5. **Relations with Others**
   Ability to get people to work together. Consideration. Interest to people.
   ☐ ☐ ☐ ☐ ☐ ☐ ☐

6. **Planning and Organizing**
   Development of work plans and schedules. Organizing others to get an effective job done.
   ☐ ☐ ☐ ☐ ☐ ☐ ☐

7. **Sense of Responsibility**
   Dependability. Assuming and discharging duties. Training and developing subordinates. Considering effect of actions and decisions on company.
   ☐ ☐ ☐ ☐ ☐ ☐ ☐

8. **Resourcefulness**
   Ability to improvise, to find ways to get things done without specific instructions. Ability to overcome obstacles.
   ☐ ☐ ☐ ☐ ☐ ☐ ☐

FIGURE 17–2 Employee Appraisal

out with a "good" average. Austin then began to wonder whether he should not do some scaling—up and down—according to what he knew of the employees. He decided against this, however, for it would be short-circuiting the executives who did the rating.

After some more thought Austin decided he'd call a meeting of all the people who had filed ratings with him. He'd show them the ratings, explain

EXHIBIT II (Cont'd)

Name _____ Appraisal Date _____

AREAS OF CONSIDERATION

	Doubtful		Satisfactory		Good	Outstanding
9. Self-Confidence Self-assurance. Self-reliance in meeting new situations and developments.	☐	☐	☐	☐	☐	☐	☐
10. Adaptability Flexibility. Acceptance of changed procedures. Ability to cope with the unexpected. Ease in shifting from one assignment to another.	☐	☐	☐	☐	☐	☐	☐
11. Willingness to Delegate Sharing work load with his people. Entrusting responsibility to others.	☐	☐	☐	☐	☐	☐	☐
12. Drive Basic urge to get things done. Ambition. Energy applied to job. Self-starting ability.	☐	☐	☐	☐	☐	☐	☐
13. Foresight Vision. Forward thinking and planning. Consideration of the broad aspects of management decisions.	☐	☐	☐	☐	☐	☐	☐
14. Cost Consciousness Awareness of costs to company. Efficiency within organization.	☐	☐	☐	☐	☐	☐	☐
Self Control 15. Self-restraint. Control of emotions. Eveness of temper.	☐	☐	☐	☐	☐	☐	☐
16. Attitude Enthusiasm, optimism and loyalty toward associates, job and company, and its objectives.	☐	☐	☐	☐	☐	☐	☐

Appraiser's Signature_____   _____
Concurred by _____   (Title)
        (Next level of supervision)   (Title)

FIGURE 17–2   Continued

the problem, and ask for suggestions. He had a feeling the Lomax system lacked objectivity, but he was still hesitant. All officers and department heads attended Austin's meeting. During the afternoon, a sharp altercation took place between Austin and Cohn, though not as heated as the exchange

PROMOTIONAL STATUS
(Based on Current Appraisal)

A. ☐ Promotable 2 or more levels (outstanding performance and potential)

B. ☐ Promotable next level (outstanding performance)

C. ☐ Possibly promotable to next level (acceptable performance; capable if needed)

D. ☐ Not promotable (satisfactory performance but nor promotable; unsatisfactory
performance)

SUGGESTED COURSE OF DEVELOPMENTAL ACTION FOR
PRESENT SURVEY YEAR

Note: Normally only one of the four boxes below should be checked. If "promote" and
"rotate" are both checked, indicate reason or preference.

☐ Promote
     (within present department or field _____
     {   or
     (in other departments or fields (specify) _____

☐ Rotate for experience
     (within present department or field _____
     {   or
     (in other departments or fields (specify) _____

☐ Consider other assignment (specify) _____

☐ Continue on present job

Reasons for Proposed Assignments for Development and for Testing Potential

_____
_____
_____

Other Developmental Needs

_____
_____
_____

Proposed Management Training

_____
_____

FIGURE 17–3   Promotional Status Based on Current Appraisal

in the latter's office several days back. Cohn suggested that, because there
were so many bugs in the idea, the whole thing ought to be delayed. The
ratings should not go into the employees' personnel files, for they certainly
would cause a lot of hard feelings.

Austin was determined that he would have a performance appraisal program instituted, and at the conclusion of the meeting (which got almost
nowhere) he sat in his office pondering what his next step would be.

CASE DISCUSSION QUESTIONS

The Amherst Insurance Company Case

1. How good is the Lomax-Austin plan for personnel appraisal?

2. What is Austin's next step?

3. How should he handle Cohn? What is his problem with Cohn in the first place?

Index